The South
Central States

TIME-LIFE Library of America

The South Central States

Arkansas Louisiana Oklahoma Texas

By Lawrence Goodwyn
and the Editors of
TIME-LIFE BOOKS

Time Incorporated, New York

The Author: Lawrence Goodwyn, writer, essayist and social critic, has lived most of his life in Texas. He received a B.A. from Texas A. & M. University in 1949 and an M.A. from Trinity University in San Antonio in 1956. Most of his writings have concerned the American South and Southwest, covering both the post-Civil War period and the contemporary scene. Mr. Goodwyn has contributed to national publications such as *Harper's Magazine* and to scholarly journals such as the *Southwestern Historical Quarterly*. A contributing editor of the *Texas Observer*, a Southwestern journal of opinion, he is a resident of Austin.

The Consulting Editor: Oscar Handlin, Charles Warren Professor of American History at Harvard University and director of the university's Charles Warren Center for Studies in American History, is one of America's foremost social historians. His work on U.S. immigrants, *The Uprooted*, won the Pulitzer Prize in 1952.

South Central States Consultant: William Ransom Hogan, Chairman of the Department of History at Tulane University in New Orleans, received his M.A. and Ph.D. degrees at the University of Texas. A contributor to many historical and literary journals, he has also written a number of books, including the authoritative *The Texas Republic* (1946).

The Cover: Offshore oil derricks, reminders of the single most important economic influence in the South Central States, rise from Galveston Bay off Baytown, Texas.

TIME-LIFE BOOKS

Editor
Maitland A. Edey

Executive Editor
Jerry Korn

Text Director   **Art Director**
Martin Mann   Sheldon Cotler

Chief of Research
Beatrice T. Dobie

Picture Editor
Robert G. Mason

Assistant Text Directors:
Harold C. Field, Ogden Tanner

Assistant Art Director:
Arnold C. Holeywell

Assistant Chief of Research:
Martha Turner

Publisher
Rhett Austell
General Manager: Joseph C. Hazen Jr.
Circulation Director: Joan D. Manley
Marketing Director: Carter Smith
Business Manager: John D. McSweeney
Publishing Board: Nicholas Benton,
Louis Bronzo, James Wendell Forbes

TIME-LIFE Library of America

Series Editor: Oliver E. Allen
Editorial Staff for *The South Central States:*
Assistant Editor: David S. Thomson
Picture Editor: Sheila Osmundsen
Designer: John Newcomb
Assistant Designer: Jean Lindsay
Staff Writers: Jonathan Kastner,
Marianna Pinchot, Peter Yerkes
Chief Researcher: Clara E. Nicolai
Text Research: Ruth Silva, Don Nelson,
Vista Grayson, Evelyn Hauptman
Picture Research: Nancy Jacobsen,
Judy Gurovitz, Ella Anderson, Myra Mangan

Editorial Production
Color Director: Robert L. Young
Assistant: James J. Cox
Copy Staff: Marian Gordon Goldman,
Patricia Miller, Dolores A. Littles
Picture Bureau: Margaret K. Goldsmith,
Merry Mass
Traffic: Douglas B. Graham
Art Assistant: Mervyn Clay

The text chapters of this book were written by Lawrence Goodwyn, the picture essays by the editorial staff. Valuable aid was provided by these individuals and departments of Time Inc.: LIFE staff photographers Ralph Crane, John Loengard, Leonard McCombe and Stan Wayman; the Chief of the LIFE Picture Library, Doris O'Neil; the Chief of the Bureau of Editorial Reference, Peter Draz; the Chief of the TIME-LIFE News Service, Richard M. Clurman; Bureau Chief Benjamin Cate (Houston); Correspondents Holland McCombs and Patsy Swank (Dallas).

Contents

Introduction

I have been waiting a long time for someone to write a book like this about our part of the Southwest. In writing it Lawrence Goodwyn has done us all a service.

In a sense, this is personal with me. I was born in Arkansas in the other century (1898), and I cannot remember when I first began to be jealous of that much larger state of Texas, and to speculate on what kind of magnet was drawing settlers from and through Arkansas to Texas, to that new state to the west of us, Oklahoma, and to Louisiana as well. The settlers were looking for "land and wood and water" (the refrain of the late Senator Robert S. Kerr of Oklahoma). Since Arkansas had all three of these things in abundance, the citizens of my state felt neglected.

I am old enough for some memories that few men now living can share. I can remember the wagons, horse-drawn and covered with tarpaulins, moving west, seeking the bare necessities of life; and I have lived long enough to see another sort of covered wagon, motor-propelled and covered, not with tarpaulin, but with a hard metal top, and looking not for land and wood and water but for homes and jobs and opportunities. Some are headed for industrial cities of the North and East, but a surprising number are going to New Orleans and to the great, growing urban centers of Texas.

This kind of activity has bred a certain spirit of rivalry in the citizens of my native Arkansas, and their mood occasionally shows through. Anyone knowing of the football hysteria that occasionally overtakes the four states discussed in this volume will appreciate the feelings of the big fullback sitting by me in history class at the University of Arkansas in the days of Oklahoma's football ascendancy when the instructor commented, "And so, in 1907 we took Oklahoma into the Union." The football player said, *sotto voce*, "*That* was a big mistake!" But it was anything but a mistake, for Oklahoma has added a glorious chapter to American history.

And may I brag on Texas, too? Though here I have some difficulties not encountered in the case of Oklahoma, which is near to Arkansas in size and population. A Texan said to me once, "Don't try to brag on us—you are so patronizing! You sound like the owner of a Ford saying to the owner of a Cadillac, 'You have a good car, too.'"

That does it! The poorer and more modest Arkansans have had to take talk like that for a century. But of course there is justification for the awareness of size and greatness exhibited by Texans; their state is vast and wealthy. Mr. Goodwyn has not allowed his Texas background to obscure one of his state's problems—a problem bred partly by Texas' size and importance—that of eliminating finally the phenomenon of separatism. Many Texans are still reluctant to "rejoin" the Union.

My favorite Texas story is of the two former Arkansans who returned for an Arkansas homecoming. One of their former neighbors inquired, "Have you boys done all right out there in Texas?"

The first one said, "I'll say I have! I got ten million dollars in the bank, six Cadillac cars and I own seven hundred and fifty thousand acres of land."

As he walked away, the Arkansas farmer said to the second Texan, "Is he telling me the truth? Can I believe that?" "Ever' word," the other man replied. "I border him on four sides."

But I must not make too much of the spirit of rivalry that the three smaller states display. It is no longer as perceptible as it once was even in Arkansas, which felt the impact more than did Louisiana and Oklahoma.

Among the most striking things about the whole region, to my mind, is not the spirit of rivalry, but the spirit of Christian cooperation. The region's church life is notable. In a sense it is the sincerest part of the composite character, if the region may be said to have such. The author's characterization, "fundamentalist," is acceptable if one word must do, but many students of the area would give it a coloration of genuine humaneness and graciousness. The church is at the center of Southwesterners' major interests, and its "fundamentalism" is not "religiosity," as some outsiders fear.

The natural features of the region—rivers, mountains and prairies—are vividly described in this significant volume, as are the growing economies of the four states. The economic development of a good part of Oklahoma and Arkansas, the mountain area in particular, now progresses steadily. Perhaps I can be forgiven for adding a footnote here about my own state: the Ozark region, once so isolated that its folklore and culture seemed like an importation, is now related by commercial ties to some of the world's great markets. An example is found in Siloam Springs, Arkansas (population 6,000). There are seven thriving young industries here, and every one of them has a sizable export business. The first order received from abroad by a canning plant was for a huge shipment of red kidney beans, and it came from Kuwait!

Modern miracles in commerce and industry have profoundly changed the status of the four states. Mr. Goodwyn's references to the poverty of many of the rural dwellers are convincing, and this poverty is serious enough to deserve the highlighting it receives. I trust, however, that the reader will grasp the full import of the tremendous forward thrust of industrial development, in Arkansas as elsewhere in the South Central region, which has brought a new prosperity.

Although it is the lowest of the four states in population and in per capita income, Arkansas still does not feel neglected nor even suffer any embarrassment, for the gaps are closing rapidly. Its pride was helped mightily when the Razorbacks of the University of Arkansas began to enjoy a series of football victories over the Longhorns of the University of Texas in 1964. Another advantage Arkansas has over Texas—one that was enjoyed in the past but tends to be forgotten now—is the attractive recreation areas provided by the Ozarks. Their importance has been obscured partly by the fact that, with oil and beef and manufacturing wealth, Texans and others can go farther for their summer diversions than they could before, and they need no longer vacation in the nearby Arkansas hills.

The telescoping of commercial and cultural history that Mr. Goodwyn has achieved in this book should sharpen the curiosity of all readers regarding the rugged frontiers of rural Arkansas and Louisiana, two areas that have seldom been credited with the remarkable basic resources, physical and human, belonging to them. And the same can be said of Mr. Goodwyn's descriptions of southern Louisiana, which has always seemed to be a cultural dependency of France rather than the legatee of the state's marvelous upriver country. It is notable in this connection that my state, too, shows evidence of early French influence. The Congressional district that I represented, for example, has the Fourche la Fave River, as well as Petit Jean Mountain, the latter more celebrated now that its best-known resident is Winthrop Rockefeller.

Even less familiar to the American people, perhaps, is the division that Mr. Goodwyn's text makes evident between the two more northern states within the South Central region—Arkansas and Oklahoma—and the two more southern ones—Louisiana and Texas. These two subregions have somewhat different social and political mores.

Arkansas, for example, drew upon the legal and religious institutions of Kentucky and Tennessee, and later, at the turn of the century, transmitted a robust political leadership to Oklahoma, many of whose people came from Arkansas and other states outside the Deep South. On the other hand, Louisiana received steady human migrations from the Deep South states of Mississippi, Alabama and Georgia. East Texas, and later all of Texas, then felt the second wave of this Southern migration.

However, Texas, like Oklahoma, also attracted people and capital from non-Southern areas. New York investors early recognized the potentialities of Texas, and as late as 1930 Professor Robert Montgomery of the University of Texas could say, "Let no one say Texas is poor—we are Manhattan's richest colony." It was an appropriate comment for that period, though hardly for today.

Further, Texas, again like Oklahoma, was the recipient of strong influences from Tennessee. Citizens of the Volunteer State (and it got that name because so many of its men volunteered to fight against Mexico) moved in great numbers to Texas during the 19th Century. Sam Houston and the late Speaker of the House of Representatives, Sam Rayburn, were among that number. The tragedy of Houston's closing days is particularly well told by Mr. Goodwyn. There are whole volumes that tell less about the pre-Civil War period than this book's moving account of Houston's courageous stand against secession.

This book tells the saga of one of the nation's most interesting and complex regions. Americans should be grateful for it.

—BROOKS HAYS
Former Congressman from Arkansas

Silhouetted by one of Oklahoma's spectacular autumn sunsets,
which shows up dramatically in a telephoto shot, farmer Herbert
Yost heads for home after a day of wheat planting. Yost's farm is
near the town of Kingfisher, in Oklahoma's rich winter-wheat belt.

1

Land, the
Enduring Value

The land rolls away from the Mississippi River, out of the eastern forests into the Great Plains, out of the Old South into the West. It is a frontier country of sharp, bleak diversities, perpetually a changeling in search of some new identity.

By reputation, its people are different from those in the rest of the nation and in many respects the land itself supports this notion. From the Atlantic Seaboard to the Mississippi Valley the topography of America, despite its many variations, has a fairly consistent greenness. Even much of what passes for poor land nurtures woods and sedge, fern and foliage. But here, on the Southern frontier, green gives way to brown.

The dank, alluvial bayou country of Louisiana dries into the tree-dotted landscape of Texas' coastal prairies and then dries further into open range, into the treeless short-grass country of the Texas-Oklahoma Panhandles. Along the blistered barrens stretching toward El Paso in far West Texas, tall cactus plants or a rare gnarled tree become treasured landmarks in a desert country long baked dry by the western sun. Cumulatively, the change is profound. In one vast sweep north and west from the Mississippi delta, the soil thins and the land rises. Louisiana swamps become Arkansas plateaus and gulf prairies shrivel into arid range.

These changes in the landscape bring with them changes in the way men live, in their style of life. For generations existence on the plains has had a precarious quality that has left its mark on both the habits and attitudes of the people. During the big period of settlement after the Civil War, recurring droughts intimidated wave after wave of immigrant Southern farmers for whom the frontier became a bleak land of frustrated hopes. Their experience perhaps explains the extravagant exultation that surfaced in a rare good year and that has, in this century, become a trademark of the region for people in the rest of the nation. Everybody is aware of the figure of the swaggering Texan—cattle baron, cotton king or oil wildcatter—brandishing the material proof of his triumph over flood and drought, disease and sand. Surely this swagger derives its intensity from a deep awareness—almost a racial memory—of just how fragile any triumph over this resistant land can be. Less noticed is this Texan's impoverished back-country cousin, defeated by the same uncompromising forces of nature, or his counterparts in the pine hills of Louisiana, in the mountainous interior of the Arkansas Ozarks or on the red-clay prairies of Oklahoma. The flamboyant style of some of the region's people may simply be an act of faith, a form of personal reassurance in a land that still yields more poverty than affluence.

The land has left its mark on the people in other ways. Its isolation has helped give them their storied lack of subtlety, and its vastness has enlarged their sense of the possible, just as its occasional prodigality has helped create their psychology of bonanza. But if the people of the South Central States have, indeed, an identifiable regional personality—at least when they are seen from a distance—they are also a highly varied people about whom it is possible to make only the simplest generalizations. To this variety the history of the land, as distinct from its physical features, has contributed a great deal.

Few Americans realize the unusual length and complexity of the history of this region. The 1,000-mile-wide sweep of land from the Mississippi delta to the High Plains encompasses not only a vast amount of space but also all the recorded history of America. Though often overlooked, this is a seminal fact: the states of Texas, Oklahoma and Louisiana—and Arkansas to a lesser extent—find their historical beginnings not in the relatively recent westward movement of Anglo-Saxons but in the ancient colonial rivalry of France and Spain.

Here, on the Southern frontier, the soldiers of Spain fought and died before the Pilgrims landed at Plymouth Rock. Here, in the 17th Century, rival adventurers from France explored the banks of the Mississippi and named the new empire Louisiana, for their sovereign, Louis XIV. Here, near the delta of the same great river, a city of energy and highly individual style—New Orleans—had already begun to rise while the rest of colonial America remained rooted along the Atlantic Coast. Here, Santa Anna's hardy armies of Mexican revolutionaries perished before a mixed Texas-Mexican army of even stouter revolutionaries in 1836. Here, too, the Indians of the Southern plains raised their last ensign of revolt against the white man in the 1860s and 1870s.

The racial complexities—and many of the tensions—of the modern frontier South are traceable to these varied beginnings. Out of the French venture in Louisiana came not only the urban Creoles of New Orleans, but also the rural French-descended Acadians, who were expelled from Nova Scotia by the British when they took over Canada and who ultimately gave the name of "Cajun Country" to virtually all of present-day southern Louisiana. A Louisiana scholar has recently put the number of modern Acadians at 500,000.

Out of Spanish ambitions in Texas came a new way of life in the saddle that was profoundly to affect the development of the cattle kingdom and, through it, the enduring legend of the American West. Indeed, one cannot speak of the Texas cowboy without conceding his almost completely Mexican origins—any more than one can generalize about the modern Texan without noting that nearly two million residents of the Lone Star State are of Mexican descent.

Additionally, some half a million Oklahomans are of Indian extraction while, to the south, heavy German immigration has long since put a permanent Teutonic stamp on sizable portions of rural Texas, including Lyndon Johnson's hill country in the center of the state. Extensive Irish and Italian immigration during the 19th Century considerably changed and enriched the strong ethnic gumbo that is New Orleans. Finally, some three million Negroes live in the four states, almost 300,000 of them in the city of Houston alone.

For those who are tempted to generalize about this part of America, these are statistics to give pause. It is by no means a region populated only by the stereotype found in tobacco advertisements on television—the tall, bony man with an angular jaw jutting below his Stetson hat. With such numbers of Negroes and Mexicans, Indians and Germans, Italians and Irish, it is apparent that a single symbolic representative of the region will not easily be found, either in the past or the present.

Not that the practitioners of the art of legend building have not tried. Throughout the 19th Century, as life in the United States became more urban-

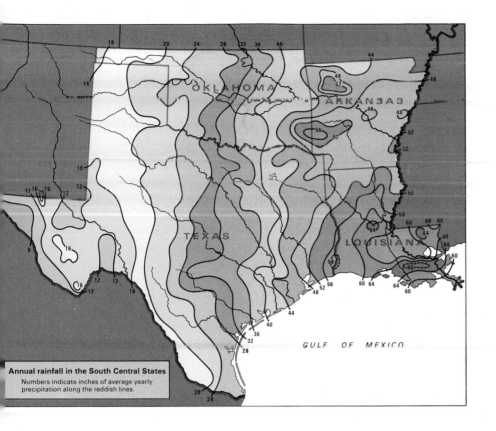

As this precipitation map indicates, rainfall in the South Central States varies widely. In general, the rainfall diminishes from east to west. Wherever it falls below 20 inches a year, the minimum requirement for agriculture, farming generally gives way to grazing. Louisiana is the wettest of the four states; its southeasternmost corner is swampy bayou country. In summer there are almost daily showers in the coastal sections, while the northern part of the state often receives prolonged rains in winter. Rainfall in Arkansas is normally abundant and fairly well distributed. In Oklahoma there is usually enough rain for crops, although the state is subject to recurrent periods of drought and even dust storms. In Texas, precipitation figures are slightly misleading, since much of the rainfall is sporadic and runs off without being absorbed. Like Oklahoma, the state is subject to drought.

Annual rainfall in the South Central States
Numbers indicate inches of average yearly precipitation along the reddish lines.

ized and more complex, writers attempted to draw a picture of the true, uncorrupted, "natural" American, as if, by describing such a creature, they could recapture a supposedly simpler, more virtuous time in the nation's life. James Fenimore Cooper invented the woodsman Natty Bumppo in his *Leatherstocking* novels and Mark Twain created Huck Finn, both utterly resistant to the charms of an increasingly confining civilization. Later writers, both good and bad, found their natural, unspoiled American on the Southern frontier in the figure of the cowboy. The cowboy's story is limitless and marvelously flexible. He is a hero, though occasionally —wearing black—he materializes as a villain. His enemies may be fence-building farmers, hostile Indians or the prairie vigilantes called jayhawkers. They harass him but somehow never defeat him. Carried to millions by the dime novel and to added millions by motion pictures and television, the legend of the cowboy is today, for better or for worse, an inescapable part of the nation's heritage.

Yet in providing a clue to the true nature of the Southern plains, the cowboy is a curiously indecisive fellow. Unlike the mythical hero of the North Woods, Paul Bunyan, the cowboy is a figure without a name, seemingly without provable traits of character. He sits on his Spanish mustang, alone in the vastness of the frontier, amid his Longhorns, his chuck wagon and his Indians, certain in his innocence to be fleeced by sharpsters in the town at the end of the trail. His only fixed reference seems to come from the land itself. The range sustains him and his enemies alike and thus nurtures his style of life. His saga is fleeting—he defeats all his foes and then in his moment of triumph remounts his mustang, gallops out of town and vanishes over the horizon.

Just what this enigmatic figure means is not at all clear, but surely part of his strong appeal for the urbanized American tied to the nine-to-five round is the cowboy's appearance of independence, his rejection of the town and its constraints, and his choice, at the price of loneliness, of the open spaces. And perhaps in some ways he does stand for the people of the Southwest. He is nameless and elusive and yet somehow inseparable from the land. He regards himself as an individualist with the strength to endure in a harsh, often hostile, environment. Both of these things can generally be said for many of the people who came to challenge the Southern frontier.

Though they were not the first, the most numerous and persistent challengers were, of course, the Americans—men from the Old South, from the

Midwest, from the East, looking for new land, new opportunities in the expanding U.S. of the 19th Century. In each state the incoming Americans adapted themselves to the local conditions—and to the resistance of the people already there. In most places the newcomers were given, or gave themselves, a name expressive of what they were or how they arrived. On the wharves of New Orleans, French-speaking Creoles watched the arrival of the uncouth rivermen flatboating produce from the newly opened Midwest and called them a variety of names, of which one of the few that is printable was "Kaintocks." Farther west, Mexican *vaqueros*, or cowboys, identified the newcomers as "gringos." The latter came like ripples of an advancing tide. There were many waves: the buffalo hunters, slaughtering the mainstay of the nomadic tribes and thus presaging the Indian twilight; the gaunt, gambling cattlemen, adapting their Spanish and Mexican land grants to new uses on the open range, becoming "barons" if successful and, sometimes, "rustlers" if not; and the cowman's nemesis, the horde of farmers, with their radical agrarian politics and their bales of barbed wire for fencing the plains. The cowmen disdainfully called them "nesters."

In Oklahoma the Americans descended on the Indians in their reserves. The Oklahoma Land Rush, which began in 1889, was theoretically under the strict supervision of the U.S. government, but it quickly became a series of wild, chaotic human stampedes. The immigrants gathered at a government-established line and were supposed to wait until an official starting time before rushing pell-mell to stake out their claims. But not all of them observed the rules. Those who left "sooner" (i.e., before the starting time) naturally tended to get the best lands. So widespread was the practice that, at least in retrospect, it became respectable, and to be a forthright Oklahoman was to be a "Sooner." As almost any native will point out, the trait has found its modern expression in the quickness and aggressiveness of the University of Oklahoma "Sooners" football team.

In Louisiana, although the Acadians managed to consolidate their hold on the southern rural portions of the state, their urban cousins, the French-speaking Creoles of New Orleans, saw their culture slowly disintegrate under the successive onslaughts of Yankee mercantile captains and riverboat gamblers, plus Irish and Italian immigrants, and the Negroes from the Caribbean and the American South who were to make the city synonymous with jazz. The northern pine-hill section of Louisiana was settled by English-speaking farmers who, in rising

degree of vilification, have been called everything from "wool hats" and "one-gallus yahoos" to "peckerwoods" and "rednecks." Counterpoised, as it were, against the Roman Catholic Acadians of the bayou south, these Protestant hill people have helped make Louisiana a state with baffling diversities of custom and outlook. As a consequence, modern Louisiana politics are among the most unfathomable in the nation.

The arrival of the Americans in Texas produced conflict with the Mexican authorities who administered the land grants. Whereupon the newcomers fought a nearly disastrous war for independence, blending poor tactics and raw courage to lose all the important battles but the first one and the last. On the foundation of Sam Houston's crushing victory over the Mexican General Antonio Lopez de Santa Anna at San Jacinto in 1836, the "Texians," as they then called themselves, built an erratic but functioning 10-year republic on the frontier, joined first the United States and later the Confederacy, and maintained their own force of Texas Rangers to smite the Plains Indians. Beginning in the late 1860s, the Texans played a vital role in the development of the Western cattle trails. They managed to endow each of these experiences with an extra measure of heroism and then, in the retelling, added a good deal of self-righteousness and just plain mythology. The resulting legacy of fact mixed with self-adulatory fiction has influenced the behavior of their descendants ever since, not always for the best, and has made a true reading of Texas history very difficult.

In Arkansas the plateau of the Ozarks fostered isolation. Neither the French and Spanish nor the Indians had seen fit to challenge the Ozarks in sizable numbers, and so the incoming Americans did not have to pay in blood for possession of the soil. During some of the most freewheeling years in American history, the settlers of the Ozarks were cut off from the frontier fury surrounding them. Working their rocky hillsides, they existed, generation after generation, almost outside of history. The nation knew dimly that the "Arkie" was a mountain man, a fine storyteller after the fashion of mountain people, and that he possessed a curious Elizabethan quality in his speech. Beyond that he seemed even more difficult to characterize than the Cajun, the Sooner or the Texian—although, like them, he possessed a capacity to endure that set him apart from such predecessors as the Spanish.

The Southern frontier, then, has had numerous claimants, but no one group, not even the Americans, has been clearly victorious for long enough to produce a kind of person that can be pointed out as representative of the whole region. Nor can the region itself be characterized by a single descriptive phrase. Texas and Louisiana share much common history—in a context that generally may be described as "Southern." In contrast, Texas and Oklahoma share a history of a later era that is almost wholly "Western" in style. In commercial and industrial outlook, the coastal regions of Texas and Louisiana are similar, prompting the phrase "the Gulf Southwest." There is really little about Louisiana that is "Western" nor much about Oklahoma that is classically "Southern." And Arkansas is fairly much a world apart, its style and history tending to be dominated by the Ozark Mountains.

In general, the people of the four states have both frontier and Southern memories. Thus, as a group, the four states of the area are perhaps best viewed as participants in great American sagas, some of them "Southern," some "Western" and some simply "Southwestern." It is the very presence of these dissimilarities that gives the region its distinct regional flavor and persuades us to talk about the people of the four states in a single book.

Insofar as this varied history has application in the present, it is well to remember that the descendants of all the various peoples who came to the Southern frontier through four centuries are still there. Ethnic and racial islands of people whose heritage is Indian or Mexican, French or Spanish, Negro or, simply, U.S. Southern, are the rule. The reason may be that in the struggles between these groups—between Indian and white man, Mexican and gringo, Kaintock and Creole, Southerner and Negro—each one has felt sufficiently threatened to cling to its own identity and the legends that sustain it. There has been no grand amalgamation in the classic American sense, no "melting-pot" fusion producing an environment of shared experience and hopeful idealism.

Rather, this region where the South moves uneasily into the West gives the appearance of a vessel permanently in midpassage, riding on currents that eddy just outside the mainstream of American experience. There persists an underlying dislocation, perhaps traceable to the quixotic nature of the land itself, or perhaps to the region's fractured, formless history, or perhaps to both. Unity is most visible on Saturday afternoons when the state university's football team plays a team from some other region. Dozens of startled opponents stand ready to attest to the psychological perils of venturing into the Ozarks to challenge the Arkansas Razorbacks or of invading Baton Rouge to play Louisiana State.

Quite simply, the visiting team is met by an outpouring of regional solidarity that, in sheer vocal intensity, may well be unmatched on the continent. But during the rest of the week the kind of cultural unity that is shared by New Englanders, for instance, is clearly missing.

Part of the reason may be geographical. The land is simply not conducive to moderate life styles of the kind that encourage cohesion and cooperation. Even that most valued of nature's gifts—water—appears in the form of capriciously placed rivers that bested strong men for more than two centuries. It was not only the Mississippi—whose destructive powers need no embellishment. The Father of Waters in fact has a singularly un-Southwestern virtue: it flows conveniently north to south. The others—the Arkansas, the Red, the Brazos, the Colorado, the Nueces—all follow the same northwest-to-southeast course that blocked the frontiersman's wagons when he migrated westward and blocked his Longhorn herds half a century later when he headed north on the great trail drives. Whatever direction he has traveled, the river valleys have always been in his way, never leading him across his country, merely deeper into it. There has always been, it seems, another river to cross. Legends aside, probably as many cowboys perished at river crossings as ever pulled a Colt revolver in anger in the saloons of Abilene and Dodge City.

The region's extreme variance in rainfall patterns (66 inches annually in the delta of the Mississippi, eight inches in the desert west of the Pecos) has bestowed on the inhabitants a permanent legacy of too much and too little. Today, after a half century of intensive dam and levee building, a measure of protection has been obtained against floods. But the problem of too little continues to haunt the western portions of Oklahoma and Texas. Burgeoning populations on the High Plains are straining the limited water resources. The West Texas city of Lubbock is still an unfamiliar place name to most Americans, yet it contains 150,000 people and is host to the 16,000 students of Texas Tech. El Paso (320,000), Midland-Odessa (160,000) and Amarillo (165,000) are all bulging islands of humanity in a shallow and depleting sea of underground water tables. Yet the people of this area find it very difficult to agree on plans for dams and aqueducts. Ancient hostilities over local control versus federal encroachment have in the past reached levels of emotion baffling to the Easterner, whatever his politics.

It is not a wholly unfamiliar pattern. For generations, Louisianans postponed the kind of decisive action needed to cope with the Mississippi River—and suffered death and destruction as a result. Today, their cousins on the nearby plains regard water programs 5, 10 or 15 years in the making as "studies" compelling no immediate implementation. In Texas and Oklahoma, as was true earlier of Louisiana, it has been virtually impossible to get the kind of broad-scale support of business, labor, farmers and plain citizens necessary to inaugurate massive engineering projects. The need is vaguely conceded, but the social energy to address it somehow does not materialize. In contrast, California is decades ahead of Texas in confronting its similarly growing water crisis.

The reasons for this continuing indecisiveness, while perhaps not easy for the outsider to grasp, are actually like refracted colors from the South Central States' enduring spectrum of land, history and heritage. They are reflections of the region's view of itself. As such, these reasons merit some inspection.

Even more than most Americans, the man of the Southern frontier regards himself as an individualist, descended from individualists. His reading of his own history sustains this feeling. And, indeed, the frontier has never given the appearance of being a friendly environment for settled conformity. The very act of "going west" was itself a definable break with the institutions and constraints of an older society. Whether responding to railroad pamphlets extolling the fertility of land beyond the Mississippi or to the spirit of adventure coursing through the dime novels that country boys read in the crossroads hamlets of Georgia and the Carolinas, the man who came west in the 19th Century had manifestly decided to cut his old ties and bet on himself. Significantly, however, he came as a man not only attuned to the soil but also convinced that he could succeed, if he could deal with the land without too many intervening middlemen of the type who seemed to sap all the profit out of farming in the Old South. His decision to head west may be seen as an expression of two tendencies—his love of the land and his desire to "be his own man."

But once on the frontier, he found that the land forced these two tendencies to war with each other. He could survive and perhaps even prosper on his land—*if* he worked closely with his neighbors to hold it against his assorted natural and human foes. Or, stated somewhat more precisely, he could get along if he conformed—if he joined with his neighbors in forming livestock associations to protect his cattle against rustlers, or if he formed agricultural cooperatives to work for decent prices for

his crops. It was more embarrassing still when the proudly self-reliant frontiersman had to seek government aid to provide drought relief in the bad years, to build railroads to give him access to markets or to send the Army to guard his fields against the Comanche. "A man can't make it alone" goes the phrase, and in his heart the plainsman has always known this. Indeed, it is a Western phrase that surfaced at "house-raisin's," when neighbors gathered to help a newcomer build his frontier home, surfacing spontaneously and generously when boll weevils wiped out a man's cotton crop or tick fever crippled his cattle herd.

Even within the ranks of the "cattle kings"—the most heralded individualists of them all—there have been pleas that the government provide a National Cattle Trail and subsidize research into the nature of cattle diseases. The individualist of the West has historically had his hand out to the East—to seek, in the 19th Century phrase, the "internal improvements" of roads, canals, levees and railroads that alone could make rational economic life possible on the plains. In short, the frontiersman has used the stentorian tones of the individualist in proclaiming his need for assistance to protect the way of life that underscored his individualism.

The Westerner has tried very hard to come to terms with this contradiction. He has justified his requests not as welfare payments but as basic tools needed by hard-working men to survive in a rough and hostile environment.

There can be no question that he has been right about his needs, and he probably has been right, too, in thinking that it is a proper function of a society to pitch in and help one of its distressed parts. The nation has agreed and the railroads and other facilities have been built. But the plainsman has never really been content to let the issue rest. For him, it has always been important to establish the fact that accepting aid does not diminish his status as a purer example of rugged American individualism than, say, an Eastern factory owner. Many regional histories emanating from Western state universities in recent decades have revealed this sensitivity, underplaying the help received from the national government while portraying the conquest of the West almost as a feat of personal will by rugged frontiersmen.

Meanwhile, of course, the special needs of the West persist, reviving again and again the tension between the belief in individualism on the one hand and the self-evident need for organized action on the other. There probably is not a more dedicated editorial defender of Southern states' rights and

American individualism than *The Dallas Morning News;* nonetheless the paper throughout the middle 1960s led an active lobbying campaign urging Congress to pass the billion-dollar Trinity River Project, which would make that stream navigable for 300 miles and thus turn the inland city of Dallas into a gulf seaport.

It would be ungenerous to term this attitude hypocritical. It is simply that the harsh, resistant land continues to spread-eagle the populace between the two impulses that brought their ancestors across the Mississippi their love of the soil and their intention to demonstrate their individual worth by mastering the forces of nature. The truth is that no matter how much love is lavished on the land, the plains are too vast and too arid to respond properly. So the people must accept help.

But despite this knowledge that both neighborly cooperation and government aid are necessary, the mystique of frontier individualism goes marching on, producing public indecision and postponing needed public works. The plainsman will some day, perhaps not too late, accept the need for cooperation to bring water to his cities and farms, but he will wait a while first, lest what he regards as a betrayal of his frontier heritage seem anything but reluctant. He will accept it because, like his fathers before him, he could hardly survive without it.

It has always been that way. Only the very first white men who pierced the region were outside this tradition. The Spanish and French explorers thought in terms of gold, quick fame and strategic slices of countryside as bulwarks against each other and the British. But those who came in their tracks, the Acadians, the free Negroes, the Arkies, and those who called themselves Texians and Sooners, all wanted simply a piece of earth—blackland to sink a plow into, grassland for cattle, bottom land as insurance against prairie drought. When the good land was gone they filled the plateau crannies and mountain valleys of the Ozarks, paddled into the remotest backwaters of the Louisiana bayous, stepped out onto the Great Plains and undertook to farm the desert.

Most of them came from the Old South states of Tennessee and Georgia, Mississippi and the Carolinas. In time, they built cities such as Fort Worth and Baton Rouge, Oklahoma City and Texarkana that appear on the surface indistinguishable from Omaha, Denver or Sacramento—the same clash of neon in the central city, the same split-level ranch houses endlessly proliferating in the suburbs. But the people who live in the ranch houses of the South Central States remain of the older time. The

rhythms of the old rural South pulse everywhere —in country towns like Crockett, Texas, and Walnut Ridge, Arkansas, and even in modern cities like Houston. Every weekend thousands of Houston's million and a half residents retreat to the "home place" in the Piney Woods of East Texas. There, in the counties where their grandfathers were born, they take their ease as they can nowhere else. Everywhere the rural ways persist behind the façades of the modern cities. The past lingers in fundamentalist churches and in Catholic parishes, in the twangy music of fiddle and guitar, in the emotion of spirituals and blues. It endures in recipes of historic gumbos and barbecue sauces, in the woodsman's passion for year-round hunting and fishing, and in the folk memories that guide his approach to politics and caste.

However, even these memories, Southern as they seem, are measurably different from the planter code of the Old South. With the exception of a few hundred families nestled in a narrow stretch of the Mississippi delta, there has never been a landed gentry in this part of America. The land has been the province of the yeoman farmer and the yeoman stockman. Today, the nostalgia for the old agrarian ways contains more of the flavor of Thomas Jefferson, Virginia's champion of the small farmer, than of Jefferson Davis, the aristocratic traditionalist from Mississippi. Land, not the caste system, has been the enduring value.

Still, the attempt to hang on to the old frontier outlook in the midst of an increasingly industrialized society is necessarily a somewhat baffling and frustrating experience. Most of the people of the South Central States never came to terms with the 19th Century and their descendants are having no little trouble with the 20th. Their frontier individualism exacerbated by the long and still continuing battle with their rugged environment, they are an impatient and even inflammable people. Although they find it hard to agree about large water-reclamation projects, they are temperamentally in favor of quick, definite solutions. Thus they are visibly impatient with the compromising half measures that are inevitable in a democracy; some have not been able to come to terms with the slow processes of democratic government at all. These have taken refuge in what might be called the "high-noon syndrome"; they see life in terms of a showdown between the good cowboy in the white hat and the villain in black.

This instinct to define human and political relationships in terms of a showdown is visible today in the lazy gulf country of Plaquemines Parish,

Louisiana, where embittered diehards proclaim old-fashioned racism as the continuing order of the day. "Don't wait for your daughter to be raped by these Congolese," warned the notorious Leander Perez during an integration crisis in 1960. "Don't wait until the burr-heads are forced into your schools. Do something about it now."

More significantly, the high-noon mentality persists in Dallas skyscrapers and vividly came to light in 1961 when Ted Dealey, publisher of *The Dallas Morning News*, shocked a White House gathering of Texas newspaper publishers and editors by telling President Kennedy that the nation was tired of seeing its foreign policy conducted by someone "riding around on Caroline's tricycle." What was needed, said publisher Dealey, rising tall in the saddle, was "a man on horseback." Though the remark stirred angry disclaimers from the other publishers present, Mr. Dealey was hardly being inconsistent with his Texas heritage. Violence, rhetorical as well as physical, has always been a part of the frontier environment.

Yet, in contrast to the tendency of the Deep South, this instinct for primitive "once and for all" solutions has only intermittently produced studied defiance of the nation as a whole; much more often, men of the Southern frontier have battled one another. Whether focused on the recurring impeachments of Oklahoma governors, range wars in Texas, class struggles in Louisiana or racial crises in Arkansas, the intramural collisions have been bitter and sometimes violent. The exuberant Oklahoma plainsman, the defiant upcountry Louisianan, the ubiquitous freewheeling Texan—all have appeared to a puzzled nation as a somewhat strange species, a bit raucous and rather clumsily dogmatic. In any case, a friendly witness might again remind the outsider that this widespread assertiveness, in times past at least, has been both an ingredient and a by-product of simple survival.

Today, the frontier South is moving with the rest of the world into an era of technological breakthrough and social transformation. The Texas-Louisiana Gulf Coast, with its industrial complexes and its changing patterns of segregation, is feeling the impact of both. Roughly half of the eligible Negroes in Texas paid the state-imposed $1.75 poll tax in 1964, and one of their number, an articulate young lawyer named Barbara Jordan, became in 1966 the first Texan of her race since the Populist era to win a seat in the state senate.

The past lingers, nevertheless. Bogalusa, Louisiana, near the Mississippi state line, serves as an eerie reminder. With its armed "Original Knights of the Ku Klux Klan" pledged to defend the Southern Way and its armed "Deacons for Defense and Justice" grimly guarding civil rights workers, Bogalusa vividly dramatizes a more general truth: for most of the three million Negroes along the Southern frontier, the new era of hope has not yet yielded meaningful changes in terms of daily existence. Nevertheless, in Arkansas and Louisiana as well as in Oklahoma and Texas, the glacial pace of change shows signs of quickening. Negroes are increasingly visible in decision-making bodies, sitting on school boards and in appointive state positions, some arguing hopefully, others with rising impatience. It is too early to judge interracial prospects with certainty—doubtless a number of storms are yet to come. If the elusive past provides any insight into this most subtle of issues, the people of the South Central States will thaw at many different speeds.

In the quest for enduring specifics, one is left with the original starting point—the land itself. The years since Appomattox have somewhat softened the hostile plains environment, but men still respond to it as their grandfathers did. When the great tide of post-Civil War migration lapped onto the Great Plains, the refugees from the postwar despair of the Confederacy either adjusted to the new ways of the West or retreated in defeat to more familiar climes. Those who remained discovered that the plains wind worked always, driving prairie sand into the houses, splintering the edges of the clapboards and opening tiny, unseen fissures in the corner posts. The sandy land sifted into the shuttered rooms, into shirt and apron, into skin pores. Things weathered to a sameness. In another time, men would spray asphalt over the long, prairie-straight wagon trails and throw up brick siding against the stabbing sand. But the effect on the people would be the same. The wind, endless, unengageable, would still haunt the women and leave the men feeling strangely diminished. The plains wind would intimidate, as in the earlier time, and restless people would feel a need to proclaim their own identities. They would want to shout, to make any kind of loud noise to assert their presence. That much, at least, would be the same.

Today, with the diversity of nearly 20 million minds, the people of the South Central States are continuing their quest to find a style of life appropriate both to their enduring land and to the changing times. Whatever the future holds for them, one knows they will agree on no single response to it. They will merely engage their fate, as they have always done, with both the energy and the diversity of purpose that is their heritage.

A region with many faces

From New Orleans, southeasternmost city in the South Central States, there sweeps to the north and west a land of constantly changing topography, climate and vegetation. Low and swampy in the southeast, the land rises into the craggy Ozark and Ouachita Highlands of Arkansas and into the vast and arid High Plains of West Texas. As the land rises, rainfall decreases, from more than 60 inches a year in New Orleans to eight inches or less in El Paso.

These changes inevitably alter the color of the landscape: the jungle green in the east fades to desert brown in the west. But the progression is not a steady one. Geographers have divided the region into nine areas, each bearing a technical designation. These areas, each with its special characteristics, are indicated on the maps accompanying the pictures on the following pages.

A hunter peers down the jagged face of Cameron's Bluff on Mount Magazine, Arkansas, in the heart of the Ozark and Ouachita Highlands *(map on page 18)*. The two rugged ranges, separated by the Arkansas River Valley *(background)*, are a center for tourism.

A serpentine earth levee separates paddies near Stuttgart, the center of Arkansas rice farming. The area not only provides the great quantities of water needed for growing rice, but also is underlaid with hardpan, a clay that forms a waterproof seal under the paddies.

A bag of cotton, the last of a long day of picking, provides a seat for a woman worker as she waits to have it weighed on a farm in eastern Arkansas. There is still much hand labor in this section, but low profit margins are forcing landowners to mechanize.

A shift of emphasis
on the lower Mississippi

The lower Mississippi Valley is a fertile alluvial plain 50 to 100 miles wide and more than 400 miles long. The silt laid down by the river, combined with the area's 50-inch annual rainfall, has made the valley west of the river into prime cotton country since numbers of settlers came in the early 1900s. The people who work the land are mostly sharecroppers who do the farming and harvesting in return for a small share—$200 to $300 a year—of the profits.

Although cotton is still a principal cash crop, a boom in rice farming that began after World War II has given the area a welcome crop diversity. In the paddies seeding is often done by airplane and harvesting is entirely mechanized. Workers generally do not live on the farms, but commute from nearby communities, and are relatively affluent compared to the cotton sharecroppers. Rice farming, in turn, has led to an even newer industry—fish farming. Every third year, when the paddies lie fallow, the flooded fields are stocked with catfish, minnows or crayfish to provide an additional source of income.

Rice, sugar and bird life in a marshy crescent

Curving 600 miles along the shore of the Gulf of Mexico from the Mississippi delta to Corpus Christi, Texas, is the Gulf Coast Lowland. The eastern portion, where rainfall averages 64 inches, contains the fields that produce one third of the nation's sugar cane. Farther west is the Texas rice belt; although rainfall here is somewhat less, the swampy land provides natural paddies and produces one fourth of the U.S. rice crop. Spotted along the entire strip are scores of bird sanctuaries that shelter the millions of North American waterfowl that use the Gulf Coast for their wintering ground.

A machine called a field loader lifts a bundle of sugar-cane stalks atop a wagon on a Louisiana plantation. During World War II, machinery designed to operate in the marshy fields was developed; today the state has the only mechanized cane fields in the world.

Waterfowl take off from a lagoon in the Rockefeller Wildlife Refuge in Louisiana. At the other end of the Gulf Coast Lowland, north of Corpus Christi, is the Aransas National Wildlife Refuge, best known as the winter home of the almost-extinct whooping crane.

The low, rolling hills of the Piney Woods

Between the swamplands of the Gulf Coast Lowland and the Ouachita Mountains to the north is the well-watered and well-drained Pine Belt, technically known as the Gulf Slope, but in Texas called the Piney Woods. Throughout most of the 19th Century, lumbering was a big business in the area, but by the beginning of World War I the forests were nearly exhausted. Following the general practice, stands of trees had been felled with no thought to selective cutting or reforestation; consequently, the lumbering industry came almost to a standstill. In the 1920s and 1930s, however, the forests partially reseeded themselves, and lumbering began again, now using scientific management techniques. Today the Gulf Slope supports an industry so profitable that many farmers are forsaking traditional crops and turning their fields into tree nurseries.

In the woodlands of the Pine Belt, loblolly pines, one of the five species common to the area, rise to heights of 80 to 100 feet. The trees, which mature more rapidly than northern varieties, are used to produce plywood, construction beams and pulp paper.

At dawn a fisherman readies his tackle for a day of angling on Caddo Lake, which straddles the Texas-Louisiana border. Hundreds of lakes and ponds throughout the Pine Belt keep the hills drained and help maintain the water table at a constant level.

23

His tractor-drawn plow biting deep into the waxy, lustrous black soil, a farmer turns the earth of his Blackland farm near Greenville, Texas, preparing his fields for the spring planting of corn. Corn raised in this part of Texas is used as cattle fodder.

The rich, productive earth of the Blackland

West of the Southwestern Prairies, which stretch from San Antonio, Texas, to somewhat beyond Tulsa, Oklahoma, the land is too dry to farm without irrigation. But the broad reaches of the prairies themselves get enough rainfall to support certain crops unaided. And the heart of this fertile belt is the Blackland, a strip of dark, rich prairie soil.

The rainfall in the Blackland averages only 32 inches a year, but this is sufficient for farming because the limy, clayey topsoil holds water tenaciously. The first crop in the area was cotton; in the early years of the 20th Century the Blackland led the nation in production of the fiber. But decades of cotton growing have begun to exhaust the soil, and in recent years farming has become diversified. Today fields of sorghum, soybeans and corn flourish there, and the soil is slowly reviving.

Perched on tall ladders, migrant workers in a citrus grove near Brownsville pick fruit from the highest branches. This warm, sun-splashed strip along the Rio Grande has yielded oranges and grapefruit since it was settled by the Spaniards in the 18th Century.

Sheep scamper from their pens after receiving inoculations at a ranch near the border town of Del Rio. The largest sheep market in the United States, Del Rio marks the end of the low prairie country; from here the land rises to the great Edwards Plateau.

26

Dry, dusty plains
spotted with greenery

Dry, dusty and speckled with the slow-moving shapes of cattle and sheep and the hurrying, wind-borne clumps of tumbleweed, the Southwestern Plateaus and Plains sweep from the Gulf Coast Lowland to northwest Texas. The sheep are found to the north, grazing on the tough grass of the high Edwards Plateau. On the prairies to the south lie the cattle ranches, none smaller than 1,000 acres and some covering several hundred thousand acres.

As a result of human industry and ingenuity not all of this area is dusty, and plant life is not limited to prairie grass and mesquite. Along the Rio Grande near Brownsville citrus groves flourish, supported by a massive irrigation complex fed by river water. Farther north, another fruit-growing area, forming a semicircle around Laredo, also draws its water from the Rio Grande. And between Laredo and San Antonio along the Nueces River is the 40-mile-long strip called the Winter Garden, where the growing season is an average of 11 months long and four vegetable crops are harvested each year.

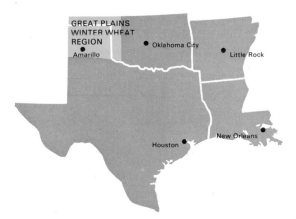

GREAT PLAINS
WINTER WHEAT
REGION
● Amarillo ● Oklahoma City ● Little Rock
● Houston ● New Orleans

The flat, dry,
productive panhandles

Forming a rectangle in the northwest corner of the
South Central States are the Texas and Oklahoma
Panhandles. Dry and isolated, the area—actually part of the Great Plains Winter Wheat Region,
which stretches into Kansas and Nebraska—was
one of the last in the U.S. to be settled, and it remains one of the least densely populated sections.

Despite a rainfall that averages only 20 inches a
year, the area has proved itself well able to support
ample crops of winter wheat, and the flour-fine soil
is laid upon a terrain so flat that fully 90 per cent
of it is arable. Farms tend to be large—the average is 1,000 acres—and highly mechanized. Because of the dry climate, half the farmland must
lie fallow each year so that water may accumulate.

Chest-deep in winter wheat, Clarence Krigbaum surveys a bumper
crop on his Hobart, Oklahoma, farm. Winter wheat is planted in Sep-
tember or October. The first sprouts appear after the first fall or
winter rainfall. It is mature and ready for harvesting in June.

On a plantation near Lubbock, a mechanical picker blows cotton bolls into a wagon *(below)*. As irrigation has opened up more land to cultivation, farms have expanded steadily on grazing land to the west—while farmers to the east diversify by raising cattle.

The Great Plains: a land transformed

Stretching northward from San Angelo, Texas, past Oklahoma's northern border and far into Kansas and Nebraska is the huge tract of land known as the Great Plains Range. The Texas-Oklahoma section of the range was long given over solely to the raising of cattle, for the annual rainfall of less than 20 inches is insufficient for agriculture.

But in the mid-1940s came the discovery that beneath the bone-dry surface lay a sandy subsoil laden with water. Since then thousands of wells have tapped these underground sources; given sufficient moisture, the thin blanket of overlying loam has been made to yield rich harvests of cotton and grain sorghum. Lubbock County, center of the area, grew from 32,000 in 1940 to 130,000 in 1960.

Irrigated fields, watered by artesian wells, form neat rectangles on farms near Plainview, Texas. The strips of green in the foreground and at right are rows of cotton. At left is the darker green of grain sorghum and at upper right is the light green of soybeans.

31

The Trans-Pecos,
unchanged by time

In the western spur of Texas is the untamed, legendary land of the cowboy, known as the Trans-Pecos, or "West of the Pecos," but technically called the Southern Desertic Basins, Plains and Mountains. Legends abound of men tough enough to survive in the dusty badlands beyond the Pecos River; "the fastest gun west of the Pecos" was the fastest gun anywhere. Monuments to those men and their times—ghost towns, abandoned stagecoach stations and ruined forts—remain, well preserved in the dry heat. It is still cattle country, and ranches average 25,000 acres. The prairie grass is tough and nutritious but so sparse that each steer needs 150 acres to graze on; local lore has it that "a jack rabbit has to graze at a lope to get enough to keep from starving."

Under the burning Trans-Pecos sun a cowboy drives a herd of white-faced Herefords through a dry stream bed, or arroyo, that serves as a passage through the rock-studded, dun-colored hills that can support only grasses and cactus, yucca and creosote bushes.

32

The storming of the Alamo by 5,000 Mexican soldiers under Antonio Lopez de Santa Anna is depicted in this 19th Century painting. It is the final day of the 13-day siege, and Mexicans are attacking from all directions. In the north *(right background)*, puffs of smoke rise following a fusillade of Mexican artillery fire; cavalry *(far right)* and infantry *(right foreground)* are nearing the walls; one detachment has already breached the outer wall and is approaching the wall ringing the inner courtyard *(left)*. The American force, numbering fewer than 200, maintains a steady but futile fire from the roofs of the two buildings.

2

An Embattled Past

The frontier South may be characterized as one vast crossroads. People have been milling about in it and passing through it for the better part of 400 years, jousting with the natives and with those who passed through earlier, and generally changing most of the traffic rules. The result is a rather disorganized history that is open to a number of interpretations. The region's sole enduring prophet has been Thomas Jefferson, whose graceful radical-progressive-conservative cast of mind has left a little something for everyone to call his own.

But whether the signposts are clear or not, the region is a crossroads. In fact, the Southwest entered upon the stage of history because it became the meeting point of two thrusts by Old World colonial powers, the French working down the Mississippi from Canada and the Spanish pushing up out of Mexico. Before they first crossed tentatively in the Piney Woods of East Texas, each had begun the long process of empire and culture building that was to deposit a lasting Latin influence on sizable portions of the Gulf Southwest.

The first meaningful exploration came in 1540 when the Spanish conquistador Francisco de Coronado first probed north of the Rio Grande on his futile search for the gold-garnished Seven Cities of Cíbola. Another Spaniard, Hernando de Soto, soon entered the crossroads from the east, making his way from Florida all the way to the Red River in 1541. These two ventures gave Spain first claim to a huge territory, but as nearly all later arrivals also found out, the Spanish discovered that the residents were an ornery lot who did not like newcomers and refused to change their ways. The Comanche Indians, and to a lesser extent the Apache, laid down a barricade of hostility across Texas. For more than 200 years the Spanish alternately battered against this barricade from the south or turned their energies toward California, where the natives were rather more hospitable.

While the conquistadors were trying to breach the Comanche barrier to the north, the French began to build in a crescent of the Mississippi River what was to be their shining New World jewel, the city of New Orleans. In the same year that New Orleans was founded, 1718, the Spaniards built as their own bastion a fortified mission at a site 500 miles to the west: San Antonio.

Thus two of America's most distinctive cities were laid down as pawns in the game of Old World colonialism. The French and Spanish founders of New Orleans and San Antonio very early launched a regional folkway their Anglo-Saxon successors were to improve upon—the art of self-promotion. They may even have had the same reason: a little deception seemed necessary to persuade anyone at all to come to this part of the world. In fact, Coronado himself was the first victim of an enthusiastic Southwestern brag. His incredible two-year, 4,000-mile journey from Mexico City to Kansas and back was directly motivated by the fanciful tales of an exploring Franciscan friar who claimed to have stood on a hilltop and seen with his own eyes the Seven Cities of Cíbola, all in gold.

As was to happen to so many who came after him, Coronado found the reality to be something less than advertised—the seven "cities" were mud-covered Indian villages, quite ungilded. Nevertheless, his conquistadors did encounter the Grand Canyon, the Continental Divide, herds of buffalo they called "humpbacked oxen" and the billowing prairies of Kansas. Though he had completed one of the great marches in history, Coronado returned to Mexico City "very sad and very weary, completely worn out and shame-faced," the first dupe of a western land tout.

It was not until the Frenchman who had discovered the mouth of the Mississippi, Robert Cavelier, Sieur de La Salle, forayed into East Texas in the 1680s that the Spanish were galvanized into a consolidation of their Texas holdings. The two colonial powers almost collided at Texas' Matagorda Bay, where the Spanish in 1689 discovered Fort Saint Louis, a small bastion erected by La Salle four years

earlier. The Spanish hurriedly built forts of their own in the area and made ready to defend their Texas claims. But they were spared this task. Whatever Texas ambitions the French may have had lapsed after La Salle was killed by his own men while leading them on a disastrous march through East Texas. After 1690 the crossroads' two claimants settled down in their own parts of the region, the Spanish in Texas and the French in Louisiana.

Spreading out along the Mississippi, the French soon tried their hand at the art of inspirational rhetoric. Promoters of the royal-chartered Mississippi Company, seeking settlers for their fledgling colony, handbilled the European Continent with rhapsodic descriptions of a new land where gold and silver were so abundant the nuggets might be used as paving stones. The frontier realities, of course, were quite another matter, as men such as the competent French colonial administrator Jean Baptiste Le Moyne, Sieur de Bienville soon learned. Sickness and hunger coursed through the French outposts in the Louisiana lowlands, presaging the deadly plagues that were to wrack New Orleans in the 19th Century. The experience of the early settlers conflicted so dramatically with the promises of royal stockjobbers that immigration faltered and the Mississippi Company collapsed.

However, the French had already found a more typically Gallic solution to the problem of settling their colony. Beginning in 1704 and continuing intermittently for more than 40 years, shiploads of girls were imported from France. Although many of the young ladies came from La Salpêtrière, a house of correction in Paris, much romantic Louisiana lore has accrued over the years to establish their genteel origins. A group of 88 girls arriving in 1721 was accompanied by three nuns, but also by a midwife who came to be known as *La Sans Regret* (No Regrets). Notwithstanding Bienville's sour appraisal of their conduct and character ("these girls were not well selected . . . whatever the vigilance exercised upon them, they could not be restrained"), the young women were allowed to stay in Louisiana and most were quickly mated. In the words of a contemporary, "This merchandise was soon disposed of, so great was the want of the country."

In 1728 Ursuline sisters of a New Orleans convent served as chaperones for another group of arriving girls who, in time, came to occupy a special place in Louisiana tradition. As each carried her belongings in a little chest called a *cassette*, the young ladies became known as "casket girls." Although horrified by the unexpectedly primitive surroundings and outspoken in their desire to return to France by the

Smoke pouring from their funnels, Mississippi River steamers prepare to sail from the central New Orleans levee, or dock. This print, made from an 1883 painting, shows the levee piled with cargo on its way to or from the many ports along the Mississippi for which New Orleans was the commercial center. This great levee—the city had many others—was divided into three parts, one handling grain, a second cotton and a third sugar. In the years before the founding of commercial exchanges, trading in these commodities took place right on the dock. The levee was also a great concourse for travelers, from sophisticated St. Louis businessmen to rough frontiersmen and trappers. Fast luxury steamers like the *Natchez (second from left)* were the belles of the river. Because of their ornate decoration, such steamers were often called "floating wedding cakes," but they were also practical craft. Drawing very little water, they could negotiate the many shallow stretches of the Mississippi.

next boat, the casket girls settled for the simpler alternative of finding husbands. The rush to the altar was, in fact, precipitate. The abundance of surplus men in the colony insured a number of controversies, and an armed sentinel was finally employed to protect the "merchandise" from overeager suitors. Finally, when all but one of the girls had been spoken for, two young men challenged each other to a duel to decide who should get her—although an ungallant observer described the girl as being so ugly she looked "more like a soldier on duty than a lady." The Commandant-General of New Orleans settled the affair peaceably by having the rivals draw straws for her hand.

In something like this manner the French gradually subdued the Louisiana wilderness. New Orleans became a lively transportation center—a crossroads within the crossroads. Wheat, corn and whiskey floated down the Mississippi on flatboats and out to the world in New Orleans-based ships. Meanwhile, human commerce flowed in from all directions. The Code Noir, or black legal code, of 1724 attested to the presence of Negro slaves; German colonists settled along a 40-mile stretch of riverfront, Spanish migrants poured in from the Canary Islands; and, in the 1750s, French-speaking Acadians began their fabled flight from British rule in

Nova Scotia, immortalized in Longfellow's poem *Evangeline*, and settled in southern Louisiana. Finally, in the years after 1776, die-hard American Tories fleeing the Revolutionary 13 colonies settled in Feliciana Parish, adding a bit of English flavor to the Continental milieu of Louisiana.

The cosmopolitan tone of modern New Orleans dates from these years when a new kind of American was created in the mid-continent wilderness: the Creole. With the French-speaking Creole, the modern Southwest begins. His quixotic stubbornness and penchant for myth making established a style of life that has characterized the frontier South down to the present.

The Creole is a curious anomaly, his origins shrouded in some controversy and his history encased in nostalgia. In the words of one Louisiana historian, "romantic folklore, filial pride and uncritical if effusive writings have hidden these people behind a mythological fog which even today it is socially dangerous to try to penetrate."

Most proud old New Orleans families still look back on a heritage of Creole glory when men and women of grace and culture ruled the Mississippi delta before being overwhelmed by crude, money-grubbing *Americains* from upriver. According to tradition, the Louisiana Creoles are supposed to have been descended from French and Spanish aristocrats. But it seems clear that the Creoles were the products of French and Spanish colonists from all levels of society, including those untouched by aristocratic refinements. When the Spanish assumed control of the colony in 1763, they were able to establish only the most fragile authority over their resistant French subjects, and the French language and French customs—altered by several generations of raw frontier living—continued to dominate the life of the city. Always outnumbered, the Spanish tended to be assimilated through the intermarriages that occurred among all segments of the population and its occupying soldiery. Perhaps the clearest Spanish influence came after 1788 when four fifths of New Orleans burned down and its rebuilding incorporated several styles of Spanish architecture.

Whatever the impact on them of the Spanish, the Creoles made a distinct, indeed unique, impact on the history of the South and Southwest: they fathered *les gens de couleur libres*—free men of color. Beginning in the 18th Century and culminating in the "Quadroon Balls" of the 19th, the Creoles developed an elaborate and contradictory policy toward the Negroes. Perhaps it can be said that the Creole men developed one policy and the Creole women another. At all events, contact between people of different color became so common and so total that at least one modern Louisiana historian has concluded that "very few full-blooded Negroes are to be found in the state." In the South, *liaisons sans mariage* with Negro women were not unusual; what distinguished the Creoles' approach was their sense of responsibility toward the children of such affairs. At a time when it was a serious offense anywhere else in the South to teach a slave to read, the mulatto children of Creole men were given educations, sometimes in France, and were recognized as free men when they reached manhood.

In time a literary magazine, *L'Album Littéraire*, was published by free Negroes in New Orleans, and *Les Cenelles* became the first anthology of Negro verse published in America. But to some free Negroes, a life of half dignity in a white society was unbearable under any terms. Colonies of mulattoes developed at Leonville in southern Louisiana and at Isle Brevelle on the Cane River. The mulattoes lived apart from both the white planters and Negroes around them and some owned large plantations staffed with slaves.

At the time the *Américains* began descending on New Orleans after the Louisiana Purchase, the city's population was a potpourri of free Negroes, Negro slaves and whites who were mostly French-speaking.

As with the abortive Spanish effort 40 years earlier, the Americans' attempt to introduce a new language and strange customs met a rather stubborn Gallic resistance. Responding to the threat of Americanization, Creoles clustered in their own part of the city, the Vieux Carré, or Old Square, that subsequently became famous as New Orleans' French Quarter. Incoming Americans lived upstream in an area then called the Faubourg Ste. Marie, which remained for a time a completely distinct suburb.

Dominating the commercial life of New Orleans, the Creoles continued to make French the language of commerce and simply ignored wherever possible the bureaucrats dispatched by the U.S. government. Creole men gathered in saloons or coffeehouses known as "bourses" after business hours and kept abreast of world events through their own French-language newspapers.

The first American census, taken in 1810, underscored the city's continuing function as a frontier crossroads. The census revealed that the already mixed population of 17,000 included some 6,000 Negro and white refugees from recent civil strife in Santo Domingo. The U.S. Congress had to ponder the fact that in the proposed new state of Louisiana, with its Creoles, Acadians, Canary Islanders, Spaniards, Germans and Dominicans, a great majority of the population could not speak a coherent English sentence. Congress overlooked this detail and made Louisiana a state in 1812. The terms of statehood gave striking evidence of the Creoles' tenacity. Louisiana came into the Union trailing the French judicial system, the Code Napoléon, which remains the basis of Louisiana law to the present day.

The War of 1812 brought the Creoles and Americans closer together, united against the common British enemy. When large bodies of British troops approached New Orleans, a great patriotic fervor swept the city. The "*Marseillaise*" and "Yankee Doodle" both rang through the streets, a bilingual harbinger of the most bizarre army ever assembled on the continent. General Andrew Jackson's forces included a battalion of free Negroes, scouts who were Choctaw Indians, regiments of Creoles and a group of Tennessee mountaineers. As added leavening, Jackson counted among his warriors all the available pirates from Jean Lafitte's band of French-Spanish-American-Portuguese-English rogues.

On January 8, 1815, these 5,000 assorted Americans broke the assault of 8,000 to 9,000 British infantry with well-placed artillery fire. The British casualties were 291 dead, 1,262 wounded and 484 missing. Jackson's force of amateurs counted 13 dead, 39 wounded and 19 missing. From that day forward, Creole preferences notwithstanding, New Orleans' place was secure in American history.

The great days of New Orleans were yet to come —and they would not be exclusively Creole days. The first steamboat docked in the city in 1812. By 1830 almost a thousand craft were plying the Mississippi, and the 1840 population of 102,000 ranked New Orleans as the fourth-largest U.S. city. As the steamboat traffic poured wealth into New Orleans, more and more American merchants became leaders of the city's commerce, and built for themselves a suburb of elegant town houses in the Garden District, upriver from the Vieux Carré. During these last ante bellum years, the Creoles fought a losing battle against these businesslike Americans and against the sheer numbers of English-speaking immigrants. After the Civil War their plight became worse. Amidst the postwar poverty that afflicted the entire South, an impoverished Creole gentry had to forego trips abroad and was forced to place its sons in the public schools of New Orleans. There, American youngsters laughed at the curious accents of the Creole children, ridiculed their dress and manners, and, to some degree at least, undermined the pride the Creoles had long felt in their French heritage. Soon, the Vieux Carré was occupied by Negroes, who subsequently were to give the world the gift of jazz. Then, one by one, the bourses were shuttered. Pride alone sustained the final bastion— the last French-language newspaper, *L'Abeille*. It hung on until 1925. New Orleans had become English, Irish, Negro and Italian—that is to say, it had become an American city.

However, in passing, the Creoles established what appears to be a permanent place in the affections of Louisianans, perhaps one that transcends even the nostalgia felt for that other famous "Lost Cause," the Confederacy. One Louisiana historian says flatly: "The commiseration . . . for the death of the ante-bellum South has been as nothing compared to [the] mourning over the fate of the Creole."

Now that all the wars and occupations, commercial dislocations and Quadroon Balls are past, we can ask what kind of person was the Creole. Was he exclusively French, or Franco-Spanish, or part Anglo-American? Aristocrat or frontiersman? Orthodox Southerner or man of the Western world?

Scholarly inquiry into Creole history in recent years has done considerable violence to the traditional picture of a race of Latin Louisianans who specialized in good wine, fine food, handsome women, the ball, the opera and the hunt. In the early years the Creoles were a frontier people who, though largely of French extraction, were not immune to such rustic shortcomings as illiteracy and primitive manners. They themselves seldom used the term "Creole" to denote a person of aristocracy. Writing in the *Journal of Southern History*, Joseph G. Tregle Jr. quietly observes: "It is abundantly clear that in the 1820s and 1830s 'Creole' was generally used in Louisiana to designate any person native to the state, be he white, black, or colored, French, Spanish or Anglo-American." Even though they were increasingly outnumbered by newcomers, the Creoles endeavored to speak for all the "natives," even including Anglo-Americans who had been born in Louisiana. The irony of Creole history is that the days of Creole eclipse were the great days of New Orleans—when the city thrived on its Yankee-run river traffic and built the stately theaters and opera houses that, in retrospect, have been seen to symbolize the flowering of Creole culture.

In short, the mystique of the aristocratic Creole dates from the time the *ancienne population* first felt threatened by the Americans, and it gathered emotional force over the years as the threat became all too real. Thus the romantic tradition of a graceful, charming Creole past may be viewed as evidence of the determination of a proud and embattled people not to become forgotten in their own land. Part of their method of preserving their identity was a conscious disassociation from the Americans they saw around them, however much their grandfathers might have resembled, in frontier manners as well as commercial aspirations, those same Americans.

No aspect of Creole life has attracted more nostalgia, or discussion, than the Quadroon Balls. Over the years these balls have grown in dimension so that today they are remembered as opulent affairs where urbane, French-speaking mulatto mistresses could make "arrangements" for their daughters to insure a certain maintenance of status into the next generation. And it is true that at least some of the Quadroon Balls matched in politesse the white affairs that were held in the same ballrooms. A visiting German Duke attended both the quadroon celebrations and the fashionable masked balls at the Orleans Ballroom and pronounced the quadroon soirees the "much more decent" of the two.

It is difficult to assess, however, the degree to which Louisiana tradition is correct in affirming that many Creole men lived openly with their mulatto mistresses in little houses on Rampart Street while maintaining separate town houses and plantations for their legal spouses. There is, in fact, ample evidence that many of the contracts consummated at the nightly revels were of far shorter

MONTANA
NORTH DAKOTA
MINNESOTA
CANADA
WYOMING
SOUTH DAKOTA
NEBRASKA
IOWA
Louisiana Purchase 1803
COLORADO
KANSAS
MISSOURI
Added to Oklahoma Territory 1890
Sold to U.S. by Texas 1850
OKLAHOMA 1907
Indian Territory 1834-1890
ARKANSAS 1836
Arkansaw Territory 1819
NEW MEXICO
Republic of Texas 1836-1845
(State of Texas 1845-1850)
Territory of Orleans 1804
Added to Louisiana 1812
TEXAS 1845
MEXICO
San Antonio
LOUISIANA 1812
New Orleans
Original Texas settlement 1690s
GULF OF MEXICO

Louisiana Purchase
Arkansaw Territory
Republic of Texas
Texas boundary line of 1816
Line of Adams-Onis Treaty 1819

This map shows how the South Central States were shaped by settlement, treaty and purchase. Spanish settlers in the 1690s occupied a small tract between the Sabine and Trinity Rivers, which they called Tejas, or Texas. By 1816 Spanish holdings had increased considerably. After declaring their independence, the sanguine Texans claimed a still larger area, including parts of New Mexico, Wyoming, Colorado, Kansas and Oklahoma. In 1850, after Texas had become a state and war with Mexico had settled the Texas-Mexico boundary, the present limits of the state were set and Texas ceded disputed lands to the U.S. for $10 million. The other South Central States were carved from the Louisiana Purchase of 1803, indicated above by the thick dotted line. The following year the Territory of Orleans was established, and in 1812 this territory was admitted as Louisiana, the 18th state. In 1819 the Adams-Onís Treaty with Spain fixed the western boundaries of the purchase, and the lands just north of Louisiana were organized into the "Arkansaw Territory" (the name having been misspelled). This territory was reduced in the 1820s to the present area of the state, which was admitted to the Union (the original spelling readopted) in 1836. The area to the west was to remain Indian Territory until 1890 when the twin Oklahoma and Indian Territories were created *(page 64)*. In 1907 these territories became the state of Oklahoma.

duration than tradition would have us believe. A traveler described an 1805 ball as a "Babylon where Creoles, English, Spanish, French, Germans, Italians and Americans drink, dance, and gamble." That ubiquitous French observer of American life Alexis de Tocqueville described the balls as scenes of incredible immorality.

It is certainly true that in the city's complex racial milieu of slaves, free Negroes, Creoles and Americans no group was excluded from participation in the custom of public balls. And these "tricolor balls," as one citizen called them, became a permanent part of New Orleans' social life throughout the first half of the 19th Century. The famed Washington Ballroom divided its time evenly: Mondays, Wednesdays and Saturdays were for whites only; Tuesdays, Thursdays and Sundays were set apart for quadroon dances. The Chartres Street Ballroom on the other hand reserved only Sundays "for white ladies," a circumstance that seems to have reflected the workings of the law of supply and demand. As one participant explained, the white balls were rendered "very boring" by the "dry stiffness of the fine ladies." Quadroon Balls, in contrast, were "marked by gaiety."

In self-defense more and more white women attended Quadroon Balls, at first masked, but soon openly. In 1837 a city governing body made it a penal offense to admit white and colored women at the same time. But there was always recourse to the mask. As the New Orleans *Picayune* frankly admitted: "They go so habited that there is no discovering whether they are black or white." In the 1830s and 1840s efforts were made to hold "chaste and civil" Quadroon Balls for "gentlemen of distinction," but the evidence is conclusive that only the second adjective could have applied.

The political passions that led to the Civil War doomed the Quadroon Balls. In 1855 the police closed the Globe Ballroom, where mixed dances had until then taken place. The further estrangements that came with the war and Reconstruction consigned the custom to its present elusive place in the Creole legends of Louisiana.

In retrospect, the Creoles' tolerance for "tricolored integration" seems to have diminished as their own position in the hierarchy of New Orleans was increasingly threatened. By the time their permanent eclipse by the Americans had become an accomplished fact in the 1870s and 1880s, the Creoles had adopted orthodox Southern racial phobias. The legend of the "chaste and civil" Quadroon Ball, with its implicit aristocratic overtones, then flowered, and with it the modern assertion that no

Negro could have been a Creole. But in their more self-confident days prior to the Civil War, these frontier Frenchmen quite blandly referred to light-skinned Louisiana Negroes as "Creoles."

Before fading from view, the Creoles inaugurated, in addition to a number of myths about their own past, a folkway of frontier assertion that was forever to color the life and politics of the Southwest. For generations they had ignored as best they could the laws of both Spanish and American regimes, and they had installed their own French-based judicial code in the statutes of Louisiana. The same cavalier indifference to laws not of their own making is detectable in the early settlers of Texas. The difference was that in Louisiana, Creole chauvinism was employed as a tactic to hold back the American tide. In Texas, on the other hand, American aggressiveness became the instrument of overwhelming the Spanish.

The men of Spain tried to colonize Texas—the name derives from that of an Indian tribe that the Spaniards called the Tejas—with their own people, but the hostile Western environment seems to have been unsuitable to the Spanish colonial temperament. For one thing, the nomad Comanche remained a far less manageable foe than the Aztecs the Spanish had conquered in Mexico. As late as 1821 only three outposts of civilization existed in all of Texas from the Rio Grande to the Red River. Spain justifiably began to fear that this near-vacuum in Texas would inevitably draw in people from the expanding young American Republic—especially after a series of expeditions into Texas by various frontier adventurers.

Prodded by an enterprising American named Moses Austin, the Spanish decided on a bold gamble. They would permit American immigration on terms so hopefully liberal that the incoming colonists would become loyal to their new Spanish rulers and thus act as a kind of American-Spanish bastion against the U.S. Though Spain lost its hold over Mexico in a series of revolutions ending in 1821, the new Mexican nationalists, facing the same problem of an expansionist U.S., agreed to honor the desperate Spanish expedient.

Led by Moses Austin's son, Stephen F. Austin, thousands of Americans poured into Texas to take advantage of the spacious Mexican land grants. These Americans, who soon began to call themselves Texians (a name later shortened to Texans), quickly spread up and down the river valleys. The liberal constitution promulgated by the victorious Mexican revolutionaries in 1824 gave provinces such as Texas rather full autonomy, a circumstance that suited the land-hungry newcomers just fine. Trouble shortly arose, however, when another coup d'état in Mexico City installed General Antonio Lopez de Santa Anna as dictator in 1834. Moderates such as Austin worked for restoration of the 1824 constitution, which Santa Anna had cast aside, but other Texans called for a declaration of independence that would open millions of acres to speculation and settlement free of Mexican law and Mexican supervision. By 1835 even Austin had bowed to the Texas clamor for armed revolt. Santa Anna promptly moved to quell the uprising.

The Texans won the first major battle late in 1835, capturing San Antonio, but the revolution appeared wrecked by a series of military disasters early the following year. Faced with the task of defending farmland stretching over thousands of square miles, the Texans made the understandable but fatal mistake of spreading their forces too thin, and squabbles among ambitious generals prevented corrective consolidations. Marching up out of Mexico, Santa Anna engaged the scattered detachments piecemeal and won smashing victories.

One of these triumphs, at a small mission near San Antonio, has gone done as one of history's famous battles of annihilation. Late in February 1836 Santa Anna's army of some 5,000 besieged a mission fort known as the Alamo. Among the 150-odd defenders were James Bowie, reputedly the inventor of the all-purpose frontier weapon known as the Bowie knife, and the legendary Davy Crockett. The garrison was commanded by a courageous and stubborn martinet named Colonel William B. Travis. The Texas government ordered the defenders to abandon the fort, but riven by internal disputes between Travis and Bowie, they stayed. As the Alamo's historian Amelia Williams has written, the place "seemed to cast some sort of spell over the Texan leaders." Bowie fell ill with pneumonia on the day Santa Anna arrived before the fort. Travis, in firm command, dispatched couriers with a letter to the people of Texas "and all Americans in the world," appealing for aid and ending with the announcement, "I shall never surrender or retreat . . . Victory or Death!" On March 1 thirty men from Gonzales, answering Travis' call, slipped through the Mexican lines to raise the garrison inside the fort to about 185 men. For 13 days the Alamo defenders withstood the tightening siege. Finally, on March 6, 1836, after repeated bombardments, the walls were breached and Travis' men were overwhelmed. All of the defenders perished.

Before the month was over, other Texas forces were beaten at Refugio and at Coleto Creek. Under

Adventurer, speculator and statesman, the grand old Texas war-horse Sam Houston is shown here in two views. The romantic miniature above was painted in 1830 when Houston, a white Virginian by birth, was serving in Washington as ambassador from the western Cherokee Nation, a post to which he was appointed after spending several years living with the Indians. The cane he holds at right in a photograph taken in 1857, when Houston was a U.S. Senator from Texas, was more than a modish accessory; Houston had been wounded in the leg while leading the Texans in their fight for independence from Mexico in 1836. Houston became first President of the Republic of Texas and served as governor of the state after it was admitted to the Union in 1845.

Santa Anna's orders some 350 Texans who had surrendered in those battles were marched to Goliad and summarily executed. By spring all of East Texas seemed wide open to the mercy of Santa Anna.

Into this desperate situation stepped one of the most unusual men ever to appear on the American frontier, Sam Houston. Houston lived in the midst of controversy and disorder most of his long life, a strange, driven man of incisive intelligence and mercurial passion. An early protégé of Andrew Jackson's and later Governor of Tennessee at the age of 34, he appeared headed for national prominence when he disappeared to live among the Cherokee after an ill-fated 11-week marriage to the daughter of one of Tennessee's most prominent families. Among the Cherokee, Houston enlarged upon his lively passion for strong liquor, developed a deep respect for the Indians' outlook and values, and took an Indian wife. Eventually he showed up in Texas, where his commanding presence and his earthy, no-nonsense manner fitted in well with the frontier—as did his capacity for drinking, fighting and dabbling in land speculation.

Houston was appointed commander in chief of the Texas revolutionary forces while the siege of the Alamo was still in progress. With most of the population fleeing before Santa Anna in panic, the government repeatedly urged Houston to make a stand with his pickup force of 400 men, but he bided his time and ignored the mounting criticism. Hastily training volunteer reinforcements while retreating eastward, he waited for a moment to strike. Meanwhile, Santa Anna overconfidently left large numbers of troops along his lengthening supply lines and divided the remainder.

Near the San Jacinto River on the afternoon of April 21, 1836—six weeks after the Alamo—Houston's army of 900 attacked Santa Anna's main body of 1,200 at siesta time. Gaining complete tactical surprise, Houston achieved that military rarity—total destruction of the enemy army on the field of battle. His report listed 630 killed and all but a handful of the remainder captured, including that self-styled "Napoleon of the West," Santa Anna. The rest of the Mexican troops, leaderless and separated from the defeated main body, fled to Mexico. With one stroke Sam Houston had won Texas its independence.

Several months after his victory at San Jacinto, Houston took office as President of the Republic of Texas. He soon furloughed almost the entire army, which had taken to living off the countryside and, full of frontier bravado, was threatening to invade Mexico. The move effectively halted the incipient threat of a military dictatorship, but it also created among the ex-soldiers the nucleus of political opposition to Houston and soon the republic was divided into Houston and anti-Houston parties. Since the Texas constitution prohibited the President from succeeding himself, Houston could not run after his first term was up, and a candidate of the anti-Houston faction, Mirabeau Lamar, won the 1838 election. However, Houston could legally run after Lamar's term was over, did so, and became President a second time. Thus during its 10-year life, the Texas republic functioned on the alternating currents of contradictory politics. In the years that he was President, Houston avoided Indian wars by the simple expedient of keeping troops out of Indian country, and he took advantage of his experience with the Cherokee to shepherd the young Texas government toward a conciliatory Indian policy. Lamar, on the other hand, pursued an aggressive expansionist program that led to a military disaster at the hands of the Mexicans, war with the Comanche and governmental bankruptcy.

Houston's attitude toward land speculation was typical of the ambivalent style of the man himself. Before his election as President, he had participated in dubious land promotions; as President, he vetoed land schemes and held to a policy that was positively reformist compared to those of other Texas politicians. Indeed, his career appears as an interesting exception to Lord Acton's famous dictum that "power corrupts."

The Texas republic was an experiment in autonomous frontier democracy unique in American history. The resulting chaos was in keeping with the adventurous crossroads temperament of the region. The republic's leaders, from Houston on down, were grandiose in method, irreverent in style and frequently drunk. A Protestant minister who lived in the republic during the postrevolutionary years concluded sadly that the population as a whole was not much interested in "the institutions of Christianity." Presumably to guard the public against designing circuit riders, a clause in the constitution forbade ministers of the Gospel from holding high public office.

But neither this measure nor all of the new republic's laws produced an observable stability. In the Presidential campaign of 1838, two of the candidates committed suicide, including the Chief Justice of the Supreme Court, who had just completed a seven-day drinking bout. In 1838 the Vice President and Attorney General were arraigned for what one observer characterized as "riotous conduct" after "much carousing." In the halls of Congress, fist

fights among the people's representatives further assaulted the dignity of the new democracy.

Throughout the life of the Texas republic, gambling vied with drinking as the chief recreation of the people and land schemes were the principal economic enterprise. But the U.S. government's anti-inflation Specie Circular of 1836, which drove paper money out of circulation and contributed to the nationwide depression of the 1840s, had disastrous consequences for both Texas farmers and land speculators. Almost everyone who had bet his stake on rising land prices was ruined. Thousands had land that they could not give away. The common Texas expression of insolvency—"I'm land-poor" —adequately describes the economy during the days of the republic.

The prevalence of land speculation, gambling and drinking is not, after all, difficult to explain. In Texas during the 1830s and 1840s the very presence of a man was proof of his willingness to take a chance. The frontier did not attract cautious introverts.

On the contrary, such outbreaks as the Shelby County war testified to the ascendancy of uninhibited knavery. By 1839 a number of land pirates, including not a few fugitives from justice, had gained political control over a whole region of East Texas centering on Shelby County. For years they shamelessly manipulated fraudulent land transactions. Finally, a murder growing out of traffic in worthless land certificates created so much tension that friends of the accused and his victim formed rival armies called the Regulators and the Moderators. Though organized ostensibly to suppress crimes, both groups took the field to waylay each other and burn houses and farms. Pitched battles involving hundreds of men took place and, in the words of a local resident, a "reign of terror and dread of impending evil spread themselves like a nightmare over the land." The affair was not ended until 1844 when Sam Houston, serving his second term as President, declared martial law, dispersed both factions and arrested the leaders.

The Shelby County war dramatized, in a vivid fashion, a fact about the Texas frontier that had a thousand individual examples—the simple truth that property was more precious to the frontiersman than human life. As a Texas doctor wrote at the time, "the killing of a fellow was looked upon with greater leniency than theft." The frontier aversion to stealing was reflected in the harshness of the criminal code, which prescribed death for horse theft, robbery or burglary and whipping and branding for larceny. Grand larceny (such as the theft of a hog) was punishable by 39 lashes, while crimes of

Two fearsome frontier weapons commonly used in the 19th Century are shown in the drawings at right. The Bowie knife, designed by an Arkansas blacksmith, was named for Jim Bowie, a smuggler, speculator and all-around fighting man; it had a formidable 14-inch blade with a sharpened, curved top edge designed for ripping and slashing. Legend says that Bowie, en route to Texas with the first model of the knife in 1831, fell into an ambush and escaped from it by using the weapon to behead one assailant, split the skull of a second and disembowel a third. After that gruesome story got around, the knife became extremely popular; few frontiersmen went without one. The Bowie was useful primarily for hand-to-hand combat, however; when a man wanted a knife that could also be thrown, he often chose a stiletto-like Arkansas Toothpick, the second most popular fighting knife on the frontier.

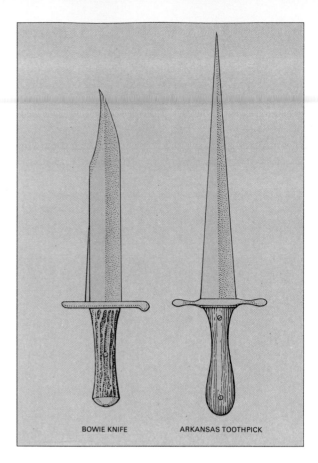

BOWIE KNIFE   ARKANSAS TOOTHPICK

petit larceny drew five to 20 lashes. The absence of jails led to an "either-or" psychology of kill 'em or whup 'em and the dearth of local police gave rise to vigilantes and lynchings. The attitude of quick revenge persisted long after the institutions of justice came to the frontier, and its residue is not hard to detect in the states of the Southern frontier today.

Yet for all its rascality, intemperance, violence and official corruption, the Texas republic established a workable, though impoverished, frontier democracy. Gradually, the land titles were sorted out, peaceably or otherwise, and the river valleys filled with settlers from the United States. The times were hard, but people assured one another that their circumstances were only temporary. Since money was scarce to the point of being nonexistent, trading in goods was elevated to a high art. An awed visitor from Germany wrote: "Boys from eight to ten years old participated in bartering . . . and showed a shrewdness seldom found in boys of the same age in Germany. A Texan is ready at any moment, even while traveling, to trade or sell anything he wears, whether it be his coat or shirt. . . . He has no conception of becoming attached to an article."

No one moved more easily through this environment than the republic's most esteemed public man, Sam Houston. He once made a "grand speech" to a temperance society by the simple device of focusing upon his own extensive and continuing case history. Summing up his sodden past, he admonished his hearers to do as he advised, not as he had done. On another occasion, the President's temperance message was reported—possibly by an overzealous political ally—as "chaste and appropriate and many passages were eloquent and thrilling." Sometimes, however, the duality of public life and private habit merged inauspiciously, the salutary effect of Sam's words being somewhat diminished by his subsequent conduct while intoxicated.

Drunk or sober, Houston represented as much as any Texan the conscience of the frontier republic. During President Lamar's crisis-ridden term, Colonel James Morgan, an observer of Texas politics, colorfully summed up the case for putting "Old Sam" back in office: "We have a bad state of affairs here now—Lamar the poor imbecile could not hold out and had to give up the helm of State to Burnet —who is even more worthless . . . Old Sam H. with all his faults appears to be the only man for Texas —He is still unsteady . . . but drunk in a ditch [he] is worth a thousand of Lamar and Burnet."

The era of the republic ended in 1845 when Texas entered the American Union. But the annexation of Texas had sweeping national ramifications, leading to the Mexican War of 1846 and finally to the addition of much of the West to the territory of the United States. It also heightened the tensions caused by the slavery issue, which moved toward a climax in the late 1850s.

Sam Houston watched with unease the growth of secessionist sentiment in the South. As U.S. Senator from Texas, he supported the admission of Oregon as a free-soil territory and voted against the Kansas-Nebraska Bill opening new territory to slavery. Both votes made Houston a special target of Southern proslavery forces, and in 1857, when he returned from Washington to run for governor, he got no support from his own Democratic Party and had to campaign as an independent. The effort failed, but two years later, with civil war threatening the nation, he again announced for governor in a desperate effort to rally Unionist sentiment in Texas. The political climate was passionate and brutal, but though nearing 70 Houston stumped the state, braved hecklers and energetically recited his case against war. Incredibly, considering the emotions of the times, he was elected and took office determined to hold Texas for the Union.

In early 1861, as the Southern states seceded and devoted Unionists fell silent, Houston continued to speak for the Union across the state. In Galveston the crowd that gathered for his address was in such an ugly mood that friends begged him not to appear. He shrugged them off and an admiring observer later described the result: "There he stood, an old man of seventy years, on the balcony ten feet above the heads of thousands . . . leaving the hearers impressed with the feeling that more of his power was hidden than revealed." Houston's presence had always had a certain power over Texans and now, in the unexpected silence, his words carried clearly: "Some of you laugh to scorn the idea of bloodshed as the result of secession. But let me tell you what is coming. . . . Your fathers and husbands, your sons and brothers, will be herded at the point of the bayonet. . . . You may . . . as a bare possibility, win Southern independence . . . but I doubt it . . . the North is determined to preserve this Union. They are not a fiery, impulsive people as you are, for they live in colder climates. But when they begin to move . . . they move with the steady momentum and perseverance of a mighty avalanche; and what I fear is, they will overwhelm the South."

But though Houston could still make Texans listen, he could no longer convince them. On March 14 a secessionist convention voted 109 to 2 to require all Texas officeholders to swear allegiance to the Confederacy. Sam Houston refused, the office of governor was declared vacant, and Lieutenant Governor Edward Clark, pledging loyalty to the Confederacy, was declared governor.

On his last day in office before being deposed, the aging warrior wrote for the last time as leader of the Texans. In words that recalled his old mentor Andrew Jackson, he said: "I have seen patriots and statesmen of my youth one by one gathered to their fathers and the government which they have reared rent in twain. . . . I stand the last almost of my race." Then, increasingly alone, he retired to his home near Huntsville, in East Texas. In March of 1863, as the nation made ready for the bloody third summer of civil war, he made his last public speech: "Once I dreamed of an empire, as vast and expansive for a united people as the bounds of American civilization. The dream is over. Let us gather up the links that remain to us and encircling them with our hearts, swear to resist to the last that worst of all tyranny, fraternal hate."

Four months later, he died—in the same month that Vicksburg fell to Ulysses S. Grant and Pickett's charge expired in the artillery hell of Cemetery Ridge at Gettysburg. In both eastern and western battle areas the fate of the Confederacy was sealed, although the war Houston tried to prevent—and whose outcome he had predicted—dragged on for two more years.

The Texas of Sam Houston's day changed rapidly following the Civil War. The destructive four-year conflict did more than end the institution of slavery; it made the South little more than a colony of the North in the reconstituted economics of the nation. Lacking capital for seed, impoverished farmers pledged their crops to the "furnish merchants," who furnished their needs at high interest. When they lost their land in the agricultural depressions of the 1870s and 1880s, they descended into the humiliating world of landless tenantry. In desperation Negro and white farmers by the thousands drove down the plank roads and rutted trails of the rural South, westward across the Mississippi and into the Arkansas plateau, into the Louisiana back country, out onto the Texas prairies. The population of Texas and Arkansas soared in the decade of the 1870s —Texas alone leaping from 800,000 to 1,600,000— and still the caravans of the poor came on.

Finally, the wagons moved farther west until they entered the treeless world of the Great Plains. There, the men and women of the South discovered that Georgia plows flattened when they struck the outcrops of limestone on the plateaus; settlers waited in vain for the familiar rains they had known in the Old South. There seemed no remedy for the rampant poverty; in an era of declining farm prices, hard work only produced greater debt to the banks and furnish merchants. A great wave of anguish swept the Texas frontier. Out of that pain grew a new species of American political animal—the agrarian radical bent on revolutionary change.

The revolt of the farmers that culminated in the Populist movement of the 1890s had its origins in the frontier county of Lampasas, Texas, in the year 1877 with the founding of the Farmers' Alliance. This movement of cooperative self-help against the hated "bankers and capitalists" spread like wildfire up and down the frontier, then gradually eastward across Texas. By 1891 the Texas alliance had organized the poorest class of farmers into a vast structure of suballiances that counted more than 200,000 members. The movement uncovered an array of talented, evangelical orators of dissent. Men with names like "Stump" Ashby and "Cyclone" Davis fanned out across the South, West and Midwest to lay before the nation's farmers their vision of a complete restructuring of the U.S. economy, including the curbing of monopolies, the revamping of financial institutions, and government ownership of communication and transportation facilities. With the alliance as its organizational nucleus, the People's Party was formed in 1892 on a national basis. But a third-party movement founded on agrarian radicalism was doomed by the sheer vigor of the industrialization that had already begun to turn America into an urban-oriented society. The Populists, with all their wild and generous dreams, soon passed from the American political scene.

However, Populism along the Southern frontier left one positive legacy that was to help the region over some difficult hurdles in the mid-20th Century. This was the tradition of interracial political activity that the Populists daringly sponsored among white farmers. Negro and white Populist speakers worked together through the decade of the 1890s. On the Southern frontier, where this interracial character of Populism had been particularly strong, it became possible for 20th Century political dissenters to challenge the entrenched one-party statehouse regimes without resorting to the race issue.

To outsiders, firebrands such as Huey Long of Louisiana, "Alfalfa Bill" Murray of Oklahoma, and "Farmer Jim" Ferguson and "Pappy" O'Daniel of Texas all appeared to be classic examples of the Southern redneck demagogue. But each of them differed in at least one important particular from such Southern kinsmen as Theodore Bilbo in Mississippi, Thomas Heflin in Alabama, Cole Blease in South Carolina and Gene Talmadge in Georgia:

the men of the Southern frontier did not indulge in the Deep South ritual of stirring the race issue. They all found other routes to political office. The rhetoric of Ferguson, who managed to fight the Ku Klux Klan while at the same time directing his political appeal at tenant farmers, was typical. "You have only three friends in the world," Farmer Jim was fond of saying, "God Almighty, Sears Roebuck and Jim Ferguson." Whatever else can be said of these men, they were to bestow upon their region a degree of flexibility that became especially evident when Negro discontent boiled over in the 1960s.

The frontier South emerged into the 20th Century carrying old antagonisms and nursing old glories, and a little out of step with the rest of the nation. Neither Northern nor purely Southern, its style had the virtue of being free of permanently disabling maladies. During the years when Arkansans, isolated on their Ozark plateau, troubled the nation scarcely at all, and when Oklahoma remained Indian Territory, the states of Louisiana and Texas gradually developed somewhat non-Southern identities. The Creoles shaped the way Louisianans regarded themselves, and the frontier had a similar impact on Texans. Other Americans could express astonishment—as, from the Civil War to the present, they invariably have—at the undisguised public knavery and private peccadilloes in the life style of the Southern frontier. But such observers rarely tramped along the back roads of rural Louisiana or Texas. There, the people had much of the same provincial innocence and pride that characterized the other sections of rural America.

There was one difference: history had happened to them. The historian Arnold Toynbee once asserted that Americans, outside the South, seemed to regard history as "something unpleasant that happens to other people." The people of the Old South, both black and white, knew better. Their romanticism was a cover for their pessimism and both were a product of the loss of illusion that derived from social humiliation or from military defeat and occupation of their homeland. The people of the Southern frontier knew better, too. But their "history" was not confined to the Lost Cause. If the Civil War was part of their background, so too were the French and the Spanish and Texas' War for Independence—and the frontier itself. Out of their embattled past, perhaps the most recognizable characteristic was the way the people viewed themselves and their future—with the frontiersman's eternal optimism. In their awareness of the past, they were distinctly Southern; in their optimism, they were unmistakably American.

Handsome relics
of old empires

The influence of the two great colonial powers that helped to shape the South Central States —France and Spain—is still evident today in two of the region's oldest and most distinctive cities, New Orleans and San Antonio. New Orleans is distinguished by its French Quarter, where town houses dating back one and two centuries reflect the tastes of the French who originally settled the city and of the Spanish who for a time ruled it.

At the same time that New Orleans was being founded, the Spanish, advancing northward from Mexico, were establishing the outpost in Texas that they called San Antonio. There they erected a series of missions, some of which still exist. The most famous, because of the battle fought there in 1836, is the Alamo, but the other four that survive provide a remarkable record of the skill of Spanish builders in the New World.

Cast-iron railings in the French Quarter, a graceful reminder of New Orleans' early French and Spanish colonial days, throw their shadows on the second-floor porch of the Philip Steegman House. The railings are in the delicate "oak-leaf-and-acorn" pattern.

The peaceful interior patio of a house
on New Orleans' Royal Street is
reached from the street by a flagstone
walk leading under a tall archway.
The heavy but graceful iron gate seals
the court from the street. As New
Orleans' houses became increasingly
elegant in the 19th Century, some of
the wealthier citizens had such
enclosed courtyards built so as to
make the best use of the cramped
city's small building lots, and also to
gain privacy. The outer walls of such
houses, facing the street, were blank.

Elegant details from New Orleans' past

The imaginative men who built early New Orleans gave a thousand individual and beautiful details to the houses that still line the streets of the city's oldest district, the French Quarter. The earliest inhabitants lived in small wooden cottages, but as the citizens' taste and the builders' technique developed, more elaborate structures were put up. The elegant houses of the mid-19th Century are the culmination of these later craftsmen's impressive skill.

A house with walls of cypress planks set on a foundation of plastered brick is an example of an early French building style.

A fan window caps four upright windows to form a simple but elegant frame for a view of former slave quarters.

Brick-and-timber construction, more durable than earlier all-cypress walls, shows through on the wall of a house built in 1772.

A graceful curved staircase made of cypress wood leads to the upper floor of a house erected in the early 19th Century.

49

The varied splendor
of New Orleans ironwork

Standing out amidst the distinctive architecture of the older districts of New Orleans is the city's ironwork. Porches, gates and fences bloom with delightful designs, often marvelously light and almost alive. The earliest ironwork was imported from Europe, but native craftsmen quickly mastered the art of working wrought iron, creating graceful and simple designs with it. The growing popularity of cast iron in the mid-19th Century gave the artists greater freedom, for with the new technique they could undertake more ambitious and intricate projects, including the representation of a variety of native plants. Many of New Orleans' most glorious works, including the lacy screens that decorate the façades of some French Quarter houses, date from this era.

A functional air vent becomes an ornament of a French Quarter home, perforated in a pattern and provided with a worked border.

A sturdy railing presents the viewer with a pattern of fruit clusters in the midst of intertwined arabesques of cast iron.

Like infernal pitchforks, these wicked iron spikes still appear graceful as they guard a Bourbon Street building from prowlers.

A shimmering, shadowing façade of cast iron decorates the tiered porches of a Royal Street home *(right)*, one of the French Quarter's finest. It is often called the "lacework" building because of its ornamental grille, which is done in the oak-leaf-and-acorn pattern. A wealthy sugar planter built the house in 1840.

The wrought-iron initials of Bartholemew Bosque on the porch of his home are reversed from the street.

Ghastely simple wrought-iron supports seem to hold up the balcony of a home on Royal Street.

A funereal design in cast iron *(left)* stands in front of an aboveground tomb in a New Orleans cemetery.

The tranquil, arched cloister of the 200-year-old Mission San José casts shadows on the ground below. The large dome of the mission's church looms above the arches, while just to the left of the dome the tower of the belfry rises, topped, like the dome, with a cross. The door in the background leads to a vault behind the church.

The Spanish buildings of San Antonio

The distinctive architectural style of the Spanish settlers of San Antonio is best seen in the four missions that lie south of the city, and in the Alamo and the Spanish Governor's Palace within the city limits. The missions were established in the early 18th Century by the Franciscan friars sent by King Philip V of Spain with the dual aim of converting the Indians to Christianity and securing the area for Spain by protecting it against French colonization and expansion. In 1794 the missions were secularized and their brief career was ended; Spanish rule itself ended in 1821, leaving only a few buildings behind as reminders of its past empire.

A geometric fresco painted in 1752 on the ceiling of Mission Concepción has a hole for the mission bell rope.

Built without nails, the stairway at Mission San José is made of oak blocks set neatly into a wall.

A graceful swirl of mosaic made of colored pebbles enlivens the patio of the Spanish Governor's Palace.

The frame of a door, judged to be some 200 years old, forms an abstract pattern at Mission Concepción.

Delicate stone carvings
in the Texas wilderness

Parts of San Antonio's Spanish missions are richly decorated with stone carvings, creating a strange touch of European grandeur on the Texas plains. The finest stonework of all is in the Mission San José, a building whose façade is so beautiful that it has been called "The Queen of the Missions." One of the most ambitious and successful Spanish buildings north of Mexico, its façade has detailed carvings of ornamental devices, holy figures and plants. It is believed that almost all the mission's carving was done by one master, Pedro Huizar, a Mexican sculptor who is reputed to have worked five years on the mission's rose window alone.

The elaborate rose window at Mission San José is considered a gem of carved-stone ornamentation.

A ritual basin set in the wall at the mission once was used by priests to wash their hands before Mass.

The main portal of Mission San José, depicting holy figures amid a profusion of ornamental detail, stands out vividly from the stark walls on either side. Although the identity of several of the figures is disputed, the one above the window is that of Saint Joseph, the mission's patron saint, called San José in Spanish.

The keystone at the Governor's Palace shows, on a royal seal, that the building was finished in 1749.

A carved head with a cherublike face decorates the interior of the sacristy of Mission San José.

Carefully restored, an intricate stone portal at San José *(left)* frames the original wooden door.

3

The Indian Twilight

Although it was among the last of the states to enter the Union, Oklahoma has in one sense the most unusual history of them all. It centers around the still unresolved fate of the continent's first occupants, the American Indians. Before it became a state, Oklahoma was "Indian Territory," one of the last and certainly the largest of all the reservations set aside by the federal government as a final haven for the tribes. When the "haven" proved something less than promised, the Indian fought some of his last battles, political as well as military, against the white man, desperately seeking to avoid removal to the Southwestern plains. Evidence of their defeat is the fact that almost one third of all Americans of Indian descent live in Oklahoma today.

To describe the history of Oklahoma and its Indians is thus to recount a centuries-long saga of peoples who once inhabited almost every part of the United States. It is a history, therefore, not only of nomadic plains peoples, such as the Comanche of Texas and Oklahoma, but also of sedentary village

A gallant Comanche chief, Quanah Parker sits proudly astride his pony in front of a tribal tepee in the 1890s. Parker guided his people even after they had been forcibly settled in Oklahoma, becoming a judge and a delegate from the Indians to the U.S. government.

folk and of isolated groups that resisted the white man and that, nevertheless, were all eventually gathered into one area for the convenience of the nation's white majority.

The American Indian was a victim of one of the great migrations of history, the western expansion of Europeans across the North American continent. The white man's treatment of the Indian was not an exercise in concerted cruelty or in genocide, although it sometimes appears that way and the effect on the Indian was often the same. Rather, it grew out of the immense, relentless pressure of this white advance, which levered Indians ever westward toward the Great Plains, sometimes with a measure of consideration for the Indians as human beings, more often with little or none. It is heartbreaking that the long process took place amid so much mutual misunderstanding. As one of America's pioneer Indian authorities, Dr. Clark Wissler, has written: "The white man defeated the Indian, traded with him, sometimes married his women, usually held his opinions and ways in contempt, but never understood him." For his part, the Indian has always found the white man's repeated failure to keep his promises utterly unfathomable.

In recent years a growing number of historians, anthropologists and other scholars have undertaken to learn about the Indian, to sort out his history and to probe that fertile but elusive entity called the Indian mind. It has proved a challenging study, since Indian myths, white versions of Indian myths, Indian interpretations of white customs, the absence of written tribal histories and the unreliability of partisan accounts have all left a confused tangle of fact and legend. But one thing is becoming clear: none of the old stereotypes constitute a reliable starting point—neither the cavalryman's caricature of the Indian as completely untrustworthy ("The only good Indian is a dead Indian") nor the romantic view of the Indian as a "noble savage."

The 20th Century verdict is at once simpler and more inclusive: there never was a "typical" Indian. Instead of being alike, the red men of America were a complex assortment of rustics, statesmen, orators, warriors, scholars and wanderers who evolved naturally from one of mankind's more delicately balanced social organizations. They responded to the white man in many ways, fear alternating with trust, hope with disillusionment and admiration with hatred. Except when they were defending their ancestral lands, they were frequently gentle and usually formal in their personal relations and instinctively mystical in their approach to life.

If these findings bear almost no resemblance to the traditional Hollywood portrait of the Indian, this is precisely the point stressed by modern authorities. Americans still know little of the far-flung Indian civilizations that stretched from Massachusetts Bay to the California coast nor of the courage and dignity that imparted such tragic dimension to the long Indian twilight—nor even of the life of the descendants of these Indians today. The result, scholars agree, is a sizable net loss to the sum of American experience that constitutes the national heritage. Beyond this, they assert, the continuing "Indian problem" that is once again surfacing in Oklahoma and many other places cannot be adequately addressed by the nation until, as a starter, authentic history replaces legend. For paradoxically, one of the strongest features of the culture of today's Indians is a fierce will to survive; though many of the forms of their way of life have disappeared, the drive to survive *as Indians* has not.

It is not that the Indians stubbornly refuse to assimilate. Many of them have. Many others simply value their Indian heritage too highly to wish to. And still others find that they are unable to, at least without a great deal of highly informed assistance and tolerance from their conquerors.

One reason for this dislocation is the very fact that the American Indian is not now and never has been a stereotype. Although the various Indian tribes did share a number of habit patterns (the characteristic of training children through gentle suggestion and admonition rather than physical punishment was one of them), they also approached ultimate questions of life and morality from many different perspectives. Even such relatively similar tribes as the Sioux, Cheyenne and Comanche, who jointly ruled the plains from Canada to Mexico, worked out remarkably different tribal methods of coping with such vagaries as the vanities and desires of the individual. The Cheyenne, for example, enforced a strict sexual code laced tight with taboos. Virginity was prized among adolescents and monogamy among married women. By comparison, their immediate neighbors to the south, the Comanche, regarded marital fidelity as an eminently dispensable virtue. The Sioux seem to have been somewhere between these two poles; their code allowed a warrior to give his wife to a friend, all parties considering the procedure not only honorable but also proof of the highest mutual esteem.

In war and politics, as in affairs of the heart, the Indians followed a variety of approaches. Some regarded armed resistance as hopeless while others fought knowing it was hopeless. Physical environment was a definite factor: Indians living in forests were somewhat different in outlook from mountain tribes and neither had much resemblance to the hard-riding nomads of the plains.

During its long death agony the Indian culture produced a large number of remarkable leaders. Their routes to fame—war, oratory, scholarship and sometimes the legends created by white men—were as varied as their personalities. Some became renowned because of the scope of their military aspirations: Tecumseh of the Shawnee, Pontiac of the Ottawa and Stand Watie of the Cherokee all dreamed of vast confederations of previously hostile tribes and set forth to weld them into war coalitions. Others won widespread notoriety through a single apocalyptic event: the Battle of Little Big Horn made household names of the Sioux triumvirate of Sitting Bull, Crazy Horse and Gall. Some owed their renown to lyrical white admirers: the fame of Hiawatha and King Philip was embroidered to near-epic proportions by Henry Wadsworth Longfellow and Washington Irving. On the other hand, the great Cherokee, Sequoyah, rose to prominence solely through his intellectual capacity—he invented an 85-character alphabet and created a written Cherokee language.

Clearly there was little uniformity in the careers of famous Indians, just as there was little uniformity

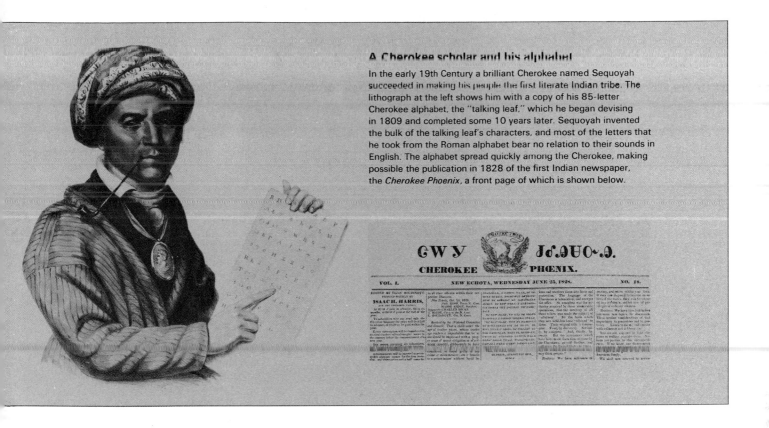

in their attitudes and tribal customs. But almost all of them were caught up in the same long process of war with the white man followed by retreat before the settlers' inexorable advance. All faced not only removal from their ancestral lands, but also the danger of dispersal and the weakening of the fabric of their tribal traditions.

Yet the history of one tribe, the Delaware, illustrates that the problem of removal could derive from Indian as well as white pressure. Prodded both by white settlers and by the warlike Iroquois of New York, the Delaware began drifting westward from the Atlantic Coast—to Pennsylvania in the 1720s, to Ohio in the 1750s and to Indiana, where the Miami tribes agreed in the 1770s to tolerate them. Some 20 years later the quest for a land of their own took many of the Delaware to Missouri. There, however, pressure from Plains tribes shunted them up and down the forests on the eastern edge of the Great Plains, down to Texas in the 1820s and back to Kansas in the 1830s. Finally, in 1867, the Delaware accepted the inevitable and settled on reservations in Oklahoma, some joining the Cherokee Confederacy and others moving in with Caddo tribes.

The Delaware were a part of the Algonquian family, one of the largest of the Indian linguistic groups. Actually, the whole question of how to group Indians has always been (and remains today) a source of considerable dispute. An identifiable Indian group was generally called a "nation" in the 17th Century, a "tribe" in the 19th. Classification by languages, such as the "Algonquian family," has offered modern scholars a somewhat more precise method.

As the fortunes of the Delaware illustrated, access to land of its own was one of the important prerequisites for maintaining the tribe's traditional way of life. This was true among both the Indian nomads of the Western plains and the forest dwellers of the East. The Indian concept of land ownership, unfortunately, scarcely fitted in with the white man's system. Indians believed the land belonged to a spirit greater than man and was open to everyone strong enough to walk or ride over it, not just to the "owner." By their lights, Indians had every right to hunt on land they had "sold" to Americans. The only positive result of this state of affairs was the addition of a phrase to the English language, "Indian giver." The negative results, needless to say, were continuous conflicts between white men who were delighted to discover how cheaply Indians could be prodded into "selling" their lands and red men who continued to hunt wherever they found game. When misunderstandings led to angry disagreements and then to violence and retaliation, the arrival of the U.S. cavalry was usually not far off.

But when war did come, the mounted hunters of the great Western plains were infinitely better equipped to defend their right to the land than were the tribes of the forests, no matter how advanced a culture these Indians had attained. Perhaps nothing illustrates this more clearly than the respective histories of two widely different peoples who met a common end in Oklahoma—the Cherokee and the Comanche.

The Cherokee were one of the "Five Civilized Tribes" (the others were the Creek, Chickasaw, Choctaw and Seminole) that long flourished, some 60,000 strong, in the broad southeastern subcontinent between the Ohio River and the Gulf of Mexico, the Mississippi River and the Atlantic. Handsome and volatile, the Cherokee were known for their intelligence. During the 18th Century, they intermarried heavily with families of Irish, German, English, Welsh and Scottish descent, as the names of various tribal leaders attest: Adair, Vann, Lowry, Ross, Chisholm, Hicks and Rogers. The general cultural level of the Cherokee is indicated by the speed with which the knowledge of Sequoyah's 85-character alphabet, perfected in the mid-1820s and representing all the vowel and consonant sounds in the Cherokee language, spread through their nation. By 1828 a newspaper, the *Cherokee Phoenix*, was being published in the native language as well as in English.

The Cherokee created a relatively sophisticated political structure and employed it to win formal treaties with the U.S. government recognizing the validity of Cherokee landholdings in the Carolinas, Tennessee and particularly in Georgia. Yet, in the words of historian R. S. Cotterill, "the Cherokee sallies into political science were viewed with undisguised hostility by the Georgians, who wished to see the Cherokees not improve, but depart." Fraudulent treaties, implemented by deception and bribery and backed by armed threats, materially reduced the holdings of all the civilized tribes between 1814 and 1828.

With the advance of the frontier, the discovery of gold in Georgia and the election in 1828 of old Indian fighter Andrew Jackson as President of the U.S., pressure mounted against both the Eastern Cherokee, radiating out from the southern Appalachian Mountains, and the Western branches of the tribe. These Western branches had already undergone an unsettled period during which they wandered into Arkansas and there fought some notable battles with bands of Osage Indians as well as with white men. Eventually these Cherokee signed a treaty with the U.S. government relinquishing their rights to their Arkansas lands in exchange for a Western tract of seven million acres that included what is now northern Oklahoma. They were also granted a "perpetual outlet west" that extended from the main tract westward to the limits of U.S. territory. In 1829 the Western Cherokee began their long march to Oklahoma—uncounted thousands of men, women and children plodding in misery toward the Western plains.

An even harder fate awaited their Eastern kinsmen. After gold was discovered in Cherokee territory in Georgia, both President Jackson and the Georgia legislature took steps to assert jurisdiction over the tribal lands. On December 19, 1829, the Georgia legislature enacted the first of a series of laws annulling all Cherokee statutes, forbidding further meetings of their tribal council and legislature within Georgia, declaring all contracts between white men and Indians invalid unless witnessed by two white men, providing for the survey and distribution of Cherokee land, and excluding the Cherokee from digging for gold in the newly discovered fields. The Cherokee tried legal remedies, but the U.S. Supreme Court settled the sovereignty question in 1831 by concluding that the Cherokee were a "domestic dependent nation" under the guardianship of the federal government and therefore legally incapable of maintaining actions in state courts.

After additional legal maneuvers failed, the Eastern Cherokee Nation lost its political unity and split in its turn into two groups, each one headed by an able chief. The majority supported John Ross, who wanted to stay in Georgia and continue the fight; the remainder sided with John Ridge, who regarded acceptance of a removal treaty as the only way out of a desperate situation. In 1836 the U.S. Senate ratified a pact in which the Cherokee Nation ceded some eight million acres of land to the U.S. for about 50 cents an acre. The fact that tracts in the gold fields were shortly thereafter selling to speculators for as high as $30,000 an acre fortified the resolve of Ross's followers to resist removal. While his group stayed rooted in Georgia, 2,000 people followed Ridge on the long journey to Oklahoma early in 1838. The reports of sickness and death on the march that filtered back to Georgia if anything stiffened Ross's determination to hold out in the ancestral lands. But the U.S. Army under General Winfield Scott forced these remaining Cherokee from their farms and homes and herded them into stockades. A Baptist missionary who watched the sad proceeding was moved to angry words: "The Cherokees . . . were allowed no time to take any thing with them, except the clothes they had on. Well-furnished houses were left a prey to plunderers, who, like hungry wolves, follow in the train of the [soldiers]. . . . Many of the Cherokees, who, a few days ago, were in comfortable circumstances, are now victims of abject poverty."

Under these circumstances, Ross bitterly accepted removal in the fall of 1838. Some 13,000 people started out on the 800-mile exodus to Oklahoma, divided into marching groups of about 1,000. The caravan, begun in despair and heartbreak, disintegrated into a dreadful winter tragedy. White frontiersmen in Arkansas, watching the starving families crossing their state, readily accepted the name the Indians gave to the wilderness roads, the "Trail of Tears." In the spring of 1839 the survivors straggled into Indian Territory. Behind them, on the roads of Arkansas, Tennessee, Mississippi, Alabama and Georgia, were 4,000 graves.

Yet the hardy Cherokee managed to maintain their tribal integrity in their new home and, with difficulty, their morale as well. They adopted a new constitution and created an unusual civilization on the plains, basically American Indian yet Anglo-American in many of its customs and usages. In the ensuing years almost all the surviving Cherokee Indians were united in Oklahoma, as scattered bands trickled in from all over the southeastern U.S.

In the American Civil War the Cherokee supplied troops to both sides and suffered heavy losses. Three Cherokee Home Guard units won fame for their service with Union forces; the tribal chieftain Stand Watie became a brigadier general in the Confederate Army. John Ross, who stood with the Confederacy, died shortly after the war was over, and his nephew, William P. Ross, a graduate of the College of New Jersey, now Princeton University, became Principal Chief of the Cherokee Nation. One of his advisers among the tribal elders, Clem Rogers, fathered a boy named Will, who was to become one of America's foremost folk humorists. Today, of all the tribes in Oklahoma, the Cherokee is the largest.

The Comanche Indians of Texas and Oklahoma, unlike their brethren the Cherokee, were inclined to resort to open warfare when their lands were threatened by white men. The Comanche had methodically snipped off the tentacles of Spanish advance into Texas even before English settlers had founded colonies of any consequence on the Atlantic Coast. They had continued to resist the Spaniards while the Cherokee had remained shielded from white advance by the Appalachian Mountain barrier. So pervasive was the Comanche's military suzerainty in the latter half of the 18th Century that they often thronged the streets and squares of San Antonio "with insolent bravado and defiance." In approved guerrilla fashion the Comanche seldom let their enemies select the time and place for battle. For generations that extended into centuries, they raided and harassed, almost always extracting greater losses than they suffered, and remained, with rare exceptions, undefeated to the very end.

The pride and sense of place needed to sustain this enduring belligerency within the relatively small Comanche nation was traceable to a unique blend of European and Indian military influences that produced one of mankind's most adroit artists of mobile warfare: the mounted, rifle-equipped Comanche brave. For the horses, he could thank the Spanish; for the rifles, French and later American traders. But for his individual horsemanship and his sure sense of cavalry tactics, he could credit his own heritage as a nomadic hunter on the plains.

Migrating southward from the Idaho-Wyoming Rockies, perhaps in the 17th Century, the Comanche encountered Spanish settlements in New Mexico and from them acquired the instrument that was to change the history of the plains: the Spanish mustang. These hardy ponies, originally brought to the New World by the conquistadors, proliferated northward over the great prairie-plains area between the Mississippi River and the Rockies. Tribe after tribe learned to capture, breed and ride them until even the far-north Sioux were mounted. But the southernmost Comanche were the first to tame the mustang, the first to adapt him to the hunt and the first to realize the opportunities for expansion that he afforded.

The results were truly revolutionary. To a man on foot, plains life was precarious. Tribal hunters frequently had to trek for days to find game, and a misstep that caused a herd of bison to bolt often meant privation, even starvation, for the tribe. The population, static in good years, suffered inevitable decline when drought deflected the nomadic buffalo herds and put them beyond the reach of even the hardiest hunter.

All this changed with the coming of the mustang. Mounted, a Comanche hunter could range over thousands of square miles. In league with his brothers, he could surround herds and even stampede them into cul-de-sacs at the ends of canyons where they could be picked off at leisure. Food became plentiful. Loads were shifted from dogs to horses, and tepees became larger because the travois poles, now carried by ponies, could be longer and heavier. Stealing horses became a part of life and a test of manhood. The population expanded, and more leisure was available for hunters to develop other skills. In the 18th Century, Comanche warriors became among the finest riders on the North American continent, and thus formidable foes even before they acquired rifles. With one leg slung over the back of his pony and the other gripping the underside, the Comanche could lean out under the animal's neck and—fully protected by his horse from opposing fire—aim and fire his arrows with remarkable accuracy and rapidity.

Children of the tribe usually had their own ponies when they were four or five; youngsters competed in trick-riding contests that enhanced their prestige in the adolescent world and insured their artistry as warriors later; harnesses and sleds were fashioned to enable the entire tribe—people and dwellings, supplies and utensils—to become part of a single tactical team. To the consternation of their enemies, settled Comanche villages could vanish in as little as 30 minutes and the whole tribe might be miles away within hours.

Gradually, the Comanche asserted their supremacy over the whole of the Southern plains, driving the Apache westward into New Mexico and Arizona, forcing Texas tribes into a narrowing belt along the Gulf Coast and sending raiding parties deep into Mexico. The sonorous, flowing Comanche tongue became the court language wherever Plains Indians met, and the whole Texas-Oklahoma area justly came to be termed "Comanchería"—the land of the Comanche.

Hardened by the nomad life on the plains, secure in their prestige as warriors and hunters among all the peoples of Comanchería, ignorant of the power undergirding the American movement westward, and finally armed with the white man's rifles, the Comanche watched the intruding Americans with concern, but without the helpless foreboding of the more worldly Cherokee. Thus the advance guard of Texans, pushing out onto the plains in the 19th Century, encountered a warrior people sustained by a tradition of victory, their morale intact and their rifles ready.

There was no way for the Comanche to know that their position was utterly untenable—and for reasons that had little to do with their individual capacity to outride the blue-clad cavalry. Aside from the weaknesses in equipment inherent within any preindustrial nomadic society, the Comanche were suffering from two grave disadvantages, one common to all tribes and the second particularly afflicting the Plains Indians.

The white man's most effective weapons against the Indians were not his guns but his diseases. Initial contact with Americans invariably spread smallpox and other deadly illnesses through the Indian camps. By the time enough whites had moved into a region to constitute a serious threat, the Indian population had frequently been reduced by half or more. Estimates of the Comanche population vary widely, but it seems likely that the tribe totaled some 20,000 members in the early 1800s. This figure was drastically reduced, however, as the 19th Century progressed, and the Comanche probably numbered no more than 12,000 by 1850. Not counting women, children and men too old to fight, the Comanche's warrior strength was only about 4,000 at the beginning of their nation's greatest period of danger.

The Comanche's second infirmity lay in their dispersion. The 4,000 warriors were scattered in small bands flung across the High Plains of the Texas-Oklahoma Panhandles and throughout the vast prairie country billowing southward from the Arkansas River to the interior of Mexico. They had to be—because each band needed to hunt over a land area large enough to support sufficient buffalo to supply them with food and clothing. These economic needs made organization for war a difficult task, for each of the bands was little more than a voluntary association of a few dozen families under an able leader. When religious festivals or the annual autumn hunt brought the bands together to form a temporary national unit, the parent political institution thus created was democratic literally to the point of anarchy. Individuals participated only to the extent they deemed wise, and there was no mechanism for enforcing tribal decisions. This of course rendered political unity for either peace or war almost impossible.

Tension between generations produced further disunity. Chieftains who had had time to assess the scope of Anglo-American power tended to become more submissive as they grew older, even to the point of accepting removal to a reservation. But the justice of the tribal cause and the desire to prove their valor in battle generally drove youthful warriors to defend their hunting grounds. Most of the great "Indian wars" in American history were fought, on the Indian side, by a minority led by young warriors who were eager to display their fighting prowess and preferred death to defeat.

In Indian-white diplomacy the babble of voices was not confined to the Indian side. The palefaces had their militants and moderates too. Congressmen from the West, prodded by frontier constituents, land speculators and transcontinental railroad interests, were generally militant. Easterners, aware that they would have to put up most of the money for any punitive expeditions, were less so. Some fiscal conservatives plumped for peaceful policies in the name of economy, but others adopted an aggressive stance calling for a "once and for all" settlement through military action. Sam Houston of Texas was representative of those Americans who, knowing the Indian culture firsthand and admiring it, favored conciliatory policies. Somewhat later, books like Helen Hunt Jackson's remarkably effective attack on U.S. policies, *A Century of Dishonor*, further rallied humanitarian sentiment in behalf of the Indians.

But almost all the arguments were submerged in the sheer clamorous energy of the white man's surge westward. No matter how far west the Indians were prodded, the frontier always caught up with them. A period of tension would lead to crisis and perhaps to bloodshed, and then to a new removal treaty. Treaties ceding new lands to Indians "in perpetuity" did not last long, usually less than 10 years, before pressures for new removals reappeared. In 1839 various Comanche bands came to terms in Texas, agreeing to lay down their arms in return for a stretch of plains land. But pressure for another removal built up quickly and the Comanche were forced to sign another treaty in 1851. The ink was hardly dry on this pact before the white men were again maneuvering these Comanche bands toward Oklahoma.

Some of the most bitter fighting coincided with the Civil War. When the war temporarily denuded Western Army garrisons, the Comanche attacked, putting settlers to flight and rolling back the frontier as much as 50 miles in some places. By 1864 the victorious Union armies could spare some troops for frontier duty, and Colonel Kit Carson launched a punitive expedition on the Southern plains. But as the Spanish and Texans had before him, Carson received a basic education in plains warfare from young Comanche will-o'-the-wisps. The Comanche did not share Hollywood's later fondness for cavalry charges at close quarters; indeed, a war leader's prestige collapsed if his policies led to severe battle losses, regardless of the damage he might inflict on the enemy. The Comanche simply did not believe in losing lives for strategic purposes. Basic Comanche tactics centered on the guerrilla techniques of ambush and riposte. They raided and harassed reconnaissance columns, always striking swiftly and always withdrawing before seriously engaged. When Carson returned home from his exasperating expedition, the Comanche were still undefeated.

In the same era another cavalry officer, Colonel J. M. Chivington, descended on a band of peaceful Cheyenne in southwestern Colorado and indiscriminately killed hundreds of women and children. The "Sand Creek Massacre," as it came to be known, stilled whatever voices of caution might have prevailed among other Indian tribes. As cavalry regiments were advanced against the Sioux in the north, too, the rattle of rifle fire increased along the whole of the Western frontier.

Finally, in 1867, the U.S. Department of the Interior arranged a huge parley at Medicine Lodge Creek in Kansas, just across the border from Indian Territory. Several thousand chiefs and warriors, representing scores of tribal groupings, attended the council, their herds of war ponies consuming prairie grass for miles around. The instructions carried by the American officials were almost completely contradictory—to produce peace along the frontier and to move all the plains tribes onto reservations where they could be taught farming. To achieve both results, the Americans tried to secure the signatures of tribal leaders to a removal treaty without spelling out the meaning of the agreement. Most of the Civilized Tribes, which had already settled down, after a fashion, to farming in Oklahoma, accepted this sleight of hand with philosophical resignation. But the Plains Indians listened to men like the Comanche chief Ten Bears, who announced: "The Comanche are not weak and blind. . . . They are strong and farsighted, like grown horses. I was born upon the prairie, where the wind blew free and there was nothing to break the light of the sun. I want no blood upon my land to stain the grass. . . . I know every stream and every wood between the Rio Grande and the Arkansas. When I was at Washington, the Great Father told me that all the Comanche land was ours . . . so, why do you ask us to leave the rivers, and the sun, and the wind, and live in houses? The Texans have taken away the places where the grass grew the thickest. . . . Had we kept that, we might have done the things you ask. But it is too late."

And so the frontier continued to bleed through the late 1860s and early 1870s as the Comanche, Cheyenne, Sioux and Kiowa clashed with cavalry detachments deploying into Indian country.

However, the white men won their ultimate victory not so much with Army cavalrymen as with guerrillas of their own—the buffalo hunters who literally destroyed the Indians' way of life. After

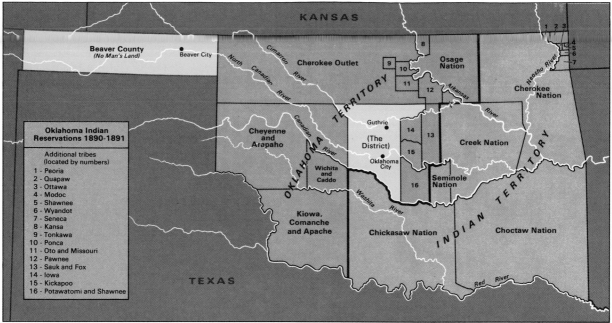

After Wright, *A Guide to the Indian Tribes of Oklahoma* © 1951 University of Oklahoma Press.

This map shows how the area of today's Oklahoma was divided among the Indian tribes "removed" there by the U.S. government. The first Eastern Indians settled in the area were the Choctaw (1820), and they were soon followed by the other four Civilized Tribes—the Cherokee, Chickasaw, Creeks and Seminole. These tribes, or nations, had Oklahoma pretty much to themselves until after the Civil War, when they were forced to give up their Western lands as a home for other tribes. The center of Oklahoma, sometimes called The District, was not assigned to any tribe and was the scene of the first Land Rush in 1889. By 1907 all of the reservations had disappeared.

Eastern tanneries discovered in 1870 how to work buffalo hides into leather, the skins suddenly became valuable. The slaughter on the Southern plains promptly reached almost incredible proportions—in the years 1872 to 1874 some 7.5 million animals were killed—and by the middle of the decade the once-vast herds had all but vanished.

The morale of the Plains Indians plummeted as tribal hunting parties came back into camp empty-handed and reported finding thousands of skinned buffalo carcasses rotting on the plains. One by one, starving Comanche bands rode into Fort Sill and surrendered. But there were stubborn holdouts, groups in each of the plains tribes that refused to give up. Alone among the Comanche to continue the fight were the proud Kwahadi Comanche of the desolate "Staked Plains" of far-west Texas. Led by a young chieftain named Quanah Parker, son of a Comanche chief and a white Texas captive girl, Cynthia Ann Parker, the Kwahadi pleaded with their tribal brethren to remain on the land and continue to resist the white man. The answer was always the same, that the hunters with the long rifles had destroyed the buffalo and there was nothing to eat.

Nevertheless, in this third act of the long Indian drama, the Kwahadi and a few isolated bands from other tribes put up a spirited resistance, winning a number of skirmishes with the cavalry. They even dreamed of annihilating the white intruders. But the end was near. Perhaps symptomatic was the famous attack on Adobe Walls, a buffalo hunters' camp in West Texas, on June 27, 1874. Several hundred Indians, including Quanah Parker's Kwahadi and some Cheyenne, Arapaho and Kiowa warriors, decided on a frontal assault against the hated killers of their buffalo. The fact that the Indians even contemplated such a direct attack against expert marksmen armed with long-range buffalo guns, in direct contravention of the basic military principles of the Plains Indians, indicates the extent of their desperation. The attack was a dismal failure. The Indians found they could not dislodge a mere 28 white men from their stronghold; on their part the sharpshooters showed they were able to pick off Indians almost a mile away. Soon Quanah Parker had had enough, and he led his band off to another futile season of hunting the vanishing bison herds.

Parker also had to cope with a large punitive expedition led by Colonel R. S. MacKenzie, who was bent on either driving these last Comanche insurgents onto a reservation or exterminating them. MacKenzie's summer-long campaign netted only three Comanche dead and no prisoners, but he did succeed in destroying Comanche and Cheyenne campsites in Texas' Palo Duro Canyon and in stampeding a herd of 1,400 Indian ponies off a cliff to their deaths. The 1874-1875 Texas winter was one of great privation for the Kwahadi, and the next spring Quanah Parker accepted his fate. In June 1875 he led his surviving people into Fort Sill—400 men, women and children, and 900 ponies, in a mile-long surrender procession.

Two years before, in 1873, the Apache, despite the efforts of their renowned leader, Cochise, had been removed to the Chiricahua Reservation in Arizona, and although the Sioux nation won its victory of annihilation over General George Custer in the summer of 1876, Crazy Horse gave up the hopeless struggle the following spring and led his Oglala Sioux warriors into captivity. A general peace came to the plains.

The Indian's spiritual troubles had only begun, however. While his own society flourished, he had managed to reconcile a system of communal economic life with a retention of individual liberty. The Indians accomplished this, in the words of R. S. Cotterill, "by reducing their government so nearly to anarchy that it operated only by practically unanimous consent. . . . Communism freed the Indian from ambition to acquire wealth as anarchy freed him from temptation to seek power. It made him improvident of the future . . . [but it also] promoted tribal solidarity."

The morale of the individual Indian was thus inescapably bound up in the continuance of tribal life, especially since what religion he had was private, not organized for public expression and wholly unrelated to his morality, which he drew from tribal custom. In direct consequence, the Indian has resisted assimilation in the larger American society because, with the loosening of his tribal moorings, he has problems of the soul. He has, in addition, suffered from prejudice because his skin is not white. Furthermore, the Indian has been able to exercise little political power and because of this has seen no way out of his difficulties, the worst of which has been a widespread and in many cases overwhelming poverty.

For more than a generation following final military defeat, waves of Indian nationalism glorifying the old ways alternated with attempts to learn the white man's techniques. Quanah Parker consistently urged his people to modernize and adopt the white man's ways, not because he admired the social and economic arrangements of the whites but because he believed that any other procedure was hopeless. But even when the Indians followed Parker's logical advice, confusion resulted. Many of the whites with whom the Indians dealt, including government agents, were hardly models of moral rectitude. They frequently cheated the Indians, stealing the crops the Indians managed to grow, rustling their cattle and embezzling funds intended for Indian welfare. These experiences produced a confusion and aimlessness among the Indians, and a sort of torpor came to characterize life on the reservations of Oklahoma.

For half a century the government's Bureau of Indian Affairs, which started out as a branch of the War Department, attacked these problems of Indian dislocation by trying to force red men to become fully assimilated within the American system. Agricultural agents swarmed over Oklahoma to teach the Indian male how to plow a straight furrow. This policy, however well intended, involved a direct assault on tribal organization and on Indian ways of thinking. It did not work. Many Indian males considered labor in the fields humiliating and fit only for women. A well-tended crop gave them neither a sense of accomplishment nor peace of mind. Though their lives as hunters had passed, the ideas derived from the old ways persisted.

In 1934 the federal government reviewed its Indian policies and passed the Reorganization Act. This act set forth an enlightened program, but it was not always carried out wisely at the local level. This problem plagued subsequent government efforts, as has the Indians' ingrained suspicion of all the white man's doings. As a result only a minority of Indians have learned to make their way in modern America. Furthermore, the simple fact is that the "vanishing American" is no longer vanishing: from a peak of over one million before the coming of the white man and a low of some 270,000 in 1901, the population of American Indians is today more than 600,000 and growing rapidly.

Learning to cope with English grammar in reservation schools or to perceive the substance of Christianity has, for most Indians, been only a halting first step toward a new and acceptable identity. Thousands have learned, after a fashion, to travel what the Apache warrior and prophet Geronimo called "your Jesus road," and some have become successful in the modern American sense as farmers or businessmen or in the professions. But an underlying dislocation continues. Poverty and despair remain widespread. The series of questions asked by Cochise three generations ago as white settlers poured into his Arizona hunting grounds remains relevant today: "Why is it that the Apaches want to die—that they carry their lives on their fingernails? They roam over the hills and plains and want the heavens to fall on them. . . . Tell me, if the Virgin Mary has walked throughout all the land, why has she never entered the lodge of the Apache?"

Today, anthropologists and cultural and art historians are the Indians' chief admirers. Indeed, the gulf between public and scholarly opinion has been so vast that some students of Indian history have been moved to extremes of despair. In his recent study of Indian leadership, *The Patriot Chiefs*, the writer Alvin M. Josephy sharply criticized both the "television image of what Indians were never like" and the popular presumption that Indians should "hurry up and get assimilated. . . . The forces in American life that want Indians to get off the reservations and be like other Americans may have their way. But the Indians will resist patiently for decades still to come and it will not happen easily or soon. When it does, much of the greatness and majesty and wonder of the United States will have disappeared. Indian culture and Indian thinking, so untreasured by the unknowing, will be gone and only the history books will be able to tell us of it and make us wonder why we did not enfold it and make a place for it in our national life."

One place to start, of course, is to make a genuine place in our national life for the Indians themselves. A number of dedicated people, some of Indian extraction, have been trying to do just that. One is Muriel H. Wright, the granddaughter of a Choctaw chief, who has devoted much of her life to Indian scholarship, especially the history of the Oklahoma tribes, and has been the president of the National Hall of Fame of Famous American Indians. Another is W. W. Wheeler, who is chief of the Cherokee and has long been active in the National Congress of American Indians. Mrs. James Cox, herself a Cherokee and the wife of the grandson of Quanah Parker, has been instrumental in helping the Indians preserve their cultural and artistic heritage.

The efforts of these people and others are being continued by members of the younger generation, including a handsome, intelligent and determined young Oklahoma woman named LaDonna Harris, the half-Comanche wife of Fred Harris, who was elected U.S. Senator in 1964. With tireless energy, Mrs. Harris has tried to induce the nation to look at the raw statistics of Indian heartbreak. Average Indian life expectancy is 43 years compared with a national average of more than 70. Forty to 75 per cent of all Indians are unemployed, depending on the areas in which they live. The average income of Indian families is $30 a week and half of the children drop out of school before the eighth grade. The economic position of the Indians is, in fact, worse than that of any other American minority group. In most Indian communities the pattern is one of bare subsistence. Moreover, the avenues to improvement are often blocked—by poor education that fits most Indians only for unskilled labor, by white prejudice, by the clash of alien cultures.

But Mrs. Harris has done more than simply publicize these tragic facts. As president of Oklahomans for Indian Opportunity, she has seen to it that OIO directly addresses problems of Indian dislocation by working with the people themselves, both the youngsters in trouble in school and the older people who still shy away from any participation in non-Indian life. The task, as she well knows, is huge. After centuries of distrust, the walls of prejudice on both sides are high enough to block the vision of less determined people in the two races. But her work is a hopeful sign that the nation at long last will, in the words of her Senator-husband, "clearly define and state our national policy and our responsibility to Indians."

The passion of LaDonna Harris is but the latest expression of a long and eloquent tradition. Some of the most moving words ever uttered on the American continent were spoken by Indians—out of the agony of their fate and through their haunting capacity to articulate despair without rancor. This special quality of Indian thought provides perhaps the permanent epitaph to their days of grandeur. The surrender speech of Chief Joseph, the Nez Percé leader who did everything he could to prevent war, and the words spoken by the great Sioux chieftain Crazy Horse as he lay dying are a measure of the strange mixture of courage and gentleness that suffused Indian civilization.

Said Chief Joseph, as his 1,300-mile winter retreat ended almost within sight of freedom in Canada: "Tell General Howard I know his heart. . . . I am tired of fighting. Our chiefs are killed. . . . The old men are all dead. It is the young men who say yes or no. He who led the young men is dead. It is cold and we have no blankets. The little children are freezing to death. My people, some of them, have run away to the hills, and have no blankets, no food; no one knows where they are—perhaps freezing to death. I want to have time to look for my children and see how many I can find. Maybe I will find them among the dead. Hear me, my chiefs, I am tired; my heart is sick and sad. From where the sun now stands, I will fight no more forever."

And Crazy Horse, bayoneted in captivity, gazed up from the floor of an Army barracks and said to the guard who had mortally wounded him: "Let me go, my friend, you have hurt me enough."

Dashing across the flat Oklahoma plains on horseback and in buggies, some of the 100,000 people who poured pell-mell into the part of Oklahoma opened for settlement in 1893 raise a fearful cloud of dust. The former Indian Territory was opened in successive sections.

The saga of early Oklahoma

The famous "Land Rush" into Oklahoma was actually a series of controlled migrations: the government allowed white settlers to move into one part of the territory after another between the years 1889 and 1906. As the whites moved in they took over land that had supposedly been set aside in perpetuity as reservations for the Indian tribes removed to Oklahoma from their tribal holdings elsewhere. After each "rush" the white settlers quickly staked claims in classic frontier fashion and established farms and towns.

Some communities, such as Guthrie, sprang from the plain overnight and became settled commercial centers with astonishing speed. These mass incursions by white men drove the Indians into ever smaller areas of the territory and disrupted what little the Indians had preserved of their traditional ways of life.

The town of Guthrie
takes root on the prairie

Guthrie is one of the Oklahoma communities that sprang into being within hours after a signal gun had started the first land rush into the Indian Territory in 1889. Almost 15,000 settlers arrived on the first day, and open-air offices, tents and even wooden frame houses soon dotted the flat western landscape, completely transforming what recently had been a tiny depot on the Santa Fe railroad line. The lure of free land was so compelling that many of the settlers had come from thousands of miles away. On the evening of Guthrie's first day a roll call revealed the presence of people from 32 U.S. states, three U.S. territories and six foreign countries.

A lawyer and a land agent set up shop in Guthrie on the first day of the opening of Oklahoma, April 22, 1889. Lawyers were kept busy helping to settle the disputes that arose when, in the confusion of the rush, more than one person claimed the same piece of land.

A large, curious crowd gathers outside the makeshift Guthrie jail a month after the first settlers arrived. Some of the prisoners in Guthrie were "Sooners" who had claimed land sooner than the law permitted. Today Oklahoma proudly calls itself the "Sooner State."

Guarding his claimstake, a settler from Kansas named Pearson sits by his tent puffing a pipe while a friend clowns with a gun behind him. During the first days of Guthrie's settlement, most of the settlers lived in tents or inside their wagons *(background)*.

Living in a boxcar, the family of a railroad worker roughs it during Guthrie's first days. A number of Oklahoma towns developed along the line of the Atchison, Topeka and Santa Fe tracks, which had been laid down across the territory in 1887.

A signmaker's wares indicate some of the diverse businesses that sprang up in Guthrie within a few weeks of its first settlement. Besides its numerous lawyers and real-estate agents, Guthrie soon had a drugstore, barbershops and several doctors.

A new, rough but prosperous community

Guthrie lost much of its makeshift look during its first month and settled down to business. It was still not a place for the fainthearted: housing was rough-and-ready, and the town's entertainments were crude. The heart of Guthrie was its shops, which flourished almost from the outset. Within four months it boasted three newspapers and electrically lighted streets. Although Guthrie was later surpassed in size and importance by Tulsa and Oklahoma City, it served briefly as the state capital.

70

The Reed Brothers Gambling House is shown as it flourished in June 1889, less than two months after Guthrie's founding. Gambling was popular in Guthrie, nor was there any problem getting a drink: by the end of the town's first week, it had 50 saloons.

A large crowd of traders and onlookers mills around the main street of Guthrie on a market day in 1896, seven years after the town was first settled. Guthrie was the principal trading center for the smaller communities and the farms that surrounded it.

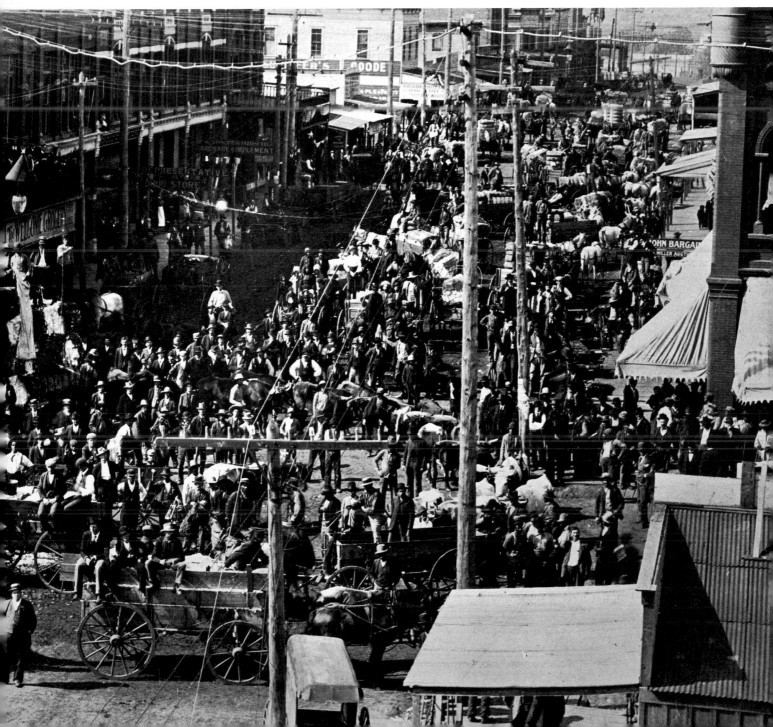

Indians following "the white man's road" in Oklahoma

Indians from more than 30 tribes lived in Oklahoma when the Land Rush began, most of them having been forced to move there by the U.S. government. Once proud and independent peoples, they increasingly had to learn to "walk the white man's road." Some gave up their tepees and other native shelters to live in frame houses, and worked at such mundane tasks as making bricks, splitting and hauling rails, and doing farm chores. Despite crusades for better education and other attempts to draw them into the mainstream of American life, the lot of many Indians today is not much better.

Little girls of the Kiowa tribe pose for an 1891 class picture at a U.S. Government Indian Agency school northwest of Anadarko, Oklahoma. Agency schools were set up by the Bureau of Indian Affairs in an attempt to acculturate the Indians on reservations.

No longer a sight to inspire fear, the great Apache leader Geronimo sits at the wheel of a stylish touring car accompanied by three onetime warriors. Geronimo was captured in Arizona in 1886 and spent his last days under military supervision in Oklahoma.

On a reservation in Oklahoma,
a Cheyenne husband and his wife stand
in front of their wooden home. Behind
them is their farm wagon, necessary
for the chores of their new life.

4

A Legend
That Will Not Fade

Long before the last Indians were settled on reservations, they had become part of a larger story that was to grow and change—and keep on changing as each generation of Americans took its turn at interpreting it—until today the story has become part of the national memory. Its title: The Legend of the West.

The legend of the American West may be viewed as reflecting colors in a spectrum. Most visible is purple—as in the prose of Zane Grey:

He had said straight out that he loved the girl—he had asked her to marry him—he kissed her—he hugged her—he lifted her upon his horse—he rode away with her through the night—and he married her. In whatever light Florence reviewed this thing, she always came back to her first natural impression; it thrilled her.

In the hands of Zane Grey, the legend sold more than 50 million copies. A good part of the legend's landscape was as purple as Grey's rhetoric: the sage on the plains, the distant hills at sundown, the profanity of the trail boss. Etched against this backdrop were sharper tones of black and white to help identify the cast—dark Stetsons for the bad guys, white ones for the sheriff's men. Once this line-up was clear, other blacks and whites could be mingled; both the good and bad gunslingers sported black-barreled Colt revolvers with gleaming pearl handles.

Even before the turn of this century, the legend had reached full and colorful flower. For kids all over America there were dime novels about *Red Ralph the Ranger* and *Wild Bill, the Whirlwind of the West*. Later, in novels for adults, like Owen Wister's *The Virginian*, a cloying romanticism was offered to lady readers who preferred their cowboy stories without cows. And, of course, the indefatigable Zane Grey, who churned out stories for 35 years, offered something for everyone—stampedes, gun fights and love affairs. It was a time when the authors, the public and the saga had all reached the same plateau of innocence.

Under the pressure of world leadership, modern America is manifestly losing its innocence, yet the legend gallops into more homes today via television than in the hardest-riding days of the dime and dollar novelists. How to account for this apparent contradiction? One explanation is that the frontier West contained enough authentic elements of drama to survive almost any kind of literary or dramatic maltreatment. But in a larger sense, the legend

The face of a working cowboy, Clarence H. Long, is tanned and weather-beaten after a lifetime on the ranges of the Texas Panhandle. Long, now a landowner after spending his youth working as a "hand" on big ranches, wears the traditional Stetson and neckerchief.

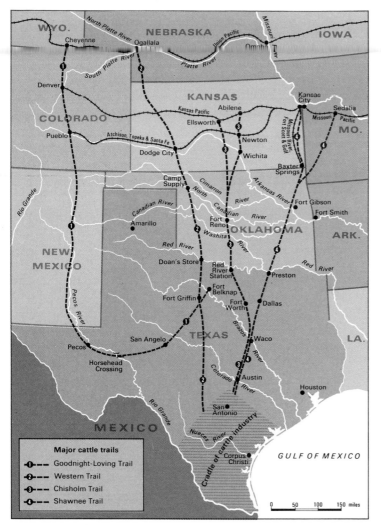

The four major routes taken by cowboys on their months-long cattle drives from southern Texas to cattle markets and railheads in the North were the Shawnee, Chisholm, Western and Goodnight-Loving Trails. The first, the Shawnee, which connected with the early railheads in Missouri, was largely abandoned when new railheads were established in Kansas. The Chisholm Trail, which saw its first cattle drive in 1866, was heavily traveled for 10 years, until the farmers of southern Kansas succeeded in making it off limits to the often disease-ridden Longhorns. A route farther west, the Western Trail, then came into general use. The Goodnight-Loving Trail, which went through dry and desolate Western areas, connected Texas with the cattle markets in New Mexico, Colorado and Wyoming.

is durable because it is essentially a primitive morality play. The triumph of the white hats over the black hats is more than an expression of America's view of the beneficence of its own continental development. It answers longings in men everywhere. Because of its universality, the struggle between the bad gunslinger and the sheriff has been elevated out of legend into myth. From there, it is not likely to be dislodged. In the words of the philosopher Ernst Cassirer, "A myth is in a sense invulnerable. It is impervious to rational arguments."

So the legend of the West goes on, growing with time. It is a kind of eternal granary containing seeds that can be selected and planted in any period. Thus, although it is a product of the 19th Century, the legend has little difficulty adapting to the social climate of the second half of the 20th. In the age of the civil rights movement, a Negro cowboy can simply be added to the cast of the television Western. Since some highly accomplished cowboys were, in fact, Negroes, the legend and the Longhorns can both march on unconcerned. Should a civil rights movement develop at some future date among American Indians, the legend's storehouse has another kernel ready to ripen: Indians may have been the most intrepid cattle handlers of all.

We have been calling the saga of the cowboy a legend and a myth. But, as we have seen, it is based —albeit not completely and none too solidly—on fact. There were cowboys—Negro, Mexican and Anglo-American—and cows and open range and rough cattle towns. In fact, the whole legend is deeply rooted in American history. For the legend to be best appreciated, however, the history must be kept in focus. It is not, for example, a legend that grows out of America's total frontier experience. Every region of the U.S. had at one time or another its frontier era: western New York State was once a frontier with a quite adequate supply of hostile Indians. The cowboy legend grows out of one specific frontier, the one that ran north into the Great Plains from Texas and that was truly frontier only for little more than a single generation. But for a while, the day-to-day events that transpired along this soon-to-disappear frontier had a grandiose quality that is the raw material of legend. The crucial uniqueness of this particular frontier is embodied in the trail-driving cowboy.

Without the cowboy, there could have been no Chisholm Trail and no roundups, no rustlers, stampedes or rodeos. Wyatt Earp could not have become marshal of Dodge City for the reason that there probably would have been no Dodge City (nor could that other famous cow town, Abilene, have sprung up to hire Wild Bill Hickok as its marshal).

The cowboy, then, is at the center of the legend's universe. Railroads were built to transport his cattle, and water and land customs and laws evolved in response to his needs. Yet, curiously, he was not solely a creation of the West; he owed much of his existence to the victorious North. To a large extent, his era was created out of the Civil War.

In the spring of 1865, when General Robert E. Lee surrendered his Southern armies, most of the war-weary nation viewed the American West (when it thought about it at all) as a rather distasteful place—a wilderness where cavalry was sent to put down Indian depredations; somewhere for people to go when they got in trouble or failed in business; a repository for outlaws, incompetents and surplus immigrants. True, a little seepage of the flood of romanticism that was to come had begun to trickle through—Davy Crockett had extended the Daniel Boone legend some distance westward and dime novels had appeared telling of Davy's barehanded exploit of wrestling a bear.

But the West of the fables and the Saturday night television drama, a land peopled with gunslingers, rustlers, U.S. marshals, sodbusters, cattle barons, hardy cowhands riding herd on stampeding Longhorns, *that* West had not yet been born. It was, however, about to be.

It all began in the first postwar spring of 1866.

The returning soldiers of Texas, like their impoverished counterparts throughout the defeated South, had to fall back on the most elemental resources of nature to find the substance for a new start. For those in South Texas, nature had provided an unusual bounty. Wild Longhorn cattle and mustang horses, both originally brought to the New World by the Spanish, had proliferated spectacularly in the plains environment. Millions of these animals roamed the open prairies; if a man was sufficiently strong or hard-working or ruthless, they were his for the taking.

The returning Confederate veteran did not need the price of a horse, merely the skill to find and break a mustang. For a few dollars he could avoid even this chore. Unbroken mustangs were rounded up and sold inexpensively, and a "gentled" horse could be had by paying four or five dollars to a "broncobuster." The service provided by the latter, while cheap, was also of limited utility; it proved only that, as was said in Texas, the animal could be mounted and ridden without death to either horse or rider. A thoroughly trained horse with "cow sense," the basic tool of the open-range cattleman, could be procured for from $10 to $18.

Also requiring little or no capital outlay was the crop itself. The Longhorns were everywhere. The originals of the breed had roamed the plains of North Africa and the province of Andalusia in Spain for a thousand years before a handful were brought to the New World on Columbus' second voyage. They and others that were subsequently imported multiplied rapidly. At the end of the 16th Century an enterprising Mexican cattleman was reported to be branding 30,000 head a year. By the 1850s, wild herds roamed the entire area between the Rio Grande and the Red River and in that same decade some cattle drives to Louisiana and Missouri were made. The Longhorns of the virgin North American plains had long legs and lanky bodies that lent them surprising speed. They have been accurately described as being "tall, bony, coarse-headed and coarse-haired, flat-sided, thin-flanked, sway-backed, big-eared, with tails dragging the ground and legs that belong to a race horse." Centuries of running wild on the range had bred a remarkable toughness and vitality, inuring them to both drought and blizzard and to the resulting by-products of thirst, hunger and cold.

The penniless ex-soldier thus had as much access to horses and Longhorns as his ambition and his strength permitted. At the outset, land ownership was not a problem either, as the range was largely unfenced and open. The only problem was that the Texas cattle were not worth much of anything in Texas. But elsewhere in the nation four years of wartime destruction had diminished livestock herds at a time when large new markets were opening up. In the North cattle brought from $30 to $40 per head as the people of the victorious Union clamored for beef. If a man could only get these Texas Longhorns to market. . . .

The Spanish culture of South Texas helped provide the answer. It not only furnished the product (the Longhorn) but also the basic tools of the trade (a herd of cow ponies, or a remuda). In addition, Mexican *vaqueros*, or cowboys, had pioneered the technique of roping cattle from horseback through the use of *la reata*. When the gringos of Texas pronounced the two words, it came out "lariat." With those inheritances, all that was needed was a marketing device. The American contribution: the long-distance trail drive.

The first of the great trail drives north out of Texas came in the spring and summer of 1866. To obtain mounts, cattlemen went "mustanging" in the brush country of South Texas and stocked their *remudas* from the range-running horse herds. This accomplished, they proceeded to round up

wild cattle, often through the use of small decoy herds of "gentle" Longhorns (a gentle Longhorn was described as a wild Longhorn that could look at a man on horseback without stampeding).

Out of the boot of Texas, starting near the mouth of the Rio Grande, came the great restless herds of Longhorns, trekking northward toward San Antonio, the first town of any consequence along the way. Fledgling trail hands learned that the Longhorn was an exceptional trail animal with a long, swinging stride and a temperament that grew more cooperative with each day on the move. The semiwild cows could walk 15 miles to water and make one drink last two days. Gradually, a kind of order evolved. Two men called "pointers" rode at the head of the caravan, then swing riders and flank riders and, in the rear, drag riders. A cowhand quickly learned to value both a horse trained for night herding and a trail outfit that provided a good chuck wagon. He learned that high-topped boots gave needed protection against rattlesnakes and brush and that high heels gripped the stirrups better. A neck handkerchief was helpful in combating trail dust; indeed, when riding drag behind the herd, virtually the only way a man could breathe was by pulling his bandanna up over his nose. The tall-peaked Mexican sombrero was the best defense

against the plains sun, its broad brim doubling as an umbrella when it rained. The cowboy's lariat was his most indispensable trail tool besides his horse and his gun, though it compelled him to wear gauntlets to protect his hands and wrists from rope burns. In the mesquite country of South Texas, he discovered that a rough leather covering worn by the Mexicans was ideal to protect his legs while on horseback. Many wore these *chaparejos*, or "chaps," all the way to Kansas. Each article of clothing had its own special purpose, yet the sum of them all heralded a new way of life.

That same spring of 1866, gradually, almost imperceptibly, San Antonio became the first of the cow towns of the legendary West. Its development had none of the spectacular boomtown aspects of its sister cow towns that were shortly to arise in Kansas at the other end of the cattle trail. But San Antonio was to prove the most durable of them all, performing its special function during the entire period of the cattle drives. Created by the Spanish as a fortified outpost, the old city had endured uncertain times at the hands of Comanche raiders, frontier freebooters and land-seeking Americans before its Alamo became a symbol of revolution and freedom in 1836.

Now in the aftermath of the Civil War, restless

How the range really looked

A priceless, authentic record of the life of the cowboy at the turn of the century is provided by Texan Erwin E. Smith's photographs, two of which are shown here. Born in 1886, Smith was too late to photograph the great trail drives, but his work shows what herding cattle was like in the era when many steers were still Longhorns, and Jeeps and pickup trucks were far in the future. The photograph at left captures one of the cowhand's worst enemies, the choking clouds of dust that a herd on the move kicked up, and that especially afflicted the men riding "drag" behind the stragglers. The picture at right shows a cook inspecting an iron pot of stew over a log fire, while a cowboy sleeps in the shade of a temporary tent strung from the side of the chuck wagon. The chuck box at the rear of the wagon, facing the camera, was fitted with drawers and compartments for food: the staples on the range were coffee, beef and sourdough biscuits.

herds of Longhorns, the scent of the open range still fresh in their nostrils, were driven to the city from the south of Texas. As they came, the old city began to be transformed into a frontier town trading in commodities virtually unknown outside of the cow country. Men who were determined to try the long cattle drive to the north bought Longhorns from more cautious citizens who preferred a small profit to the risks of the trail. Fledgling cowboys discussed their footwear needs with local bootmakers and the craft of fashioning trail boots began to take form. For as long as the cattle drives lasted and for generations thereafter, men were to demonstrate their Western credentials by pointing to their high tops and remarking proudly, "Had 'em made myself, down in San Antone." Although no one seemed to take special notice of it, the city was to take on the aspect of a hiring hall that dealt in the practitioners of other new crafts—horse wranglers, cowpunchers and trail bosses.

In the plains surrounding the city, and elsewhere in the South Texas area that was soon to be known as the cattle kingdom, mixed groups of cows were merged into huge trail herds, and a strange new custom had its primitive origins, the cattle being marked with fresh "road-brands" for identification along the trail. One by one in the spring and early summer of 1866, the herds were nudged into line and the first of the great drives had begun.

It was a 1,000-mile push from the tip of Texas to the railheads in Missouri where the "trail outfits" hoped to market their herds. From the outset there were many hazards—the restlessness of the Longhorns and the subtle barriers of shallow, unpredictable plains rivers that could flood into torrents over shifting quicksands. Some herds began to suffer heavy losses from bad river crossings or from sudden stampedes that were beyond the control of the trail hands.

Across the Colorado and the Brazos they went, and then over the Red River into Indian Territory. The huge herds seemed to consume prairie grass like locusts, and the civilized Indian tribes, with their vast holdings in eastern Oklahoma, let it be known that they expected to be paid grass rentals. Farther west, the prairie was open—but in that direction there was always the danger of damaging raids by the Comanche, widely known as elite rustlers of livestock. Most trail bosses veered eastward that first year, heading for the Missouri railheads, and tried to bluff or bargain their way through the lands of the Civilized Tribes. The losses to drownings, rustlings, sickness and stampedes mounted.

North of the Arkansas River, the cowboys, almost

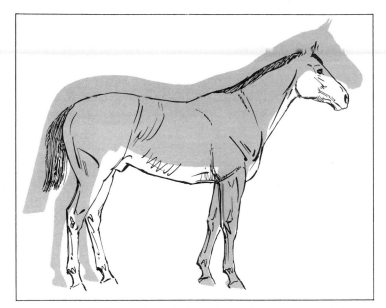

The Quarter Horse, the horse that can "turn on a dime and give you a nickel in change," was developed by 17th Century Southern colonists and named for its ability to beat other steeds in a quarter-mile race. Short, stocky and heavily muscled compared to the Thoroughbred (on which it is superimposed above), it is nevertheless a graceful animal. By the 19th Century the Quarter Horse had reached Texas, and crossed with the descendants of
• Spanish mustangs, it has produced some of the finest cow ponies.

all of them former Confederate soldiers, picked up rumors of Northern hostility ahead on the trail. To many staunch Union men of Kansas and Missouri, the high-pitched trail cries sounded disturbingly like the rebel yell, evoking grim images of the recent war. Who could say these mounted men had not ridden for the swift-striking Confederate cavalry of Jeb Stuart or Joe Wheeler or Nathan Bedford Forrest?

Other farmers who nursed no grudges noted that their own domesticated cattle became sick and died after the tick-ridden Texas herds passed through. The disease, to which the range-hardened Longhorns had become immune, was known in Texas as "Spanish fever." The Kansans and Missourians had another name for it: Texas fever. As the news spread in 1866 that Texas herds were heading their way, bands of armed men formed to block the trail, demanding that the herds be detoured farther west around farming and livestock country and away from the few existing Missouri railheads.

Even more ominously, other armed bands, composed not of farmers but of border ruffians, began to appear on the fringes of the herds. For a price, the herds could go through; otherwise, they would be stampeded over miles of plains where the numerous strays could be rustled at leisure. Even trail

bosses who paid tribute had no security against the reappearance of their blackmailers, signaled by shouts, gunfire and a sudden, fearsome nighttime stampede. Inevitably, there was gunplay with these bandits. Some outfits gave up in despair. Turning loose what was left of their herds to winter on the prairie, they returned empty-handed to Texas.

Would-be cattlemen thus discovered that the entire route was one of unending peril. They braved the assorted dangers for the simple reason that a Longhorn worth about three dollars in San Antonio brought up to $40 at the railroad terminal in Sedalia, Missouri. But inexperienced as they were in the world of the cattle trail, outfit after outfit suffered disaster. The drive of 1866 became a colossal failure. Of the quarter of a million Longhorns pointed northward in 1866, only a handful ever reached Eastern markets. With the coming of winter, Texas cattlemen knew they were not exempt from the poverty that coursed through the other states of the defeated Confederacy. No one could guess a legend had been born.

Yet the Southern plains remained alive with Longhorns—six million of them. And in the spring of 1867 the price of beef in Northern markets was still high. The Texans puzzled over the possibilities.

They were not alone. The first postwar drive had been a revelation to a tall, loud-talking Illinois visionary named Joseph G. McCoy. Correctly concluding that trail drives through the unpopulated country somewhat farther to the west might avoid farmers, bandits and other perils, McCoy persuaded officials of the Kansas Pacific Railroad, which ran across Kansas, to grant him special freight rates for cattle. He then went looking for a railroad that would agree to carry the cattle from the Kansas-Missouri border to Midwestern market outlets. Thrown out of the offices of the Missouri Pacific Railroad in St. Louis, McCoy doggedly touted his vision to the officers of the Hannibal and St. Joseph Railroad, a line that ran from St. Joseph, Missouri, to Chicago. They heard him out and agreed—a decision that made Chicago rather than St. Louis the stockyard capital of the U.S. Going back to the people of the Kansas Pacific, McCoy selected a spot on their line that he thought might be convenient for the Texas drovers. An agent was dispatched southward to spread the word through Texas that a cordial welcome awaited all trail herds at a place in Kansas called Abilene.

Abilene was little more than a dozen log huts, some newly fenced corrals, a pair of cattle scales and two iron ribbons snaking eastward across the plains. But it was enough: a substantial number of

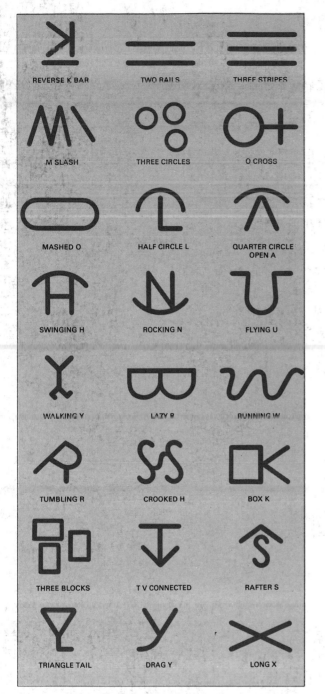

As distinctive as royal coats of arms, cattle brands identify ranches and their herds. They are essentially pictograms and there is a special —and somewhat confusing—vocabulary that describes them. For example, a horizontal line may be called by three different names: a long line is a "rail"; a short line placed beneath a letter or symbol is a "bar"; three or more lines are "stripes." Similarly arcs, called half or quarter circles in some brands, take different names when attached to letters in other brands. The addition of wings or legs can make letters "fly" or "walk" while other terms such as "drag," "long" and "running" describe letters that, to render the brands distinctive, have been distorted in one fashion or another.

cattle reached there in 1867, proving the feasibility of the long-distance cattle drive. The legend had its second cow town. Packed into freight cars at Abilene, huge numbers of Texas cows jostled over the rails to Chicago and thence to markets all over the Midwest and East. The numbers multiplied geometrically—75,000 in 1868, 350,000 the next year and 700,000 by 1871.

The people of the cattle country of Texas increasingly practiced a strange new folkway, a wild free-for-all that went by the name of "mavericking." As a folkway it was added abruptly to the other springtime custom of mustanging. The term derived from the actions of an early-day cattleman named Samuel Maverick who let his unbranded cattle roam over the prairie, mixing in with other herds so that all unbranded calves in the area were said to be "Maverick's." The term spread until it came to apply to all unbranded cows, as well as to each year's crop of calves, whoever the owner might be.

In the loose frontier life of the unfenced range, the spring roundups of "mavericks" became a test of stealth in which virtually everything afoot was fair game for the branding iron. "Mavericking" was thus a genteel Texas term for cattle stealing by the pillars and would-be pillars of the community. The universality of the custom is indicated by the cattleman who only half jokingly told folklorist J. Frank Dobie that "any cowman of open range days who claimed never to have put his brand on somebody else's animal was either a liar or a poor roper." In those first postwar days, at least, cattle rustling was about the only workable method of capital accumulation for men who had no other resources. Less easily explained, of course, are the loose values and primitive cynicism that wholesale stealing inculcated into the way of life; few objective Texans would claim their land has yet fully escaped this darker aspect of its heritage.

But in the heady days of the open range, cattlemen had little time for such ethical considerations. Once the mustanging and mavericking had been completed each spring, the drive itself became the final challenge. The 90-to-120-day trek northward was an unromantic experience of lonely hard work, often for 20 hours at a stretch. As the cowboys became more adept at controlling stampedes and managing river crossings, trail outfits were able to cut the number of hired hands. By 1880 eight good men were all that were considered necessary for handling 1,500 head for 1,000 miles. At $25 per month for ordinary cowpunchers, the turnover in the work force was high.

When water was scarce and the cattle restless,

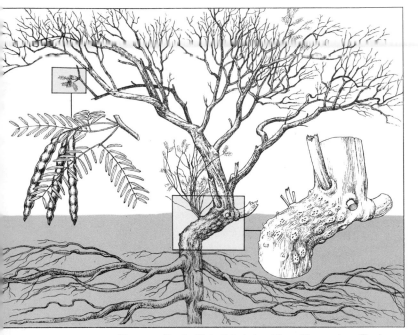

The mesquite plant is both hated and feared by ranchers. The beans *(left)*, which spread the plant, are harmful to cattle. Further, mesquite is almost impossible to exterminate: even if it is cut off at ground level, the stump *(right)* will sprout again. The plant also has a huge root system that leaches large amounts of water.

night-herding trail hands tried to quiet their cows by singing to them:

Oh say, li'l dogie, when you going to lay down,
And give up this shifting and roving around?
My horse is leg weary and I'm awful tired,
But if you get away, I am sure to be fired.
Lay down, little dogie, lay down.

To drown the wild sounds of the night, trail hands talked to their cows and, less frequently, to one another. When they reached Abilene after three months on the trail, they were ready to unleash a few wild sounds of their own. Abilene and the railheads that succeeded it were ready to accommodate them; if San Antonio dealt in new commodities, the cow towns at the other end of the trail thrived by satisfying the oldest instincts in man. All were rich in saloons, saloon girls and gambling halls.

The Atchison, Topeka and Santa Fe Railway reached Newton, Kansas, in July 1871, soon consigning Abilene to an oblivion that only the legend was to overcome. In the next year the rails marched on to Ellsworth and Wichita and finally to Dodge City. Each new boomtown resembled the one it replaced, with its Alamo Bar or its Texas Saloon discreetly located on the other side of the tracks from the town's permanent citizens.

Here, in these prairie boondocks, was the stuff of legend. Here, marshals like Wild Bill Hickok of Abilene and Wyatt Earp of Dodge City labored to enforce their own brand of order on the Texas cowboys. (Earp, who collected a $2.50 bonus for each Texan he arrested, earned a reputation for dedication, if not for fairness.) Here, occasionally, there was a certain amount of gunplay—not enough to justify the fusillades that assault the modern television viewer, but enough, certainly, to provide the substance of stories cowmen could expand upon during the long winter and over the branding fires at spring roundups. Most drovers came to believe that a Texas gunman named John Wesley Hardin coolly took Wild Bill Hickok's guns away from him, and perhaps he did. As all worthy students of the legend know, Hickok eventually died with his boots on while playing poker in a saloon in Deadwood, South Dakota—the cards he held, pairs of aces and eights, forever after have been known as a "dead man's hand." Hardin, for his part, developed a towering reputation as a gunfighter before being shot down on the streets of El Paso in 1895.

The emerging lore was sustained by hard economic facts. As refrigerated railroad cars made it possible to transport slaughtered Texas beef to Eastern ports and thence in refrigerated ships to European markets, prices soared from the 1877 level of $2.25 per hundred pounds on the hoof to nine dollars and more in 1882. Since matured Longhorns weighed 800 to 1,000 pounds and some went as high as 1,600 pounds, a single large herd marketed in Kansas could bring a sizable fortune to its owner. The number of Longhorns put on the trail rose into the millions, bringing wealth to many and also causing a frantic scramble for the free grass of the open range. The age of the cattle king had arrived.

Then, as now, large-scale ranching in the West hinged on the availability of water. A man's control of water resources was governed by a system of "range rights" that evolved in the West. A frontier rancher found a stream, established a headquarters camp and claimed all land facing the stream for 15 or 20 miles plus all the land back from the stream as far as the ridge that marked the water divide. Beyond the divide lay another stream and the land of another rancher. In an area without streams, the cattleman could place his homestead near a water hole and control the surrounding range as effectively as if it were tightly fenced in.

As the land became more thickly settled and men began to fence their ranches, these easy doctrines came under intense pressure. The way some

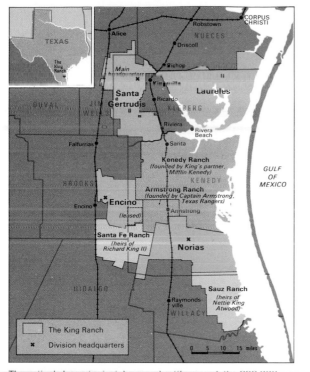

The nation's largest privately owned cattle spread, the 820,000 acre King Ranch, operated by the Kleberg family, dominates the southeastern coastal section of Texas, along with ranches run by other descendants of Richard King. The King Ranch maintains an average of 50,000 head of cattle and more than 2,100 horses.

ranchers acquired and held their grasslands became a study in courage and sometimes ruthlessness. To make sure of retaining control of the land they had claimed, a number of cattlemen bought rights to it from the federal government under the Homestead Act. They paid $1.25 an acre, first purchasing those acres on which their ranch house stood and where their water was. Some borrowed money from their cowhands to purchase further acreage. Not a few cattlemen then fenced in thousands of acres of prairie to which they had no legal right at all and proceeded to defend these holdings against all comers.

Of all the great cattle barons of fact and fable, Richard King and Charles Goodnight left their names most firmly embedded in the history of the West—King because of the sheer size of his acquisitions and Goodnight because of his courage and resourcefulness in combating the hostile land. King fled a New York apprenticeship as a boy, eventually became a river pilot, and later made a fortune out of the Confederacy as a wartime cotton agent and speculator along the Rio Grande. He used the proceeds of these ventures to buy up more and more Texas land, eventually assembling the fabulous empire of the King Ranch that today covers more than 800,000 acres of the boot of Texas.

Goodnight was an authentic frontiersman who pioneered an extraordinary "dry-drive" trail up the Pecos Valley to cattle markets in New Mexico. The trail was extended northward to Denver by Goodnight's partner, Oliver Loving. The cattle passage to the land west of the Pecos was only for the most hardy; Loving was fatally wounded by Comanche warriors during the drive through the Pecos Valley in 1867. The business of driving cattle across waterless deserts was extraordinarily arduous; the animals had to be driven without rest because their thirst made them so restless that they could not be controlled if they were allowed to stop. Goodnight's subsequent efforts to tame the arid Western ranges constitute an epic of determination and courage, quite in keeping with the legend—though Goodnight's story has been left largely unrecorded by writers of Western romances. Only the great accomplishment of his earlier years, the Goodnight-Loving Trail, has become a recognized part of the Western saga.

As the cattle barons arose and larger and larger herds were assembled, the great days of the trail drives came to their climax—and to their disastrous end. It had been a risky business from the start. Men like King and Goodnight had spent much of their energy and ingenuity trying to find some kind of insurance against the droughts, diseases and blizzards that assaulted the cattle kingdom. Finally, in 1886, they were struck by a series of droughts and blizzards that helped to bring an end to the era of the trail drive.

The blizzard of the 1886-1887 winter is known in Western history as the "Big Die-Up." Countless thousands of cows died in the Texas Panhandle, along the trails to Kansas, and on overstocked winter ranges in Colorado, Nebraska, Wyoming and the Dakotas. In an effort to combat falling prices in 1884 and 1885, both absentee-owned Eastern and English cattle companies and Texas cattlemen had frantically marketed greater amounts of beef and had enlarged their herds beyond the capacity of their grass resources. The 1886-1887 blizzard, hitting the overstocked ranges, killed as many cattle by starvation as by cold. But other factors were also helping to bring an end to the trail drives. By 1886 railroads had radiated throughout cattle country, and it became safer, though less profitable, to sell steers at nearby railheads than to drive the herds north. Further, the prairies were increasingly being fenced, making the old drives across open range all but impossible. After 20 years, the great drives were over, although the way of life lingered to the end of the century and became memorialized in the trail drivers' reunions at the Buckhorn Saloon in San Antonio. But by 1890, whatever the legend was to become, the data had been assembled and the facts were all in.

What distinguishes the real from pure fable? We will probably never get a completely satisfactory answer. There are many seeming inconsistencies. It is somewhat dismaying to discover, for example, that the Colt revolver carried by the early cowboys had an effective range of only 25 to 30 yards and was not equal in either range or deadliness to the bow and arrow until the improved version of 1870. And the quiet truth is that most cowboys never saw an Indian on the warpath. Few Texas cattle outfits braved the Trans-Pecos country of the warlike Comanche as Goodnight and Loving did. Generally trail hands worried far more about the silent, efficient rustling of their herds by deft Indians than they did about an arrow in the back. For the cowboy, the essence of life was the lonely trail between Texas and Kansas where his principal foes were the recalcitrant steers entrusted to his care and the problems of water, both too much and too little.

True, there were "cattle barons," but the battle between the cattleman and the farmer has been vastly overplayed. In the era of Populist agitation that followed the era of the open cattle range, farmers considered their chief enemies to be the banks and the railroads whose ubiquitous land lobbyists corrupted state legislatures and siphoned off the West's public lands. Farmers had relatively little to quarrel about with their neighbors the cattlemen. Other assorted tidbits that contaminate the purity of the legend are continually being discovered by modern historians.

Yet bits and pieces of information stretch across the decades to underscore the reality that, in one way or another, it all *did* happen. Trail drivers did wear high-heeled boots, sombreros and bandannas. Their mustangs were unquestionably superb trail animals. Invariably there was a chuck wagon; Charles Goodnight invented one of the earliest models. And every cowboy fan under the age of 70 can relax in the knowledge that Bat Masterson was one of the expert marksmen whose buffalo guns drove off the Indians at Adobe Walls in 1874.

Arduous as the cowboy's life was, distorted as his saga has become, the cowboy legend has nevertheless had much more than a simple appeal to incorrigible romanticism. Its telling and retelling has seemed to satisfy in all men some deep longing for clear moral definitions. A modern theologian, addicted to reading Westerns, once explained his interest in exactly these terms: "If just once I could

stand in the dust of the frontier main street facing an indubitably bad man who really deserved extermination, and with smoking six-gun actually exterminate him—shoot him once and see him drop dead. Just once to face real and unqualified evil, plug it and see it drop. . . ."

Whatever it may yet become, the legend has long since transcended national boundaries. Books on the wild West by German author Karl May have sold some 15 million copies to cowboy-and-Indian fans in the land of Goethe and Wagner. Increasingly, Oriental sharpshooters, complete with chaps and lariats, dominate the motion-picture and television screens of Japan, their twirling Colt revolvers plugging the black-hatted villains with the precision of Marshal Dillon.

Meanwhile, back in the land where it all began, the end of the long trail drives closed only one chapter of the cattle story. As access to markets was made secure in Texas, cattle raising became the province of thousands of small stockmen as well as of the great cattle barons. Today, in Texas, a number of the huge outfits like the King Ranch remain—their ranch hands using jeeps and helicopters as well as cow ponies to work with the vast herds. But significant numbers of cattle are also raised on small farms. Many residents of the state's cities have their "piece of land" out in the country where often the only visible sign of activity is a cluster of grazing cattle. The bony Longhorns are gone, replaced by stout modern breeds such as Herefords, Brahmans, Santa Gertrudis and Angus that yield more and better beef.

Oldtimers grudgingly admit that the new breeds make for better steaks. But in defense of the long-striding old Longhorn, they point out that the stubby modern cows could never have made it up the Chisholm Trail. That part of the saga of the West—the hardiness of the Longhorn—was never in the least mythological.

A few thousand Americans—probably not more than 40,000—heard the call and actually lived the life of the cowboy for a few years between 1866 and 1890; millions more all over the world have lived it vicariously ever since. Since it has captured the imagination of so many, the legend of the West cannot wholly be without value. Where is the greenhorn among us who has not dreamed of a life of personal engagement with nature, alongside generous comrades who seldom utter a discouraging word, out where the deer and the antelope play? The myth of the American West grows with time because part of it actually happened and all of it, perhaps, should have.

Cattle raising
the modern way

The Old West—where Longhorn cattle roamed the open range and leather-skinned cowboys fought rustlers as they drove their herds to the railheads—is firmly enshrined in a legend that dies hard. But in fact cattle ranching in Texas, the nation's leading beef producer, has for most of its history been more an industry than a romance. For years the range has been fenced in, and today the rancher is likely to have been to college.

Cattle breeding is a marginal business, often turning a profit no greater than could be earned by money on deposit in a savings bank. For this reason ranches use scientific methods and are run with strict attention to efficiency. Trucks and tractors are replacing the horse for some tasks, and every detail of cattle raising is carefully planned to make cattle the most efficient possible machines for turning forage into meat.

Dripping wet after a trip through a "dipping vat," a Hereford starts back to pasture on a Texas ranch. Cattle are dipped several times a year to rid them of insects. Some of the pests cause disease; others irritate the animals so much that they fail to eat enough.

SHORTHORN

These placid cattle, crossbred in Texas with the Brahman, produced the first American purebred, the Santa Gertrudis. Shorthorns are both good beef producers and excellent dairy animals.

THE LONGHORN

Nine types of modern beef producers

In the late 1870s, when railroads penetrated to the heart of Texas cattle country and barbed wire began to enclose the open ranges, the lean Longhorns around which the cattle industry had grown were doomed. The endurance and self-sufficiency that let them survive long drives across open country were no longer essential. Gradually, the Longhorn was replaced by short, stocky cattle bred mainly for the quality and quantity of their beef.

In 1873 Texas ranchers began importing stock from Britain to improve their herds. The first imports were Shorthorns, which were soon followed by white-faced Herefords and black Aberdeen Angus. The British breeds did not prove entirely successful in the Southwest, however. Adapted to a cool climate, they faltered under the heat, insect pests and diseases of parts of the region. To improve the resistance of the British breeds, ranchers crossed them with huge, humped Brahman cattle from India.

Now several breeds and crossbreeds have been developed that thrive in the Southwestern climate and still produce high-quality beef. A sampling of show bulls from these various types is shown here.

ABERDEEN ANGUS

A short, stocky black animal from Scotland, the Angus yields well-marbled beef. Hornless and resistant to eye diseases, it usually passes these desired characteristics to offspring.

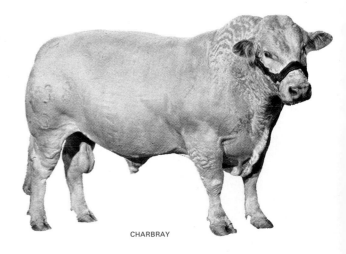

CHARBRAY

Originally developed in the Texas Rio Grande Valley, this animal is a cross between the Brahman and the Charolais. Charbrays are relatively large and easy to handle, and their calves grow rapidly.

BRAHMAN

The name Brahman is given to a breed developed from several types of cattle imported from India. Brahmans are used primarily for crossbreeding; most of them are found in the Gulf Coast.

HEREFORD

Originally from Herefordshire in England, this purebred has thrived in the United States. Most U.S. beef cattle have the characteristic red body and white face that indicate Hereford ancestry.

CHAROLAIS

A relatively recent arrival, these huge cream-colored cattle originated in France and are popular in the United States because they grow rapidly and require less feed than many other breeds.

SANTA GERTRUDIS

All Santa Gertrudis cattle stem from one bull, a Brahman-Shorthorn crossbred called Monkey. Fast-maturing, they were bred for semiarid range conditions and need little care while on pasture.

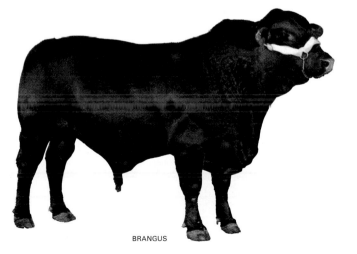

BRANGUS

Brangus cattle, first developed in Louisiana, are three-eighths Brahman and five-eighths Angus. They retain the fine beef qualities of the Angus and inherit resistance and size from the Brahman.

BEEFMASTER

This hardy animal was developed by crossing three breeds: Brahman, Hereford and Shorthorn. Beefmasters may show the Hereford's white markings. Large but gentle, they produce fine beef.

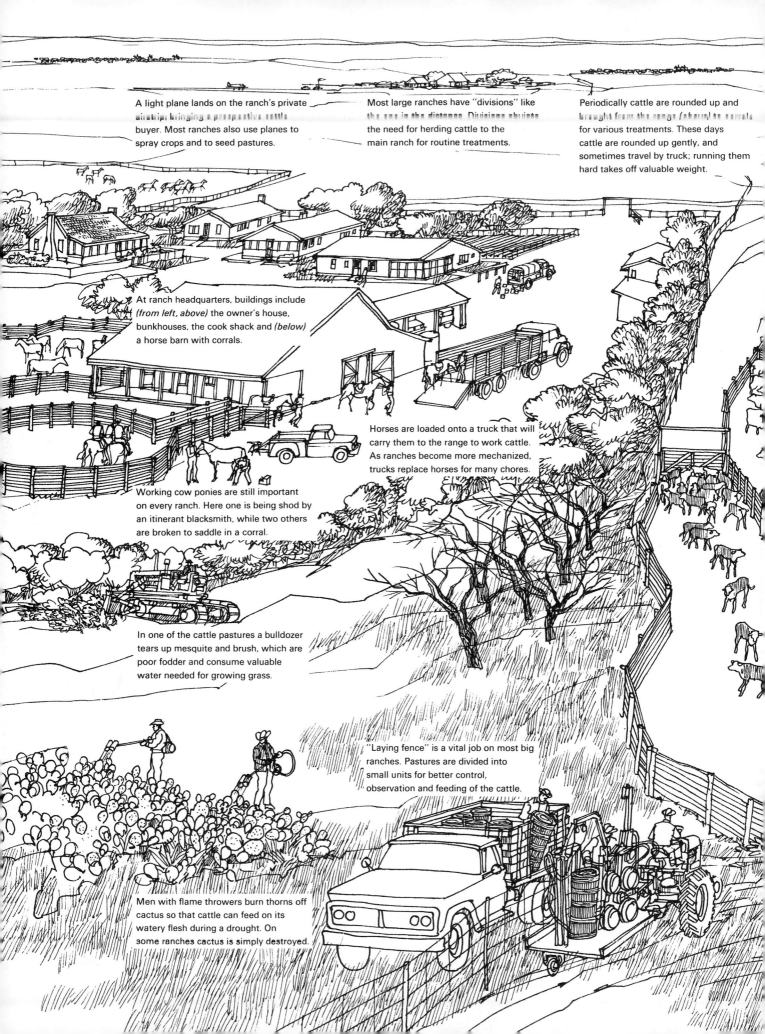

A light plane lands on the ranch's private airstrip, bringing a prospective cattle buyer. Most ranches also use planes to spray crops and to seed pastures.

Most large ranches have "divisions" like the one in the distance. Divisions obviate the need for herding cattle to the main ranch for routine treatments.

Periodically cattle are rounded up and brought from the range (above) to corrals for various treatments. These days cattle are rounded up gently, and sometimes travel by truck; running them hard takes off valuable weight.

At ranch headquarters, buildings include (from left, above) the owner's house, bunkhouses, the cook shack and (below) a horse barn with corrals.

Horses are loaded onto a truck that will carry them to the range to work cattle. As ranches become more mechanized, trucks replace horses for many chores.

Working cow ponies are still important on every ranch. Here one is being shod by an itinerant blacksmith, while two others are broken to saddle in a corral.

In one of the cattle pastures a bulldozer tears up mesquite and brush, which are poor fodder and consume valuable water needed for growing grass.

"Laying fence" is a vital job on most big ranches. Pastures are divided into small units for better control, observation and feeding of the cattle.

Men with flame throwers burn thorns off cactus so that cattle can feed on its watery flesh during a drought. On some ranches cactus is simply destroyed.

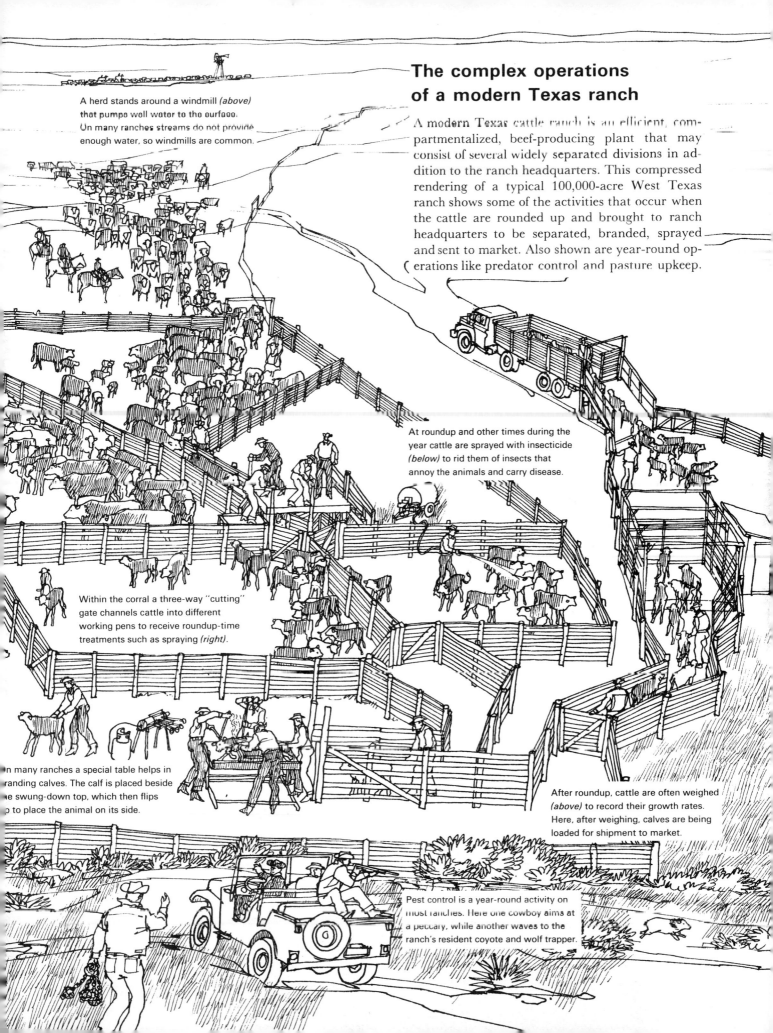

A herd stands around a windmill *(above)* that pumps well water to the surface. On many ranches streams do not provide enough water, so windmills are common.

The complex operations of a modern Texas ranch

A modern Texas cattle ranch is an efficient, compartmentalized, beef-producing plant that may consist of several widely separated divisions in addition to the ranch headquarters. This compressed rendering of a typical 100,000-acre West Texas ranch shows some of the activities that occur when the cattle are rounded up and brought to ranch headquarters to be separated, branded, sprayed and sent to market. Also shown are year-round operations like predator control and pasture upkeep.

At roundup and other times during the year cattle are sprayed with insecticide *(below)* to rid them of insects that annoy the animals and carry disease.

Within the corral a three-way "cutting" gate channels cattle into different working pens to receive roundup-time treatments such as spraying *(right)*.

On many ranches a special table helps in branding calves. The calf is placed beside the swung-down top, which then flips up to place the animal on its side.

After roundup, cattle are often weighed *(above)* to record their growth rates. Here, after weighing, calves are being loaded for shipment to market.

Pest control is a year-round activity on most ranches. Here one cowboy aims at a peccary, while another waves to the ranch's resident coyote and wolf trapper.

Technology on the range

Like all modern industries, cattle ranching depends heavily on machinery for its success. Although no machine has been developed to match a cow pony's ability to work cattle, trucks and tractors perform most of the horse's other draft and transportation work. One large Texas ranch operates a fleet of 41 vehicles, all equipped with two-way radios, and its cowboys drive about 150,000 miles a month. Agricultural technology has also played a great part in improving ranch efficiency. Cattle used to forage for whatever feed they could find. Today many eat specially developed grasses and prepared feeds.

On a ranch near Tyler, Texas *(left)*, one of the hands forks Coastal Bermuda grass into a spreader. This newly developed hybrid grass is rich in nutrients; two acres of it will support a cow and calf that normally require up to 40 acres of ordinary pasture.

Hats pulled down against the wind, two cowboys ride to work on saddles mounted on the back of a pickup truck. To save time and preserve the horses' energy for tasks only cow ponies can perform, they too are carried to the range by trailer *(background)*.

Inspecting cattle by helicopter *(right)* is a new technique used on a few large Texas ranches. Some cattle have become so accustomed to the copter that a rancher can fly low over them to observe individual animals without danger of stampeding the herd.

A group of cattle is sold off at one of the regular auctions held by the Amarillo Livestock Auction Company in Texas. Auctions take place every week, all year long. Sales of about 380,000 head a year make this the leading auction market in the U.S.

Marketing the yearly crop of cattle

Marketing beef cattle is accomplished by several different methods. For years most of the cattle were shipped by rail to be sold by commission firms at large terminal markets in major cities. In the 1930s improved trucking and decentralization of slaughterhouses reduced the reliance on rail shipments, and today increasing numbers of cattle are sold at auctions held relatively close to their home ranges. Many are also sold by what cattlemen call "private treaty": a buyer purchases directly from a rancher, specifying the type of animals he wants rather than taking whatever is available at the markets.

Cowboys at the Fort Worth Stockyards, a terminal market, use motorcycles to herd cattle into pens, where purchasers will collect them. Regardless of where ranchers sell them, most cattle are shipped elsewhere for additional fattening before slaughter.

From calf to cutlet:
the life story of beef cattle

Almost all beef cattle eventually end up as meat, but they reach the butcher in a variety of ways. Much of the good meat comes from young castrated bulls called steers, although some also comes from heifers, or young cows. Before they are slaughtered, these animals have often been fattened on special diets to make their meat tender. Canned meat and other processed meats such as sausage come mostly from older animals or inferior young ones. Only a relatively small percentage of animals are kept for breeding, and all but a very few of these are eventually slaughtered to make processed meat.

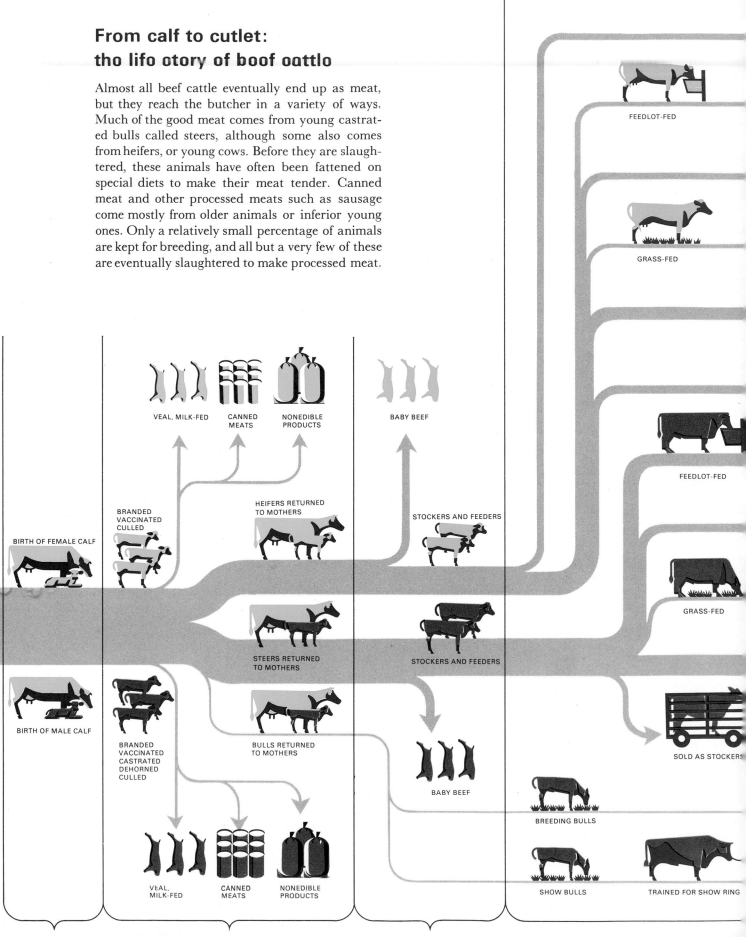

FEEDLOT-FED

GRASS-FED

VEAL, MILK-FED

CANNED MEATS

NONEDIBLE PRODUCTS

BABY BEEF

FEEDLOT-FED

BRANDED VACCINATED CULLED

HEIFERS RETURNED TO MOTHERS

STOCKERS AND FEEDERS

BIRTH OF FEMALE CALF

GRASS-FED

STEERS RETURNED TO MOTHERS

STOCKERS AND FEEDERS

BIRTH OF MALE CALF

BRANDED VACCINATED CASTRATED DEHORNED CULLED

BULLS RETURNED TO MOTHERS

SOLD AS STOCKERS

BABY BEEF

BREEDING BULLS

VEAL, MILK-FED

CANNED MEATS

NONEDIBLE PRODUCTS

SHOW BULLS

TRAINED FOR SHOW RING

FIRST TWO MONTHS   **THIRD MONTH**   **4-8 MONTHS**

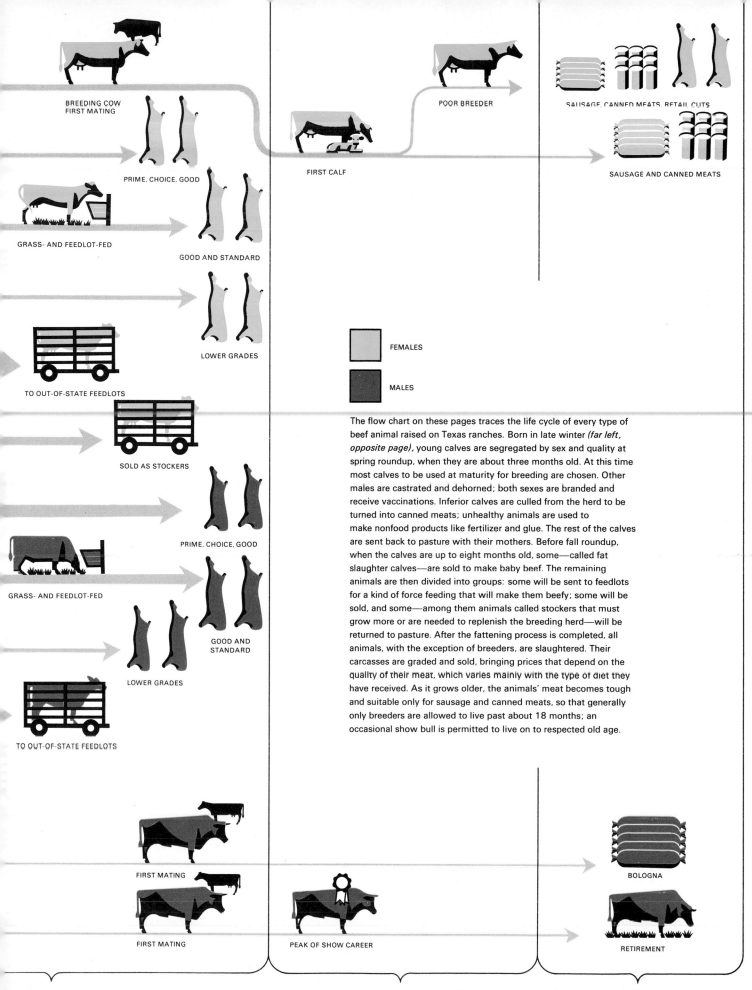

BREEDING COW
FIRST MATING

PRIME, CHOICE, GOOD

GRASS- AND FEEDLOT-FED

GOOD AND STANDARD

LOWER GRADES

TO OUT-OF-STATE FEEDLOTS

SOLD AS STOCKERS

PRIME, CHOICE, GOOD

GRASS- AND FEEDLOT-FED

GOOD AND STANDARD

LOWER GRADES

TO OUT-OF-STATE FEEDLOTS

FIRST MATING

FIRST MATING

POOR BREEDER

FIRST CALF

FEMALES

MALES

PEAK OF SHOW CAREER

SAUSAGE, CANNED MEATS, RETAIL CUTS

SAUSAGE AND CANNED MEATS

BOLOGNA

RETIREMENT

The flow chart on these pages traces the life cycle of every type of
beef animal raised on Texas ranches. Born in late winter *(far left,
opposite page),* young calves are segregated by sex and quality at
spring roundup, when they are about three months old. At this time
most calves to be used at maturity for breeding are chosen. Other
males are castrated and dehorned; both sexes are branded and
receive vaccinations. Inferior calves are culled from the herd to be
turned into canned meats; unhealthy animals are used to
make nonfood products like fertilizer and glue. The rest of the calves
are sent back to pasture with their mothers. Before fall roundup,
when the calves are up to eight months old, some—called fat
slaughter calves—are sold to make baby beef. The remaining
animals are then divided into groups: some will be sent to feedlots
for a kind of force feeding that will make them beefy; some will be
sold, and some—among them animals called stockers that must
grow more or are needed to replenish the breeding herd—will be
returned to pasture. After the fattening process is completed, all
animals, with the exception of breeders, are slaughtered. Their
carcasses are graded and sold, bringing prices that depend on the
quality of their meat, which varies mainly with the type of diet they
have received. As it grows older, the animals' meat becomes tough
and suitable only for sausage and canned meats, so that generally
only breeders are allowed to live past about 18 months; an
occasional show bull is permitted to live on to respected old age.

9-18 MONTHS

19 MONTHS-5 YEARS

6-20 YEARS

5

Liberating
a New Energy

The closing of the frontier that came about near the end of the 19th Century seemed to presage great changes in American life. With the land available for Western homesteads virtually exhausted, where would America's expansionist energy find an outlet? Historians such as Frederick Jackson Turner, who saw the existence of the frontier as the crucial underlying fact of American history and who theorized that the frontier had been the "safety valve" for the country's explosive vitality, foresaw a basic alteration in the tone and temper of American society.

As it turned out, the closing of the frontier was followed by explosive events, but not because the country's safety valve had been sealed. The events merely took new forms and new directions. Instead of pouring outward into virgin land, the nation's energy was channeled upward in new cities, in new ways to exploit natural resources such as oil and natural gas, and in new manufacturing plants. Nowhere did this assault on a new and quite different frontier take place more dramatically than in the old frontier areas of the South Central States.

Concern over the effects of the closing of the frontier may well have been stirred by the first in a series of dramatic immigrations that put the whole "end of an era" question in stark relief. Acted out with a kind of wild West grandeur, this first immigration and those that followed are lumped together under the name of the Oklahoma Land Rush.

At the time, many authorities viewed the wild goings on in Indian Territory as the final stage in the closing of the American frontier. In retrospect, however, the series of rushes into Oklahoma can be seen not only as an end but also as a beginning—an exuberant harbinger of modern industrial America. For while all the trappings of the land rush—from prairie schooners to the primitive method of officially claiming land by driving stakes into the ground—were authentically frontierish, the animating motive of these particular frontiersmen was not just to establish farms, but also, and perhaps more importantly, to build towns. The idea propelling many of these first Oklahomans was to get settled, start a business and begin to make money as quickly as possible—in keeping with a tradition that was neither Eastern nor Western, but simply American.

For sheer organized hysteria the first rush of

A thicket of oil derricks covers downtown Kilgore, Texas, the geographical center of the vast East Texas Oil Field. Site of the second well to tap the East Texas pool, Kilgore has 1,134 producing wells within its city limits, crammed into every available space.

1889 into Oklahoma may never have been surpassed—unless perhaps by the fourth rush four years later. Thousands of eager settler-speculators lined up under the gaze of the U.S. cavalry, impatiently awaiting the signal to plunge into the hitherto sacrosanct Indian lands where they had a right under the Homestead Act to claim a 160-acre plot. With the firing of the signal guns at noon on April 22, 1889, people hurled themselves pell-mell on horseback, in wagons or astride mules into the raw, empty land, dismounting with stake hammers to drive hurried claims. But by no means all the buckboards that they drove were packed with plows and other farm implements. Lashed securely to the flooring of many of the wagons were the parts of a printing press or a barber chair or the office equipment needed to establish an instant bank or real-estate office. Some even carried precut lumber that could be quickly fashioned into a house or store like a modern prefab.

In short, the eyes of these people were set not so much on wide prairie farms as on townsites where the necessities of civilization, from a haircut to a daily paper, would be immediately available. Whole towns were raised in a matter of hours; committees were formed, city charters executed and elections held in a matter of days. By evening of the opening day of the rush, several tented cities of 10,000 or more joyful, dust-covered souls had sprouted on the plains. Some of these would in time amply gratify their founders' optimism, while others would not. One new metropolis was called, simply enough, Oklahoma City. Another, of equal size, was named Guthrie. Seventy-five years later Oklahoma City would have 390,000 people, but Guthrie would be a sleepy village of 9,500, its promises largely unfulfilled.

The whole startling tableau, undeniably unique even in the remarkable annals of the frontier, marked both the birth of major Western commercial centers and the opening of a new era in the whole region's history.

The first rush into Indian Territory and those that followed were notable partly because, for all their noise and dust, they were organized migrations; everyone (or almost everyone) got there at the same time. The decision to open up Indian lands was not, in fact, hastily arrived at, but was a number of years in the making. Even while Texas cattlemen were driving their herds northward across the Oklahoma prairies to railheads in Kansas in the 1880s, other Westerners had their eyes on the millions of acres of usable farmland given various Indian nations by far-off authorities in Washington.

Celebrated South Central political figures

James and Miriam Ferguson, shown with their grandson, were called "Farmer Jim" and "Ma." Both were governors of Texas, Jim from 1915 to 1917, Ma from 1925 to 1927 and 1933 to 1935.

The Indians were manifestly not farming the land, or at least not very much of it, and white men argued that it ought to be put to use. In due course, railroad interests, seeking convenient routes in the West and the profits from selling land to settlers, helped finance several raiding expeditions across the Kansas border into Indian country to focus popular attention on the "need to open the Indian lands to settlement." The frontier adventurers, such as C. C. Carpenter, David L. Payne and William Couch, who led these promotional forays were dubbed "Boomers." Gradually, interest became focused on the "unassigned lands" held by various Indian nations but largely unsettled.

Lawyers retained by the Indians argued that their clients' holdings had been granted "in perpetuity," but the more relevant political fact was that these particular clients could not vote (no Oklahoma Indians could vote until 1901, when a few got the franchise) and the people who wanted the land could. In 1885 Congress responded to the lobbying pressure from commercial interests and from Western constituencies and authorized the purchase of the unassigned Creek and Seminole lands. Deciding just how much the Indians should be paid for their land and ironing out other details took four years, but in 1889 President Benjamin

William "Alfalfa Bill" Murray, Oklahoma Governor from 1931 to 1935, was a shrewd politician who endeared himself to his people —and masked political savvy—with his frontier speech and manner.

Huey Long, "The Kingfish," Louisiana's demagogic Governor and Senator in the 1920s and 1930s, gained widespread support with his slogans of "Share the Wealth" and "Every Man a King."

Harrison issued a proclamation opening the land, and the first great run began.

Although ostensibly well policed, this first rush did not work out entirely according to plan. The choicest lots and homesites did not by any means all go to those quickest off the mark when the signal guns sounded. The evidence is conclusive that, as one observer put it, "a considerable part of the population had appeared on the site [of Oklahoma City] within 15 minutes after the noon signal for the run was given—30 miles away!" These early arrivals who had slipped over the starting line the night before were called "Sooners."

The "Boomers"—who had helped open the way for the "Sooners" and the other, more law-abiding members of the first rush—received due recognition with the election of one of their most prominent leaders, William Couch, as Oklahoma City's first mayor. Mayor Couch, unfortunately, soon died of gunshot wounds after an argument over the title to some land that is now in the center of the city. Such instances of violence, however, were surprisingly rare. People generally settled their disputes peaceably, sometimes through the courts, sometimes simply by flipping a coin. Nevertheless, one early dispute between rival townsite development companies remains to haunt Oklahoma City's

motorists. Surveying land on opposite sides of town, the two companies discovered that the streets they had laid out failed to jibe where the survey teams met. Since neither company would yield to the other, several streets in Oklahoma's capital still jog without apparent reason.

The first great land rush set the pattern. As succeeding sections of Indian Territory were opened during the ensuing decade and a half, scores of Oklahoma towns such as Ponca City and Lawton had the same one-day gestation period as Oklahoma City and Guthrie. In 1906 the last remaining tract, the "Big Pasture" reservation of the Comanche, Kiowa and Apache tribes in southwest Oklahoma, was opened. The following year Oklahoma became the nation's 46th state.

But though the swift transition from raw frontier to settled life on farms and in towns was relatively free of violence, Oklahoma's early history cannot be characterized as one of consummate order. The state's politics flourished in a free-wheeling and frequently radical atmosphere in which orthodox Democrats found themselves assaulted from both a Republican Right and an agrarian Left. The latter was a residue of the Populist movement. Many of Populism's Texas founders had joined in the various land rushes and quickly

99

revived their militant Farmers' Alliance as the Farmers Union, injecting a socialist tone into Oklahoma's political debate. Meanwhile, the northern half of the state attracted a number of stout Republican farmers from the Midwest. These sectional and ideological differences insured the development and continuance of a three-party system that was for a time wonderfully confusing.

In easy frontier fashion the Democrats tended to employ the rhetoric of the socialists on the stump, promising the people sundry benefits, but when elected they adhered to the tightfisted policies of the Republicans. By thus appealing to both sides, the Democrats soon managed to win support broad enough to give them almost unbroken control of the statehouse and legislature. Unfortunately for governmental stability, however, some of the state's early Democratic governors seemed to take their own agrarian oratory more seriously than their more conventional and conservative colleagues in the legislature would tolerate. The result was that two early governors were impeached by the votes of their own party's members.

One governor the conservatives could not impeach, although they wanted to, was a figure who was to cast a large shadow across Oklahoma politics for years—William "Alfalfa Bill" Murray. Alfalfa Bill had learned his politics in the violent contests between Populists and Democrats in Texas in the 1890s. There he had grown to appreciate both the depth of agrarian discontent among the farmers and the benefits of Democratic Party regularity for would-be politicians. As an "agrarian Democrat," Murray was well equipped to face Oklahoma's volatile electorate both in town and on the farm. He developed a wide following and defeated Republicans and orthodox states' rights Democrats with equal impartiality. Brash, uncouth and lacking in formal education, he nevertheless had courage, intellectual power and an intuitive understanding of his Oklahoma constituency. And, in the words of an Oklahoma historian, "He broke the Oklahoma legislature of the bad habit of impeaching political nonconformists." It might be added that he did so to the accompaniment of an almost unlimited supply of rural metaphors, as when he informed the legislature: "If you've got any impeachment ideas in your heads, hop to it. It'll be like a bunch of jack rabbits tryin' to get a wildcat out of a hole."

Despite the colorful interludes provided by the state's freewheeling politics, Oklahoma soon began to resemble other parts of America. Within a decade of statehood, with roads and railways linking its proud new plains cities, a place that had been settled by a series of wild human stampedes began to be largely indistinguishable from the older sections of the trans-Mississippi region.

Thus, almost suddenly as historical time is measured, the frontier disappeared from the stage of American history, to be replaced by the sight of erstwhile frontiersmen energetically building towns and cities, rail lines and highways. In a way, however, Oklahoma and the other parts of the old frontier continued to act as a "safety valve" for the nation, for as these areas grew in population, they constituted an expanding market for the products of the country's growing industries. As lively as the frontier demonstrably was, giving a certain élan to American life, the country's resilient economic system did not depend upon it, but had other ways to expand.

If the exhaustion of virgin land did not have any marked effect on the nation as a whole, however, it certainly did have a profound influence on the ex-frontier people of the South Central States. The transition from an almost completely rural mode of life to one in which the growing cities played an increasing part was a strenuous process, marked by strain and tension. And this transition was made even more dislocating by the fact that almost as soon as the Oklahoma Land Rush had signaled the end of one way of life, a whole new source of wealth, heralding a far more complicated future, was discovered in the region—oil.

Oil-bearing formations lurk beneath every major geographic subdivision of Texas, from the coastal plains to the northwestern panhandle. Beginning around the turn of the century, recurring oil booms directly touched the lives of hundreds of thousands of Texans and indirectly affected them all. Other discoveries of oil in Oklahoma, Arkansas and Louisiana had a similar if less dramatic impact on the people of those three states.

The first important commercial development in Texas came in 1894 when officials of the town of Corsicana, northeast of the center of the state, drilled a water well and encountered oil instead. For the next several years, oil pioneers drilled in the area, finding a shallow field at Powell in 1900, but these efforts produced only a modest amount of oil and the activity remained largely of local interest.

All this was to change, however, in the following year when Texas attracted national attention with the discovery of the state's first great gusher —the Lucas well at Spindletop. Spindletop is a large, shallow mound of earth that sits on the

Texas Gulf Coast prairie near Beaumont. This mound covers a "salt dome" formation in which oil had been trapped under tremendous pressure. When the first drilling shaft punctured this formation, the resulting gusher literally covered the countryside with pools of oil. Soon other wells were sunk into Spindletop and they, too, proved to be gushers. As the news spread—the site was so rich in oil that even the most exaggerated stories could not stray too far ahead of the facts—the Texas Gulf Coast swarmed with oilmen, promoters and hopeful farmers from nearby counties. By the end of 1902 hundreds of wells were tapping the oil beneath Spindletop. The field produced more than 17 million barrels of oil in that year, a remarkable 94 per cent of the state's total production. Spindletop gave birth to two of the great corporate giants, Texaco and Gulf, in addition to dozens of smaller enterprises.

Over the next 30 years scores of fields were found in Texas, some through the growing skill of the infant industry's geologists and drillers and some by cattlemen who were simply trying to find water for their herds. Discoveries at Electra, Burkburnett, Ranger, Mexia, Big Lake, Wortham and Yates transformed these scattered localities. They also nurtured Texas' independent oilmen, as well as the major companies; and, since they provided a training ground for an increasing number of geologists and other oil technicians, they inadvertently created the conditions that made possible the greatest, wildest oil boom of them all—in a field so large that it was named not after a farmsite or a town but after an entire section of the state.

The discovery and development of the East Texas Oil Field was a historical event of the kind that has implications quite beyond the event itself. Here was more than just the discovery of an extraordinarily large pool of oil: the East Texas field recast the economy of Texas, the life style of many of its people and the procedures of the American oil industry. It provided oil entrepreneurs with the stable financial backing that led to other discoveries in Mexico and South America and, indeed, all over the world. After East Texas, the nation's oil industry would go on to new accomplishments in petroleum, petrochemicals and electronics while independent oil operators, the Texas wheeler-dealers and wildcatters of fact and legend, would emerge as latter-day frontiersmen. The discovery, of course, completely altered the lives of thousands of rural people who lived in the five counties of the East Texas Piney Woods where the oil was found. For them, the transition from the old agrarian ways came with

Spurting 200 feet into the Texas air, a black plume of oil surges from the Lucas well in the rich Spindletop field on the Gulf of Mexico. Lucas, drilled in January 1901, was not the first Texas gusher, but there was no precedent for the volume of oil that had been tapped at Spindletop. The underground deposits of oil were so vast, and under such pressure, that the Lucas well spewed uninterruptedly for days, defying the efforts of engineers to control it; by the time they had, hundreds of thousands of barrels of oil lay on the Texas prairie. The state's oil industry was born in this field, where within a year more than 100 wells were sunk.

Congratulating each other in 1930 after bringing in Daisy Bradford #3, first successful well drilled in the fabulous East Texas Oil Field, the well's "promoter," C. M. "Dad" Joiner *(left)*, and his geologist, A. D. Lloyd, exchange a handshake. Daisy Bradford #3 is on the periphery of the field; if Joiner had drilled a quarter of a mile to the east, he would have missed the oil entirely. The East Texas field has produced more than 3.5 billion barrels of oil.

traumatic suddenness, and the frantic maneuvering for a portion of the great field was the decisive event of their lives. As for Texans as a whole, the world to them has ever since looked somewhat different.

It all began one October day in 1930 when a 71-year-old man named C. M. "Dad" Joiner finally got the "wildcat" well (i.e., a well in an area where no oil had previously been found) that he was drilling in East Texas down to a sufficient depth. Joiner was one of a rather numerous breed of Texans who, after 30 years in the oil fields, had acquired all the knowledge needed to be a wildcatter but lacked the money to finance such ventures. He was a "promoter," a respectable oil-field term for an operator who acquired his right to drill on a man's land at little or no cost by giving the landowner an "overriding royalty" on the hoped-for production, and who defrayed much of his drilling costs by the same method—by signing over a one-fourth or one-half interest to the drilling company. With further deductions for percentages sold to meet operating expenses, some promoters were lucky to emerge with one-sixteenth ownership of their wildcat well.

Joiner was different from other promoters in one respect. He had a fixation about East Texas and was convinced he would find oil there. He nursed his first Rusk County well, which he called Daisy

Bradford #1, for months, selling interests in it to finance equipment needs until—with the shaft still hundreds of feet short of the goal—the drilling bit stuck fast in the hole and the well had to be abandoned. He then doggedly promoted another well, Daisy Bradford #2 (with a fresh 100 per cent interest to sell, he could get new capital), but his worn-out equipment broke down once more and again he had to abandon the well. Finally, after three long years, Daisy Bradford #3 reached a depth of 3,600 feet and struck a layer of soft, porous sandstone—called Woodbine sand in Texas—that gave promise that oil might be near.

The great day arrived on Friday, October 3, 1930. A carnival-like crowd of farmers, hamburger vendors and soda-pop peddlers looked on as Joiner's crew worked to start a flow of oil. These farmers knew something about oil, since many of them had experienced the joy of leasing their mineral rights to major companies (for example, Humble Oil)—and they had also had the disappointment of seeing the oil companies allow most of the leases to lapse untested. Now they were hoping that Dad Joiner's wheezing rig could produce at least enough oil to make their mineral rights worth something again.

And Daisy Bradford #3 did just that. When it "blew in" that October evening it produced sufficient oil to drench the surrounding pine trees. The watching farmers rejoiced. Over the next several weeks the nearby town of Henderson began to fill up with "independent traffic"—land men ("lease hounds"), geologists ("rock hounds") and some more operator-promoters like Dad Joiner. Some of the major oil companies sent young men known in Texas parlance as "oil scouts" to look into matters, but the flurry of activity remained primarily the province of the independent operators.

Through October and November of 1930, trading in mineral rights sent values up from $10 to $1,000 per acre. To the farmers around Henderson, Dad Joiner's well had indeed become a heaven-sent answer to their Depression woes. In December several wildcat wells north and west of the discovery site blew in with even greater pressure and volume, indicating that the main oil formation was west of the Daisy Bradford well. Land prices "on trend" —that is, in the direction of the new finds—reached $2,500 an acre.

Now, to participate in the "Henderson play," men of more substantial means arrived—independents from Dallas, Fort Worth and Houston who had at least one solid drilling success behind them and who could finance their own operations. Among the newcomers were Clint Murchison, Sid

Richardson, Ed Bateman, and a country boy by the name of H. L. Hunt, who had made his stake in the El Dorado field in Arkansas; all were destined to become famous in the annals of Texas oil. Their purpose was to take advantage of the fact that most of the East Texas countryside, though once under lease by major companies such as Humble, was now available. East Texas was "hot."

Late in December, almost three months after the East Texas farmers had first cheered Daisy Bradford #3, an event occurred that sent oil scouts frantically calling the home offices of such giants as Humble and Royal Dutch/Shell. A well called the Lou Della Crim #1, drilled by Ed Bateman, had blasted in at a fantastic 22,000-barrels-a-day rate. What was so surprising was not just the rate of the well's production but the fact that it was located 12 miles north of the Daisy Bradford near the tiny (population: 900) hamlet of Kilgore. Could it be that East Texas had two large pools of oil? Stunned geologists checked the bottom-hole pressure of Ed Bateman's well, compared subsurface data and shook their heads in disbelief. Something big had been unlocked in the Woodbine of East Texas.

The boom blew wide open. Leases that had changed hands three and four times in the previous weeks now changed hands again as international oil companies belatedly bought in at prices that overnight made millionaires of hundreds of Texans. Kilgore's streets began filling up with oil scouts, lease hounds, employees of oil-testing companies, independents of all descriptions and every Texas geologist who was not at the moment "sitting on his own well." A visitor estimated that there were between 1,500 and 2,000 carpenters at work in Kilgore. "Shacks are springing up everywhere," he said, "and there is literally standing room only in the town itself."

The lease on the land surrounding Ed Bateman's well went to the Humble Oil Company for $2.1 million, and derricks began sprouting at 150-foot intervals along the boundaries of the "block." Lease hounds swarmed over the countryside, buttonholing farmers for their mineral rights. Life seemed to grow in dimension every day for the citizens of Henderson and Kilgore.

Hoping for part of the action, the city fathers of Longview, northeast of Kilgore, offered a $10,000 prize for the first well in their town's immediate territory. Within a month they were out the $10,000 when a third gusher—some 25 miles from Joiner's strike and 15 miles north of the Bateman discovery —roared in on the outskirts of town. Within weeks Longview's 5,000 population had doubled and the

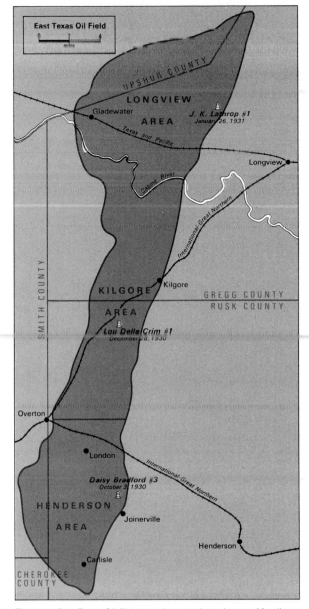

The great East Texas Oil Field wanders southward some 40 miles from the Longview Area, its widest part, to the Henderson Area, site of the Daisy Bradford #3, the first successful well drilled in the field. The man who drilled it, "Dad" Joiner, is remembered in the name of nearby Joinerville. The second well to "blow in," the Lou Della Crim #1, was near the town of Kilgore in what has come to be called the Kilgore Area of the field. The discovery of the third well, J. K. Lathrop #1, near Longview, 25 miles north of Joiner's well, made a few geologists suspect that this might not be three pools of oil but a vast subterranean lake. This proved to be the case; the East Texas pool is the largest single known reservoir of oil discovered to date in the U.S. Thirty-five years after production first started there, the field had 17,016 operating wells and was going strong.

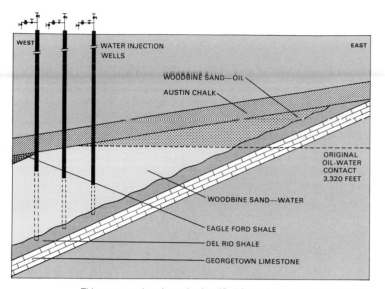

This cross section shows in simplified form the geological structure of the East Texas Oil Field and the water injection system that keeps the wells flowing. The oil is located in porous Woodbine sandstone that lies between strata of nonporous chalk, limestone and shale. These strata form what is, in effect, a wedge-shaped trap. Trapped with the oil are large amounts of water. This water, exerting pressure on the oil, pushes it to the surface when a well is drilled into the Woodbine. To maintain this underground pressure, water that comes to the surface with the oil is pumped back into the Woodbine by special wells. The oil-and-water contact line in 1930, when the first wells were sunk, was at 3,320 feet, but has risen with removal of oil.

increase in land prices had taken on the aspects of a fairy tale. Shortly before the third big discovery, a Longview real-estate man named B. A. Skipper had sold a 10-acre lease near the spot where the well came in for $750. After the strike, he offered the new owner $25,000 for the mineral rights to the 10 acres, only to be told they were not for sale.

Three great wells had been discovered—all in Woodbine sand and all 3,600 feet or so below the surface, though dotted across 25 miles of East Texas forestland. Could it be . . . not three fields, but one? The idea was too fantastic; only a few men, most of them geologists, conceived of such a possibility, and even they, at first, dismissed it. The magnitude of the oil revolution in progress was simply too great to be comprehended by its participants.

Into the spring of 1931 the discovery of "new fields" between the three strikes, and even beyond to the north and west, continued literally as fast as men could drill holes in the ground. Finally, beyond all doubt, the incredible fact was established: here were not 20 fields, nor eight, nor three, but one vast lake of oil, more than 40 miles long and three to 10 miles wide. One could drill anywhere within those limits and be sure of striking oil at the depth where the drilling bit penetrated the top of the Woodbine. Nor was that all. The oil was nestled

in porous stone that "gave up" its crude easily, was located at moderate depth in easy-to-penetrate "soft rock" drilling country and, when brought to the surface, was found to be "high gravity" crude that brought top prices. Most significant of all was the volume—East Texas was the largest oil field yet found anywhere in the world.

Soon scientists were able to explain these unprecedented and multiple bonanzas. Deep in the geologic past, much of Texas had been covered by the sea, which, upon receding, left a shoreline of sand in what is now East Texas. Over the millennia, oil developed, probably from the decaying remains of sea creatures, and the sand was transformed into sandstone by the pressure of the strata of rock forming above it. At some point the oil became trapped in the sandstone between shelves of nonporous chalk and limestone and was held there by quantities of underground water. The pressure of this water on the oil was great enough to force the oil to the surface as soon as a well was drilled into the oil from above. Thus the wells of East Texas were "flowing wells," the water pressure rendering pumps unnecessary. All one had to do was turn a spigot on the top of the well and oil was "produced." By every standard—quality and quantity of oil, accessibility and bottom-hole pressure—East Texas was an oilman's dream come true.

It quickly became a nightmare. Because of the relative slowness of its early development and the fact that little of the field had been leased at the time to big companies, literally thousands of individuals had a stake in East Texas. Local farmers and Texas oil independents—not to mention passing strangers with an eye for a deal and a talent for making trades—all had acquired a piece of at least one well. In the complicated transactions whereby drilling arrangements were made, many farms, wells, leases and even drilling equipment had been mortgaged. Repayment was to come out of the sale of oil. Time became a critical factor. Everyone, it seemed, had to produce and sell oil to pay off his obligations and retain title to his property. Thousands of wells dipped into the Woodbine. Production of oil increased wildly, and the $1.10-per-barrel price of crude began to crumble. Soon, suggestions were heard that oil production would have to be adjusted, or prorated, to market demand.

A grim controversy began. Independents cried that major companies, in reducing crude prices, were trying to drive small operators to the wall in order to acquire their acreage. Men like Dad Joiner's geologist, A. D. Lloyd, denounced proration as naked confiscation of private property. Proration

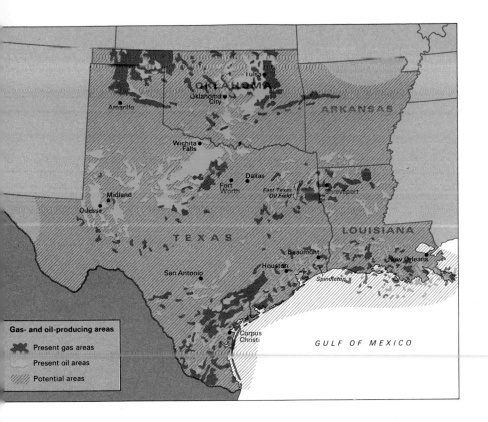

Beneath the soil of the South Central States lie vast deposits of oil and natural gas that in a single year have accounted for well over eight billion dollars' worth of products. This map shows the major deposits, including the East Texas Oil Field—the largest known pool in the nation—and Spindletop, site of Texas' first great gusher in 1901. The map also indicates deposits of offshore oil, which are being recovered in increasing quantities from land beneath the Gulf of Mexico. The cities indicated on the map are those that have grown prosperous because of nearby oil deposits or because large petroleum companies have built offices there. Gas deposits are often associated with fields of crude oil, and fields marked on the map as oil producing often produce gas as well. There are, however, a number of deposits of natural gas not associated with oil fields.

Gas- and oil-producing areas

- Present gas areas
- Present oil areas
- Potential areas

had its advocates, too. Public meetings attracted huge crowds of indignant partisans throughout the area. As the argument continued, crude prices sank to 25 cents a barrel and operators responded by increasing production all the more.

Geologists and petroleum engineers also were dismayed. East Texas was unprecedented, but even its powerful subsurface pressure could be destroyed by unrestrained production. Predictions were heard that half to three fourths of the field's oil was being needlessly put beyond the range of ultimate recovery. But thousands of heavily mortgaged operators grimly kept the oil flowing in quantities the world had never seen before from a single field.

Under pressure from all sides, the Texas Railroad Commission, which had been handed the job of supervising the state's oil production since it had long regulated oil shipments by railroad tank cars, called a hearing to consider proration. A trainload of Piney Woods oilmen clanked into the state capital and the hearing degenerated into a near riot.

In an atmosphere of growing hysteria, the commission's first proration order went into effect on May 1, 1931, a little less than seven months after Dad Joiner had started it all. The effort was a complete failure. When the commission set allowable production at 70,000 barrels a day, production

reached 150,000. When allowables were raised to 90,000, the flow exceeded 300,000.

The transportation and marketing of crude oil had by this time come to involve much of the population of East Texas. New refineries popped up, some full-blown and others little more than rough-hewn "topping plants." Oil trucks made their appearance, some equipped with special headlights and intricate back-country road maps for successful "night hauling" to avoid the railroad commission's proration agents. Operators used their relatives and friends as amateur oil marketers. Aunts and brothers-in-law sallied into adjoining counties and states to sound out filling-station operators, refineries, oil transport companies or anyone else interested in buying "sweet 39-gravity East Texas crude" at bargain prices—delivery, of course, to be made after dark. Plumbers worked around the clock erecting metal storage tanks and pipelines.

Bottom-hole pressure in the wells meanwhile continued to decline, further endangering the future life of the field. But still production soared, and as it did the price for crude continued to drop. The entire world structure of the petroleum industry was being imperiled by the flood of oil and the plummeting of prices. Finally Texas Governor Ross Sterling declared martial law and sent the

National Guard into East Texas to support the railroad commission's officials. But even with this extra help, the proration agents could not stop the flow of "hot oil." Many operators came up with ingenious new tactics, including "left-handed valves" that turned oil pipelines on when the agents thought they were turning them off. Some wells could be put into operation by turning a spigot secreted under a front porch or inside a bathroom.

Yet gradually, a kind of order began to come to East Texas. Some operators fell by the wayside, but many others reached the first essential plateau of paying off their mortgages. Others sold out for a combination of cash and a percentage of future oil production. These developments gave increasing numbers of people an immediate stake in proration and a return to normal prices.

By the end of 1932, prices had climbed back to 82 cents a barrel. Though hot-oil running became an increasingly subtle art, it had lost its near universality. Powers to inspect refineries and to trace the source of processed crude were given to the Texas Railroad Commission by the state legislature, and a further loophole was plugged with a law prohibiting the shipment of any illegally produced crude oil or any petroleum products made from it.

Meanwhile, the man who had opened up the field, "Dad" Joiner, was missing the really big money. He possessed drilling rights to three "blocks" near Daisy Bradford #3 of 4,000 acres each. He sold the rights to one of these areas to H. L. Hunt for $30,000 in cash, $42,000 in notes and the promise that Hunt would give him $1,250,000 in oil profits—if the 4,000 acres proved to contain any oil. They did. Hunt is estimated to have realized $100 million from the area he bought from Joiner. The two 4,000-acre lots Joiner retained for himself, however, did not pay off. Failing to realize that Daisy Bradford #3 was on the extreme edge of the East Texas field, Joiner kept drilling rights to property on the wrong side of his pioneering well. The property proved to be entirely outside the field and was, in Texas oil jargon, "scenery," containing not one drop of oil. Hunt later boasted, with good reason, that the transaction was his "greatest business coup." Dad Joiner was broke again within a few years.

One of the last tense scenes in the long drama came in 1934 when the Texas legislature enacted a bill requiring refineries to report the source of the crude they processed. Independent East Texas refiners bitterly opposed the law and staged a riotous demonstration in Austin to influence the new Governor, Miriam "Ma" Ferguson, against signing it.

Figures were produced charging that some refineries were processing 60,000 barrels of crude daily while the commission's allowable for the wells supplying them was only 18,000. "Ma" Ferguson signed the bill. Soon the topping plants began closing down, and by 1935 conservation officials could report that at least 98 per cent of East Texas crude was being legally processed. Complex proration and market-demand statutes such as those that evolved from the effort to cope with East Texas gradually became the basis of oil conservation practices throughout the nation.

But before it could pass to an orderly existence, producing oil in large quantities year after year, the East Texas field had to precipitate a technological as well as a legal and economic revolution in oil—and for basically the same reason: the need to preserve bottom-hole pressure. Indeed, the technical achievements in East Texas may ultimately be regarded as a greater wonder than the field's sheer size.

The difficulty lay in the fact that increasingly large quantities of salt water were coming up with the oil. The 15,000-barrel daily flow of water in 1935 rose to a staggering 200,000 barrels by 1940. Each barrel of water lifted out of the earth had the same effect that profligate oil runs had produced earlier —namely, it helped diminish the pressure toward the point below which oil in the ground would become irrecoverable. There was also a second problem: what to do with all the salt water brought to the surface. As farmers pointed out with increasing irritability, oilmen who dug large, shallow pits and let the water seep back into the ground were rendering the land unsuitable for agriculture. However, alternate methods of getting rid of the water entailed prohibitive costs.

A bold and ingenious solution was found to both problems: the salt water would be disposed of by injecting it back into the oil sands more than 3,000 feet below the surface, thus at the same time restoring the pressure of the water-drive. The East Texas Salt Water Disposal Company was chartered, and within five years of the first large-scale experiment in 1942, scores of injection wells were daily pumping almost 500,000 barrels of salt water back into the subterranean sands where nature had placed it eons before. To the astonishment of many skeptics, pressure under the huge field was completely stabilized. Today, thousands of wells in East Texas continue to yield their allotted amounts with the simple twist of a valve—after more than three decades of uninterrupted production.

For Texans, economically and psychologically,

the impact of the giant field has been so vast as to set the state apart from its neighbors on the Southern plains. The battle between the independent operators and the major oil companies for control of East Texas was in the turbulent tradition of their frontier heritage, but in a very real sense it altered the character of that heritage. With the independents managing to retain control of at least part of the field, some of the vast wealth flowing from East Texas stayed in the state—and created a revolution in the lives of its people.

Texas in 1930 had been predominantly an agrarian state, notably lacking in native capital. Its largest city, Houston, counted only some 290,000 residents. The economy, based on cotton and cattle, was drifting quietly. But after East Texas nothing was the same. Thousands of Texans were now trained in the technology of locating, testing and drilling for oil, in the subtle financial science of "putting together a drilling deal," in trading in oil royalties and mineral leases, in the professions of petroleum engineering and geology, and in the trade of "roughnecking" on a drilling rig. Most important, East Texas provided the venture capital to put these talents to work, for the field created thousands of millionaires.

These men, wildcatters by trade and inheritors of a rough-and-tumble frontier tradition, were not of a type to rest idly on their new wealth. They kept looking for oil, and quite naturally, they looked first in Texas. They found it on the Texas-Louisiana coastal plain, in deep West Texas pools and in marginal fields all over the state. They ranged into Wyoming and the Dakotas, into Canada and into Mexico, and ultimately into the Middle East and Southeast Asia. Their ventures were financed by a growing circle of Texas banks—themselves largely a creation of the East Texas field—that specialized in underwriting oil exploration. They did not outstrip the international oil giants in these endeavors, but they were successful enough to provide a massive injection of home-grown venture capital into the Texas economy. Diversified investment in oil-related industries such as petrochemicals and electronics and in insurance, modern agriculture and real estate completed the transformation of the old "cattle kingdom."

The Woodbine sands of East Texas were thus the foundation for the skyscrapers that began to rise in Houston, Dallas, San Antonio and Fort Worth. By the mid-1960s, 40 per cent of Texas' nearly 11 million people lived in these four metropolitan areas alone. In the number of cities of more than 100,000 population, only California (with 17)

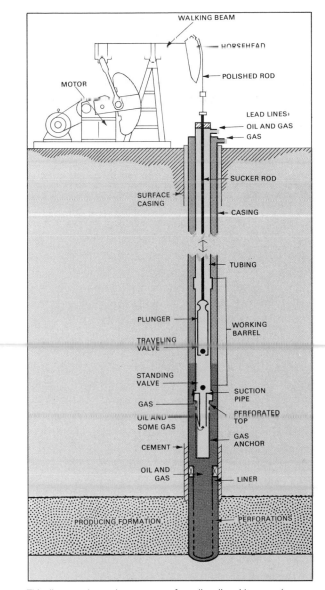

This diagram shows the structure of an oil well and its pumping equipment. In some oil fields subsurface pressure on oil deposits remains great enough to make the oil gush to the surface of the ground. In many others, however, pumps are necessary. One of the most common pumps is the "walking beam" or "horsehead" type, which dots the landscape in many oil-rich areas of the U.S.

After a well has been drilled, layers of protective casing are lowered to keep out earth and water; this casing is usually cemented in place at the bottom of the well. Next, the tubing that will bring the oil to the surface is lowered, followed by a sievelike device that allows oil to enter from the producing formation. Natural gas, separated from the oil by a "gas anchor" that keeps most gas out of the pump, rises unaided to the surface between the tubing and the casing. The pump is powered by a gasoline or electric motor that activates its "horsehead," which in turn moves the rods. The rods are attached to the plunger mechanism with its valve. As the plunger descends, pressure in the "working barrel" increases, compressing the oil. As the plunger rises, pressure decreases and oil is drawn upward. Separate outlets are provided for gas and oil at the surface.

surpassed the Texas total of 13. Houston and Dallas had become centers of finance—and no longer solely of financing oil exploration. Refineries had contributed to the emergence of El Paso, Beaumont and Wichita Falls as metropolitan centers, and the production and marketing of natural gas had similarly succored Amarillo in the panhandle, Odessa in West Texas and Corpus Christi on the Gulf Coast. Smaller cities such as Tyler, Midland, Port Arthur, Orange and Galveston had economies based in large part on the exploration, refining or transportation of oil and its by-products.

Nor could the new era be measured solely by size and statistics. There were alterations, too, in the quality of life, notably in the field of education. The University of Texas, for example, bulwarked by an endowment of nearly a half-billion dollars from oil royalties on university-owned lands, began throwing off provincial fetters and reaching for greatness among America's universities.

The changes had come quickly. The urbanized present is but the span of a single lifetime from the days of the great land rush into Oklahoma. The transition from frontier to urban sprawl is visible not alone in Texas, but in Tulsa and Oklahoma City, in New Orleans and Shreveport. Though the form was less dramatic in these states, the reason was for the most part the same—oil. Repeated oil booms buoyed Oklahoma's economy, and one of them—located in a metropolitan area—produced a form of mass hysteria rivaling the early days of East Texas. This was the "town lot boom" in the southeastern quadrant of Oklahoma City. Every homeowner, no matter how small his lot, possessed a potential drilling site. For many, the hopes of the Sooner rush of many years back were overwhelmingly realized. Tulsa became a refining center and later a home-office town, serving the many segments of the industry. It boasted that it was the "oil capital of the world."

The cumulative effect of modern oil discoveries on the South Central States has, perhaps, been too recent a thing to measure with complete assurance. Beyond the identifiable physical changes in the cities and in the land, there has been the subtler impact of the new technology on the people themselves. The economic stimulation engendered by oil discoveries has been almost universally applauded. The recurring booms gave to great numbers of people an injection of renewed faith in the American promise that had not, for many, been realized in their frontier farming communities. But a study of the impassioned controversies that accompanied the booms supports the suggestion that the changes

have not been regarded by the people themselves as an unmixed blessing. Just as agrarians of the 1890s were quick to find the cause of their poverty and other troubles in the "manipulations of Wall Street bankers and Eastern capitalists," so the displaced agrarians of the age of oil have regarded the great oil companies—and by extension, the whole Eastern Seaboard of the United States—with undisguised suspicion.

The fact that the earlier dissenters were quasisocialist farmers and the new dissenters are often conservative and well-heeled oilmen should not mask their essential similarity of view. Both speak out of the complicated mixture of hope and despair that brought men to the frontier in the first place. In this sense, firebrands of the left, like Louisiana's famous politician of the 1920s and 1930s, Huey Long, and archconservatives like Texas oilman H. L. Hunt, both in their own eras, have responded as agrarians in an increasingly urbanized world. Their rhetoric has been substantially different—Long promised in his political speeches to make "every man a king" while Hunt has been so opposed to egalitarian concepts that he once wrote a book, *Alpaca*, in which he asserted that the number of votes permitted each citizen should be apportioned on the basis of the taxes they paid, a rich man having many more votes than a poor one. But Long and Hunt, despite their radically different political views, have shared a common distrust of many aspects of the new and ever-changing world being produced by the industrial revolution. Each in his own time seems to have been sustained by the same emotion that animated the agrarians at the turn of the century, when sweeping industrialization was beginning to alter radically the daily lives of Americans. Each seems to have been saying: "The old virtues are being destroyed and we must reclaim them."

This emotion—the feeling that the world is going too fast and that the old ways must be preserved—continues to exist beneath the surface of life in the South Central region. Today, in large measure because of the forces set in motion by the East Texas Oil Field, there are skyscrapers on the plains. But the people in them cling to ways of thought that have their roots in another time. The past and present have not yet merged. This is as good an explanation as any, perhaps, of why the region's politics are so complex and passionate, or why the people are so slow to tackle education, water and other urban problems that flow from industrialization, and finally of why they have yet to settle into a pattern of daily life in which they can find comfort.

Two plains cities built by oil

The twin cities of Midland and Odessa, which rise out of the flat and seemingly endless plains of West Texas, owe their existence almost entirely to oil. Isolated in an arid and forbidding land, they sit in the center of one of the world's greatest oil-producing areas, the 90,000-square-mile Permian Basin. Once covered by an inland sea, the basin teemed with life that, buried for millions of years under layers of sediment, was gradually transformed into a reservoir of oil and natural gas.

Although they exist for the same reason, Midland and Odessa are strikingly different. Midland is primarily a city of office buildings and white-collar workers and executives. It contains one fifth of Texas' office space. Odessa, on the other hand, is mainly a workingman's town. Here live the tough, knowledgeable men who actually get the two cities' lifeblood, oil, out of the ground.

Rising like a mirage from the hard-baked plains, the office buildings of Midland shimmer in the distance, contrasting with the sharp outlines of the structure of pipes and valves in the foreground—a "Christmas Tree" in oilmen's vernacular—that tops a flowing oil well.

Photographs by A. Y. Owen

Midland oil executives walk to lunch past some of the city's recently built office buildings around Courthouse Square. Midland's residential areas, with their well-kept, substantial houses set on large plots, also reflect the high economic level of the community.

The two cities are linked by the Texas and Pacific Railway and U.S. Route 80 *(dark line, center),* which run parallel to each other across the plain from the middle of Odessa *(foreground)* to the center of Midland. A third link, Interstate 20 *(top right),* jogs midway to avoid an oil well

Odessa oil workers in hard hats wait outside the Texas Cafe for the maintenance crew they will work with to pick them up. The Texas Cafe serves not only as a restaurant, but also as an employment office, check-cashing center and mail drop for the oil workers who frequent it.

The different faces of an oddly matched pair

Midland and Odessa, just 20 miles apart, contrast sharply in appearance. Midland, which calls itself the "Tall City," has high-rise office buildings, while Odessa, grayer and with a lower skyline, is more suited to the men who drill and maintain the wells. The two cities were spawned in the same way, however, in 1881, when the Texas and Pacific Railway was laying track from Fort Worth to El Paso and put sidings in the plain about midway (thus the name Midland) between its terminals. These sidings became the nuclei of the two cities, which remained small until oil was found in 1923. Today they have a combined population of some 160,000.

A class of cheerful fourth graders graphically demonstrates a typical division of labor in Midland. The fathers of the children in the front row are occupied as indicated, but the rest of the fathers all work for oil companies. The ratio for the whole city is 4 out of 5.

The pervasive influence of oil

The area around Midland and Odessa was once part of Texas' cattle kingdom, and the prairie grasses supported wide-ranging herds of Longhorns. But now the cattle are gone and the prairie is checkered with oil wells, each one topped with a "Christmas Tree" of valves and pipes or by a quietly working "horsehead" pump. These great petroleum fields profoundly influence life in the two cities, as a large proportion of the men work at jobs connected with producing oil. Of course, many people in Midland and Odessa have occupations not directly linked to the petroleum industry. Bankers and builders, lawyers and car salesmen, teachers and policemen—and even artists—flourish here as they do elsewhere. But the fate of the two cities clearly lies with oil.

A native artist fascinated by the stark landscapes of his homeland, Woody Gwyn paints one of the big refineries near Odessa. Although he went to art school in Philadelphia, Gwyn returned to West Texas to live and has sold his works for as much as $3,000.

Dotted with neatly spaced oil wells, one to every 20 acres, the North Ward-Estes field, 50 miles southwest of Odessa, has been producing oil since the 1930s, but is still being drilled today. The heavy lines are service roads, the diagonals pipelines.

A gallery of hard-working oilmen

An oil scout for a major company, Harold Pyatt keeps track of the activities of competing outfits.

H. G. Flournoy is a "toughneck," the oilmen's name for a skilled worker on a drilling rig.

A member of a maintenance crew, L. D. Griffin, a semiskilled "roustabout," repairs a valve.

Land man Hugh Story is an independent agent who dickers for drilling rights for oil companies.

Some important figures in West Texas

Wheeler-dealer Len "Tuffy" McCormick, an ex-football player, is an independent oilman. After making and losing four fortunes in oil, he turned to natural gas for his next comeback.

Elliott Cowden worked a 25,000-acre cattle spread near Odessa when oil was discovered on his land in 1929. Although oil has made him rich, he hates what the wells have done to the land.

An enthusiastic amateur polo player, George Landreth is an oil entrepreneur. He and his partners have drilled wells as far away as New Guinea; they also own an Australian ranch.

Roustabout Geno Zinanni, a
member of a maintenance crew,
checks on an oil collection station.

Petroleum engineer Ed Anderson
advises drillers on the best
methods for extracting oil.

Jesse Turner, a roustabout who
works by the day, awaits a job call
in the Texas Cafe in Odessa.

An oil geologist, Harry Miller Jr.
determines what drilling sites are
the most likely prospects.

An independent oilman, Joseph O'Neill Jr. stands
in front of his own Midland office building.
Since becoming a success, he has been one of
the developers of a ski resort in Colorado.

Jim Hall, member of a West Texas oil family, has
become a successful racing driver and has helped
to develop the speedy Chaparral racing car,
which has an unusual winglike stabilizer.

J. P. "Bum" Gibbons, a veteran of the West Texas
oil fields, began as a roustabout and founded
his own successful oil service business in 1935.
A onetime cowboy, he always wears his hat.

The search for recreation in the isolated cities

Sitting in the middle of an immense dry plain, where furious wind and dust storms are common, Midland and Odessa are rather forbidding places to live. When their citizens feel the need for a change, they must often travel great distances. Women drive as far as Dallas, more than 300 miles to the east, to wander happily through large, cool department stores, and those in search of a variety of museums, plays and concerts often must make journeys just as long. Skiers think nothing of enduring the long ride to the mountains of New Mexico or Colorado, and boating enthusiasts range far and wide in search of water.

There are diversions at home as well. Children romp among wind-swept sand dunes. Wives join the many social clubs that have grown up. In both cities people have a passion for gardens and lawns, for creating patches of green in the midst of the dry and monotonous—if starkly magnificent—land.

An anomaly in a sun-baked land, Midland's ski shop nevertheless does a booming business with those who visit Rocky Mountain slopes. One popular resort is Purgatory, in Colorado, which oilman Joseph O'Neill Jr. *(preceding page)* helped build.

Readying his boat, L. D. Rushing, who lives in Odessa and commutes 120 miles a day to the oil rig on which he works, prepares for a weekend of water skiing. Although the nearest large expanse of water is 100 miles away, the Rushings make the trip frequently.

Beside a "horsehead" pump, oilman T. W. Kidd and his son, Tommy,
run along dunes south of Midland. Of the sandy expanse, Mr. Kidd
says, "We have a lot of beaches here. We just don't have any ocean.
But where there used to be an ocean, there's a lot of oil now."

117

6

A Vivid
and Varied People

If a single generalization can be hazarded about the people of the South Central States, it is that they are defensive about what the rest of the nation thinks of them. This feeling is so pervasive throughout the four states of the Southern prairie-plains that it is difficult to say with certainty which of the many ethnic and geographical clans is the most sensitive about its national image.

The South Central States contain more than their share of unusual ethnic or geographical "islands": the isolated backwoods of Arkansas, the "Cajun Country" of Louisiana, the hill country of Texas with its heavily German population, the Mexican-American areas of South Texas and the several big groups of urban Negroes. A majority of the region's people, of course, behave outwardly like the average run of citizens elsewhere, shopping in supermarkets and living in modest homes in neat suburbs. But almost all—whether members of the great majority or of one of the "islands"—feel that for historical and geographical reasons they are somewhat set apart from the rest of the nation. For

example, the citizens of Texas and Oklahoma resent being stereotyped as loud and boisterous fellows in big-brimmed hats who travel to football games in private planes and spend oil money with maximum ostentation. The Acadians of Louisiana, some half million strong, are weary of being pictured as boondock Frenchmen who do nothing but propagate huge families and sing songs about "*Jole Blon*" and "*Jambalaya*." The people of Arkansas have long since given up trying to convince the nation that their state is not populated exclusively by semiliterate mountaineers. And the region's five million people of Mexican, Negro and Indian descent likewise have stereotype problems that—although of course different from those bothering the bulk of their neighbors—exclude them just as effectively from the fraternal assumptions most Americans prefer to believe they have about one another.

Most of all, the people of the four states resent the simplistic notion, which they feel is common elsewhere in the nation, that the South Central States harbor very little that could be described as culture or learning. Like most states, Arkansas, Louisiana, Oklahoma and Texas have their share of country people, but to regard them all as ill-read and raucous "rednecks" is patently absurd. Several hundred thousand students are inundating the

Bilingual signs abound on a busy street in a Spanish-speaking district of El Paso, Texas, largest city on the entire 1,550-mile Mexican-American border. Almost half of the city's 300,000 residents have surnames showing either Spanish or Mexican origins.

Bob Burns, the Arkansas humorist who gained nationwide fame for radio and film performances in the 1930s, holds the pipe-and-funnel musical instrument he invented, the bazooka, a name later given to the World War II weapon of similar appearance.

region's colleges and universities, and the statistical evidence is conclusive that a substantial portion of them are from the same small towns and rural communities that are supposed to harbor nothing but ignorance and narrow provincialism.

But if the nation's view is much too sweeping, the evidence is just as strong that at some time in the not-too-distant past the peculiarities of land and history that mark the South Central States did help to shape a slightly different kind of American —or several different kinds. Indeed, the people of the Gulf Southwest would be quick to agree that they have distinct regional qualities. To acquire a better understanding of the region's people, it is essential to sift through surface impressions to see if one can get at the reality underneath.

No state has had to cope with the patronizing attitudes of its neighbors with greater patience than Arkansas. For years—indeed, for generations—the state has been either belittled by outsiders or ignored altogether. There is a reason for this. In the 19th Century the principal trails west from the Mississippi River passed north of the Ozark plateau or south of it, so that the millions who settled the West had memories of traveling through Kansas or the Dakotas or Texas but never, it seemed, through Arkansas. Then in the heyday of radio in the 1930s,

Americans came to know a fellow named Bob Burns, who billed himself as "The Sage of the Ozarks," played a "musical instrument" that he called a bazooka and told quaint, self-deprecating stories about relatives and neighbors in the Arkansas hills. This minor phenomenon seems to have settled the question, once and for all, of what kind of folk live in Arkansas—all of Arkansas. Hillbillies.

The nation next noticed the state in the 1950s when a previously little-known figure named Orval Faubus, then Governor of Arkansas, precipitated a school-integration crisis in Little Rock. After President Eisenhower sent troops into the city, the nation's television screens showed Little Rock housewives and filling-station attendants screaming at soldiers and heckling starchly dressed Negro pupils who were trying bravely to go to school. The hillbilly label seemed as appropriate as ever.

From these isolated and widely separated events, one could speculate that Arkansas harbored two million or so inhabitants who attended pine-shack churches where the Gospel was interpreted with fundamentalist fervor and who, rather less frequently, sent their children to one-room schools back in the hills where they could learn their politics according to the scriptures of the Democratic Party's southern wing.

That this image was badly out of focus was demonstrated in 1966 when the supposedly simple, Bible-quoting Southern Democrats of Arkansas trooped to the polls and elected as their governor a man who (1) hailed from that down-home Arkansas town known as New York City, (2) had once married a glamorous actress-model, (3) had divorced her, (4) had inherited a couple of hundred million dollars, (5) was running on the Republican ticket and (6) was named Rockefeller.

The election of Winthrop Rockefeller as governor undoubtedly shattered many of the Arkansas stereotypes. Nevertheless, the hillbilly tag has been affixed to the state for so long that a single event may not suffice to remove it. The truth is that the rustic image of Arkansas is more than simply an accidental by-product of Bob Burns's old jokes or Orval Faubus' opportunistic manipulation of the race issue. For while much of the state can by no means be characterized as "backwoods," the Ozark plateau, which covers about one fourth of the state's land surface, does remain remote. Furthermore, the entire state's uniquely isolated past has set it somewhat apart from its neighbors, including its Southern neighbors. Largely because of the nature of the land that produced this isolation, the Civil War had less impact on Arkansas than on most other

states of the Confederacy. As the Arkansas writer Charles Morrow Wilson records: "The great majority of the people lacked any real feeling of belonging with either the Union or the Confederacy." The reason is not hard to understand. The beautiful but rugged Ozark plateau could sustain only small farms and therefore was not suited to slave agriculture. Only in the eastern counties bordering the Mississippi River and along the Arkansas River southeast of Little Rock were big slave-cultivated plantations possible, and only in this part of Arkansas did the attitudes of the planter South prevail.

The plateau's isolation has contributed in still another way to the popular image of Arkansas as being peopled by hillbillies and little else. It has helped to preserve the Elizabethan speech habits of the natives, vestiges of which remain today. This has made the Ozarks a paradise for folklore hunters and for experts in linguistics, who have explored every cranny of the old, eroded mountains that make up the plateau. Their fascination is understandable. Clearly, a land where "dauncy" means feeling below par in health, where a bag is still a "poke," where private thoughts are so carefully hoarded that one "spends" an opinion and where to be inconvenienced is to be "disfurnished" must be irresistible to anyone who loves language. The

expert whose ear is attuned to Ozark pronunciations knows that a raffle is something to shoot with and that the part of the anatomy immediately below the neck is the chist.

The plight of local chambers of commerce and other Arkansas boosters in trying to live down these local speech habits is made more difficult by the names that sprout from Ozark maps: Figure Five, Beverage Town, Hawg Scald and Bug Skuffle. In such a land a stuck-up city fellow from Little Rock may well be suspiciously regarded as "so high-collared he can't see the sun exceptin' at high noon." A bad fate is something "worse'n smellin' whiskey through a jailhouse winder." Many of these colorful expressions, of course, are a product of Ozark originality. But many of the words the Ozark people use are vestiges of an earlier time and have long passed out of use almost everywhere else in the English-speaking world. In diction, as well as dialect, the language carries echoes of Shakespeare and Spenser. The Ozark writer Wilson rightfully asserts of his homeland that "Ozark speech is a living river which pours on through the generations . . . intermittently rising and falling . . . but never changing any principal portion of its channel."

The Ozarks constitute one of the few genuine frontier districts remaining within the first 48 states. In the remotest quarter of the area that can be characterized as back hills, people still wear high-topped "plow shoes" and calico dresses and drink "mountain dew" out of fruit jars. But while such things still happen in Arkansas, they no longer can be considered typical of the state. The most significant fact about the Ozarks in recent years is that many of the natives are pulling up stakes and leaving. As in other rural areas throughout the United States, there is a steady movement to the cities. As back-hills counties continue to lose population, Arkansas' cities and towns now hold roughly half the state's two million people. Increasingly, they aspire to such goals as revamping their archaic political and economic system, attracting new industry and upgrading an impoverished school system.

It is largely these aspirations that account for the voters' 1966 decision to elevate Winthrop Rockefeller to the governor's mansion in Little Rock. Before running for governor, Rockefeller had headed the Arkansas Industrial Development Commission and had played an energizing role in Arkansas booster programs that had produced almost 100,000 new industrial jobs in the state in a decade. Plainly the people—including many in the pine hills as well as in the urban centers—thought that this was the way they wanted their state to go. For all his Eastern ways, Rockefeller had come to symbolize the yearnings of many Arkansas natives. And the industrial beginnings he helped to inspire were badly needed. Arkansas has historically ranked near the bottom among U.S. states in per capita income and—largely because of a primitive school system that had no industrial base for taxation—in education as well.

In fact, low-paying jobs and poor school facilities have been the mutually supporting causes of Arkansas' long cycle of poverty and isolation. Even most of the new industries in the state employ relatively low-paid, unskilled workers and are far removed from the glamorous electronics industries on the Texas-Louisiana Gulf Coast and in other metropolitan centers of the South Central States. But modern Arkansans are aware of this, and even as they welcome new textile plants providing unskilled jobs, they are mapping plans for educational facilities that can supply trained graduates to staff modern growth industries.

However, the shadows of the long provincial past linger and the task will not be an easy one. Arkansas' government labors under the anachronistic restraints of the state's 1874 constitution, a document that was warped out of shape by the needs of the post-Reconstruction era and is completely unsuitable for a modern state of two million people. The constitution gives great power to local political satraps, many of whom, over the years, have grown hidebound, corrupt and unrelievedly insular. They constitute a potent force against any change that threatens their vested interests, as almost any program of modernization surely will.

Yet the man who is in some ways the symbol of the old-style Arkansas politician, ex-Governor Faubus, was also the man who appointed Rockefeller to head the industrial commission more than a decade ago—an indication that not all the elements of the state's past and present are necessarily in conflict.

It might be contended, in fact, that Faubus, like Arkansas itself, has been the victim of ungenerous handling by the nation's press, although he unquestionably brought it all on himself through his demagogic handling of the Little Rock school crisis. The truth is that the familiar portrait of Faubus as an embittered Southern racist is widely at variance with his public life before 1957 and with the progressive heritage of his people. His father, Sam Faubus, was a onetime Socialist who successively backed Theodore Roosevelt's "Bull Moose" Party, Robert La Follette's progressive "Wisconsin Idea" and Franklin D. Roosevelt's New Deal. Young Orval himself entered politics as a spokesman for the downtrodden people of the Arkansas hills, attracting the attention of Arkansas' liberal Governor, Sidney S. McMath, who appointed him State Highway Commissioner. In that capacity Faubus swept away impeding departmental debris, refused to make the traditional Arkansas kickback deals with local bosses, shunned bribes from contractors and generally ran an efficient department.

As governor, Faubus continued to try to modernize and streamline the operation of the state. Further, as his intimates attest, in the early 1950s he held moderate racial views—indeed, they could be considered advanced views for a Southern politician. But, as an Arkansas native has put it, "He dreams nobly, fights dirty." As the end of his second term approached, Faubus decided that he needed a public issue to break the no-third-term tradition and continue his political career, and this may have been the determining factor in his fateful decision to make a national spectacle out of the integration of Central High School in Little Rock.

Whatever its short-run effects on Faubus' political career—he did win a third term—the crisis was very ill-timed for Arkansas. The industrial commission soon learned that few businessmen wanted to locate a plant in a strife-torn state. Faubus himself felt ill at ease with the lunatic support his defiant stand had attracted. Meanwhile his own political organization, put on the defensive, became as encrusted with provincialism and decay as the antiquated structure he had earlier worked to overhaul. In the closing years of his tenure as governor, Faubus thus undid much of his own earlier work.

But Arkansas had enjoyed the taste of modernization too much to be content with any more home-brewed mountain dew for long. So, after a period of soul-searching, the state, with the election of Winthrop Rockefeller, took a long step away from corruption-inducing one-party politics. For this, some credit must go to the state's Negro voters, 80 per cent of whom cast ballots for Rockefeller. The fact that public Negro support for the Republican Party did not drive away white voters is a testament to the pervasiveness of the state's moderate racial climate in the pre-Faubus era, as much as to emerging new attitudes.

The Arkie of folklore is today a man in transition. But it is perhaps easy to exaggerate the speed of change. For one thing, he has a heritage of taking things at a rather relaxed pace. If he is feeling new tensions as the barriers to the outside world come down, he is endeavoring to handle them with the placidity that characterized his approach in a more pastoral era. He would like the nation to have a better opinion of him, but he will not destroy all his old habits pell-mell to achieve it. It is a question of conditioning as well as of pride. The hills of Arkansas develop long-distance runners, not sprint champions.

Among the people of the South Central States, the Arkie is, of course, not alone in trying to find, at his own pace, an acceptable *modus vivendi* with the rest of America. His neighbor to the south, the Acadian of Louisiana, has something of the same problem—although, with typical French indifference, he purports to find it even less pressing.

The Acadian of Louisiana can point to roots in the American continent much deeper than those of most U.S. citizens. His direct forebears settled in French Louisiana in the latter part of the 18th Century, after being expelled from Nova Scotia by the British, who had conquered the province during the French and Indian Wars. Hardy farmers all, the Acadians scarcely paused in Creole New Orleans before migrating into the bayou and prairie country to the west. They fanned out along the watercourses and distributed acreage among themselves, following a riverbank land pattern that gave each farmer immediate access to water.

Fewer than 10,000 Acadians originally made the long journey from Nova Scotia, but so thoroughly did they take over the countryside—and so prolific were they as family builders—that today some half million Louisianans are of Acadian descent. The fact is all the more remarkable when one recalls the fate of their urban cousins, the French-speaking Creoles of New Orleans, who have all but vanished.

The Acadians found the prairie country of southwest Louisiana to be more suitable for stock raising than farming. Two centuries after the Acadians' arrival, their "*vacheries*," or ranches, still dominate the southwestern corner of the state, and their rice- and sugar-growing farms flourish in the area around the towns of St. Martinville and Lafayette. This "Cajun Country" extends over almost the entire southern Louisiana prairie from New Orleans westward to Texas. Here, for the better part of two centuries, the Acadians have existed as an expanding French island in a sea of Americans. Even today many of the older Acadians speak only French—or at least the Acadian patois that their French has become after generations of life in Louisiana. The state's politicians have long since accepted the necessity of learning enough "Cajun" to get by with on the hustings, for the Acadian vote is too large to be ignored.

The Acadians who are most resistant to change of any kind and to Americanization in particular are called "*petits paysans.*" This breed is slowly dying as growing numbers in each succeeding generation become proficiently bilingual and in many cases cease using French altogether. Yet, as Americans increasingly cluster together in large cities and become more alike, the capacity of the Acadians to maintain their identity continues as a rare phenomenon. Part of their ability to survive *as Acadians* is, in fact, traceable to their willingness to stay on the land and resist the blandishments of such urban centers as nearby New Orleans. In the Louisiana lowlands, so similar to the Nova Scotia tidal flats that their ancestors reclaimed with dikes from the Atlantic Ocean, the clannish, rural Acadians are perfectly at home.

Yet there is more to the story of Acadian endurance in Louisiana than can be explained simply by distinctions of language and custom or even by their Roman Catholic religion. This is particularly evident in view of the failure of the urban Creoles to retain their identity in New Orleans. The two varieties of transplanted Frenchmen actually followed different courses in confronting the *Américains*. The Creole tried to hang on to all his old customs—or at least to the legends of what those customs had been. The Acadian has been more flexible. He preserves the Cajun flavor of life in southern Louisiana not by saying "No" to all things American, but rather by accepting American innovations and then reshaping them to a Cajun form. For example, one of the most enduring customs of Acadian life has been the *fais-dodo*, the all-night country dance that for generations has been the epitome of leisure activity in southern Louisiana. Modern Acadian children are, of course, exposed to American dances, such as the twist, that would have horrified the old Creoles. But the Acadians are not so horrified; they dance the twist, but they dance it at the *fais-dodo*. In fact, a modern Louisiana folk ballad asserts this:

I got a gal in Thibodaux
She does the twist at the "fais-dodo."

In this easy fashion the Acadians have laughed at themselves, tended their small but productive farms, married young, begotten large families, spoken French and English, attended Catholic Mass and kept up with modern innovations. Though few people get much closer to the Acadians than having a cup of their whiskey-strong "Cajun coffee" while pausing on a trip through southern Louisiana, Acadian ways remain dominant in more than a score of Louisiana parishes (i.e., counties) to this day. Those who do not appreciate Acadian methods sometimes ridicule them, and at such times the Acadians are not unlike Ozark people in showing some resentment. But by and large the Acadians are content. They are neither wholly American nor wholly French; they are Acadian.

Prominent in the ethnic potpourri of the South Central States is another group originally from Western Europe—the Germans of Texas. Like both the Acadians and the people of the Ozarks, the Texas Germans have been rather isolated from their neighbors, and in the Civil War some paid a heavy price for it.

The Germans have a well-deserved reputation in Texas as being the state's best farmers. Indeed, they have had to be, for large numbers of them settled in the hill country west of the 30-inch rainfall line that divides the naturally watered part of agricultural America from the dry Great Plains. In this rocky terrain of limestone outcrops in the center of the state, German farmers were able somehow to make a go of it, even in the drought years that sent some of their Anglo-Saxon neighbors recoiling back from the frontier. Today, such German towns as Fredericksburg, in the heart of the hill country, represent an impressive display of rural prosperity.

One of the causes of the first major migration of

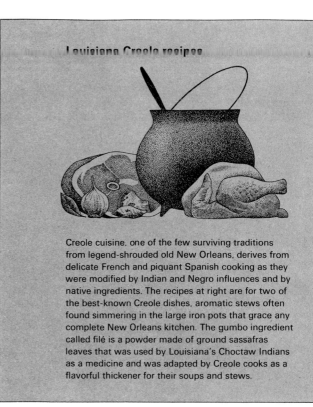

Louisiana Creole recipes

Creole cuisine, one of the few surviving traditions from legend-shrouded old New Orleans, derives from delicate French and piquant Spanish cooking as they were modified by Indian and Negro influences and by native ingredients. The recipes at right are for two of the best-known Creole dishes, aromatic stews often found simmering in the large iron pots that grace any complete New Orleans kitchen. The gumbo ingredient called filé is a powder made of ground sassafras leaves that was used by Louisiana's Choctaw Indians as a medicine and was adapted by Creole cooks as a flavorful thickener for their soups and stews.

Germans to Texas was the failure of the liberal middle-class revolutions in Germany in the 1840s. Another was the inducements of German land speculators who, touting the advantages of moving to Texas, gathered up sizable groups of German immigrants and shipped them across the Atlantic. One such operation, which called itself The Society for the Protection of German Immigrants in Texas, was formed in 1844 to bring over colonists from Hesse and, despite many disputes between the society's organizers and the colonists themselves, managed to permanently settle several thousand German families in Texas. There had been some Germans in Texas earlier in the century—the rolls of Sam Houston's army that fought and won the Battle of San Jacinto are spotted with German names—but the heavy influx began after Texas had established its independence from Mexico. By 1843 German settlement was sufficiently heavy to cause the Texas Congress to stipulate that the fledgling republic's laws should be printed in German as well as English. As the colonists arrived, they established towns all along the route from the coast near the port city of Galveston inland toward the Texas capital at Austin and beyond into the hill country. By 1854 Dr. Adolf Douai, a refugee from the unsuccessful 1848 revolution

Gumbo filé

1 large stewing chicken	3 sprigs parsley
1/2 pound lean ham	1 sprig thyme
3 dozen oysters	1 bay leaf
2 tablespoons butter or	1/2 pod fresh red pepper
1 of shortening	salt, black pepper, cayenne
2 quarts oyster stock	2 tablespoons filé (powdered
2 quarts boiling water	sassafras)
1 large onion	

Clean and cut up the chicken. Sprinkle the pieces with salt, pepper and cayenne to taste. Dice the ham and finely chop the onion, parsley and thyme. Melt the butter or shortening in a large soup kettle or deep stewing pot and add the chicken and ham. Cover closely and sauté for five to 10 minutes. Then add the onion, parsley and thyme, stirring occasionally to prevent burning. In a separate pot heat the oyster stock. When the other ingredients have browned, add the boiling water and hot oyster stock. Next add the bay leaf, chopped very fine, and the red pepper, cut in two with seeds removed. Now set the gumbo back to simmer for approximately one hour. When nearly ready to serve and while the gumbo is still boiling, add the fresh oysters. Let the gumbo remain on the stove for three minutes and then remove the pot from the fire. Drop the filé gradually into the pot of hot gumbo, stirring slowly to mix thoroughly. Pour the gumbo into a warm tureen, and serve with boiled rice.

Note: Never boil the rice with the gumbo, and do not add the filé while the gumbo is on the fire. Boiling after the filé is added tends to make the gumbo stringy. Cayenne is especially hot, and care should be taken not to use much of it unless one likes very spicy foods.

This recipe is for six. Gumbo filé may also be made with turkey, beef, squirrel or rabbit in place of chicken.

Jambalaya

1 pound fresh pork	2 medium-sized onions
1/4 pound lean ham	2 cloves of garlic
1 dozen small pork	2 sprigs thyme
sausage links	2 bay leaves
1 1/2 cups rice	2 sprigs parsley
1 tablespoon butter or	2 cloves, finely ground
shortening	1/2 teaspoon chili pepper
3 quarts beef broth	salt, black pepper, cayenne

Cut the pork, both lean and fat, into pieces about 1/2-inch square, and finely chop the ham. Separate the sausage links. Chop the onions finely and mince the garlic. Mince the fine herbs—thyme, bay leaves and parsley. In a large pot (at least five quarts), melt the butter or shortening, add the onions and pork and brown slowly, stirring frequently. When these ingredients are slightly brown, add the ham and garlic, then the minced herbs and ground cloves, mixing the ingredients in the pot thoroughly. Let all this brown for five minutes, then add the sausage links and let all cook for five minutes longer. Add the three quarts of beef broth and cook for 10 minutes. When the mixture comes to a boil, add the rice, then the chili pepper, with salt, pepper and cayenne to taste. Let the pot boil until the rice is tender, and then serve. Do not overcook the rice.

This recipe serves six.

---

in Germany, had founded in San Antonio a German-language newspaper, the *San Antonio Zeitung*, that promptly took a strong editorial stand for the abolition of slavery.

What culture existed during the early days of the Texas frontier was largely brought by the Germans. Their communities, however small, generally had a German bandstand in the center of town, and societies for the study of the classics flourished to such a degree that Texas frontiersmen often called their German neighbors "Latins" because they were forever reading the works of Cicero and other ancients in the original language. The Texans were not the only ones puzzled by the strangely fervent, idealistic immigrants. An account of the period tells of Comanche Indians creeping up to these cultural forums and "listening gravely at the open door, while one of the Latin farmers was lecturing on the socialistic theories of Saint-Simon or Fourier."

By 1850 Germans constituted a substantial minority of the populations of Galveston, Houston and San Antonio. But in the decade before the Civil War the humanistic ardor of the more outspoken German leaders began to seem dangerously out of place in a Southern state. In 1854 an organization of German idealists, *Der Freie Verein* (The Free Society), called a state-wide meeting of all Germans in Texas out of which came a far-reaching series of political, religious and social proposals. The list of resolutions included graduated income and inheritance taxes and, interestingly enough, a strong plank in support of the Monroe Doctrine. The resolution on slavery did not flinch: "Slavery is an evil, the removal of which is absolutely necessary according to the principles of democracy. . . ."

As the election of Sam Houston on a pro-Union platform in 1859 proved, Texas was by no means populated solely by hot-blooded secessionists; nevertheless, pro-Southern feeling was strong in many quarters, and the stand of *Der Freie Verein* and the unequivocal declarations of Douai's San Antonio newspaper caused many Texans to conclude that all of their German neighbors were fire-breathing abolitionists. The rumor spread that the singing societies that flourished in almost every German community were subversive organizations dedicated to spreading abolitionist propaganda. As the outbreak of the Civil War neared, the atmosphere became more and more tense. Several German communities became sufficiently alarmed to reaffirm publicly their allegiance to the laws of Texas and to recommend to their countrymen that they cease their attempts to disturb the institution of slavery. San Antonio, with a population roughly equally divided among Germans, Anglo-Americans and Mexican-Americans, was especially troubled, perhaps all the more so because the rural counties to the northwest were predominantly German. Mob violence broke out in San Antonio against the Germans, and hangings occurred elsewhere in Texas.

The war itself was a traumatic event for the Germans of Texas, forcing them to choose between their families' safety and the aspirations for freedom that had brought many of them to Texas in the first place. Some joined the Union Army and some the Confederate, and some tried to maintain a precarious neutrality. One group of 65 Union sympathizers, most of them Germans, tried to escape to Mexico from the hostile atmosphere of Texas. They were pursued by Confederate troops and 34 were killed in a miniature civil war between Texans. In the town of Comfort, Texas, there remains today a monument commemorating this event that is doubtless unique in the U.S. South. On it are engraved the words, "Our Union Dead."

Once the passions of the war had subsided, the Texas Germans soon recovered the respect of their neighbors. By 1876 the governor's inaugural address was once again being printed in English, Spanish and German. The German language was taught in Texas public elementary schools until anti-German feelings stirred by World War I largely ended the practice. The influence of the old country is still perceptible, most noticeably in rural sections throughout southeast and central Texas and also in cities such as San Antonio, which has had its German "first families" for more than a century. In the countryside the Germans still work as hard as ever, mind their own business and remain in the words of their Texas neighbors, "the best farmers in this part of the country." Yet, like the Ozark people, they see their younger generation moving to the cities, blending imperceptibly into the style of life around them.

Texas Germans, like Louisiana Acadians, are noteworthy as exceptions to the popular impression of the South Central States as a land of white Anglo-Saxon Southerners and Negroes. There is, in addition to the Germans and the Negroes, a third sizable ethnic minority in Texas—the almost two million Mexican-Americans whose ancestors were on hand to welcome the first gringos to the Southern plains well over a century ago.

The plight of Mexican-Americans in Texas has been a hard one, for these people have not only been alienated from the Anglo-Saxon majority, but have been divided among themselves. Internal division began during Texas' War for Independence,

some Mexicans giving aid and comfort to Santa Anna's armies and others emerging as soldiers and leaders of the Texas force. At the same time, these "native" Texans found that a formidable cultural barrier separated them from the newcomers from the north and east. Only three became signers (among 59) of Texas' 1836 Declaration of Independence from Mexico, and only one, Lorenzo de Zavala, got a high government post, the vice presidency of the provisional Texas government.

Zavala became involved in an incident that neatly underlines a cultural barrier that, then and now, divides Mexican-Americans and other Texans. During a crucial debate over military policy at the outbreak of the revolution, the stylish Zavala began what promised to be a lengthy oration with the words, "Mr. President, an eminent Roman statesman once said . . ." Whereupon, an impatient Texan abruptly cut him off with the observation that it behooved the revolutionary convention to give less thought to dead Romans and more to live Mexicans. This anecdote illustrates a problem that grows out of wholly different approaches to life: the *Mejicanos* of Texas are leisurely and often circuitous in their personal relations; their gringo neighbors are likely to be blunt and even aggressive. Both groups may be characterized as prideful, but they have wholly different concepts of what constitutes status, prestige and "saving face." As a result, the long association of Anglos and Mexican-Americans in Texas has not been without its abrasions.

Texas' Mexican-American population consists of a thin but venerable stratum of aristocrats, most of them refugees from various revolutionary conflicts in Mexico over the past century; a somewhat larger middle class of business and professional men; and a huge lower class composed of agricultural workers and manual laborers. Some of the agricultural workers have their own farms; many more hire out as migrant field hands. The numbers of those who have left the land to work in unskilled trades in the cities is growing steadily. If Mexico City is the focus of attention of Mexicans south of the border, the Texas equivalent for this growing number of urban Mexican-Americans is the old city of San Antonio. As a result, some 300,000 of San Antonio's population of 700,000 are of Mexican extraction.

Until recent years, prospects of climbing out of the migrant labor camps or city slums must have seemed hopeless to most Mexican-Americans of Texas. But now there is more hope. For one thing, thousands have earned college educations on the

Distinctive hats of the Southern frontier

A constellation of Stetsons illustrates a few of the hat styles beloved by Westerners. The original hat was designed by a Philadelphia hatter, J. B. Stetson, specifically to deal with the sun and wind of the West, but cowhands quickly learned that it could also be used to fan fires, carry water (allegedly up to 10 gallons) or serve as a pillow. The company went on to produce a variety of styles, and cowhands invented new ways to crease them to meet particular needs.

The original Stetson was called the "Boss of the Plains" and was first made about 1865.

The "Old Fort Worth," with its upturned front brim, has been worn since frontier days.

The "Lone Star," another oldtimer, has been creased in a variety of ways by its owners.

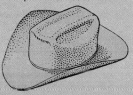

The "Brushpopper" or the "Rawlins" is most often worn in Texas' brush country.

The "High Range" is a classic "ten-gallon" hat and has either a black or a gray crown.

The "Vaquero" is a hat often worn near the border and is related to a Mexican sombrero.

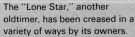

The "Longhorn," made out of straw, is especially light, cool and comfortable on hot days.

The "King Ranch Sweep" has a crease designed to cut the wind resistance of the hat.

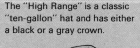

The "King Ranch Crimp," with its relatively narrow brim, is another model for wind.

The "LBJ" hat, made popular by Lyndon B. Johnson, offers a narrow brim for dress wear.

G.I. Bill, and this generation has produced a number of earnest advocates for the needs of Texans of Mexican descent. Best known of these spokesmen is Henry Gonzalez, elected Congressman from San Antonio in 1961 and since re-elected so convincingly that the office is widely regarded as his as long as he wants it. Another is Albert Peñana, an articulate and controversial county commissioner who aggressively advocates state programs to combat poverty on San Antonio's teeming West Side and in the area south to the Rio Grande.

San Antonio is a picturesque city of great charm, but it is also a city of widespread squalor. Its Latin-esque culture gives the city its uniqueness, but also its lingering atmosphere of despair. For years San Antonio has ranked lowest among major Texas metropolitan centers in per capita income and in education, and has ranked highest in the rate of infant mortality. Efforts to break the cycle of cultural deprivation, largely caused by the language barrier and its ramifications, have taken the form of state-supported preschool English classes for Spanish-speaking pupils aged five to seven. The results are promising, but the task that remains is huge. And in rural areas, where ferment among Mexican-American farm workers seeking wage increases has been growing, the cycle of father-to-son

agricultural poverty and illiteracy seems scarcely touched by programs designed to keep children of migratory workers in some kind of stable, coherent educational environment during harvest season.

In sum, the Mexican-Americans of Texas have not as yet achieved the acceptance won by other groups in the ethnic crossroads of the South Central States. Thus they face substantially the same problems as the region's three million Negroes. The latter, in fact, have at least one advantage—they are not as mired in the agricultural past as the migrant Mexican-Americans. The Negroes of the South Central States increasingly live in the region's cities—almost 300,000 in Houston, another 300,000 in New Orleans, almost 200,000 in Dallas, and 55,000 and 28,000 in Oklahoma City and Little Rock, respectively.

But there is more, of course, to acculturation than rubbing elbows with one's neighbors in large cities; the abiding problem for Negroes in this part of America, as elsewhere, is simply one of color. And in this respect, their story stands in interesting contrast—though it is hardly less disturbing, in the final analysis—to that of Negroes in the Deep South or in Northern ghettos.

As the story of Louisiana's Creoles illustrates, orthodox attitudes of separation and segregation have not always automatically prevailed in the South Central region. The exception is not restricted to the Creoles. Texas' frontier days contain intriguing instances of unusual cohesion and tolerance among free Negroes and whites. For example, the military success of the early Texas armies depended in large measure on the competence of army guides. Two of the best known were Erastus "Deaf" Smith, Sam Houston's favorite guide, and Hendrick Arnold, who guided Texas revolutionary detachments from the banks of the Medina River to San Antonio during one of the sieges of that city. The significant point is not that Deaf Smith was white while Hendrick Arnold was Negro, but that Arnold married Smith's daughter and later was granted land by the Republic of Texas for his service in the Texas army. Deaf Smith was hardly considered *déclassé* after his daughter's marriage: a Texas county was named after him.

Another prominent Texas Negro of the revolution was William Goyens of Nacogdoches, a blacksmith who became successful enough to acquire considerable wealth. Goyens served as Sam Houston's emissary and interpreter in dealings with Texas Indians. Texas historians have been intrigued to discover not only that Goyens was highly respected by his fellow Texans but that he, too, married a white woman.

Just as a sizable collection of historical data attests to the activities of free Negroes in the service of the Texas revolution, so there is a growing body of information about the performance of Negro cowboys on the cattle trails to Kansas. In his book *Cow People*, Texas historian J. Frank Dobie tells of a Negro trail boss named Al Jones who "went up the trail to Kansas and beyond with Texas cattle thirteen times, four times as boss, with white men as well as Negroes under him." Jones was not an isolated example. Many Negroes rode the cattle trail across the Red River, and in some outfits they constituted the majority of the trail hands.

Still later, in the Populist era near the turn of the century, Negroes played a prominent role in the People's Party along the Southern frontier. The founding convention of the party in Texas in 1891 elected two Negroes to the State Executive Committee, and later during the tense election battles with the Democrats, a Negro Populist leader, J. B. Rayner, stumped the state with, among others, the white party chairman. Rayner was ranked as an orator only behind "Cyclone" Davis and "Stump" Ashby, the two Populist evangelists from Texas who toured the nation.

Whatever violence these facts do to the classic stereotype of race relations in Southern states, they are perhaps most instructive as examples of what could happen under favorable circumstances. They cannot, however, be considered typical. Rayner was subjected to violence on more than one occasion, and it cannot be imagined that Negro trail bosses had a consistently easy time of it.

Still, some prominent historians feel that racial attitudes hardened with the passage of Jim Crow laws near the end of the 19th Century. Now that those laws are being removed from the statute books, it should prove interesting to see what kind of interracial climate develops among the people of the old Southern frontier. The preliminary evidence is both too fragmentary and too contradictory to permit much of an assessment.

The reason for the contradictions is not hard to find. Through the generations, the Anglo-Saxon majority in the South Central States has been too deeply engaged in trying to work out its own way of life to give much thought to the special problems of the other tenants of the giant crossroads. These people have battled the floods of the Mississippi, the rocks of the Ozarks, the dry plains of Oklahoma and Texas. They have battled the oil sands underneath their land and grappled with the rustlers and freebooters who have ridden over it. Not many Americans have had to cope with such a complexity of historical imperatives, and in such a hostile physical environment. There has not been much time for introspection. The idea of "shoot first, and ask questions later" still has its hold on the people and only now is beginning to give way to more prudent methods of social intercourse.

This being true, a friendly observer of the Texans, the Sooners, the Arkies, and all the other Southerners and plainsmen of the region may perhaps be excused for considering the rest of the nation a bit self-righteous in its impatience with the boisterous ways of the area. The people, like the place itself, may lack subtlety, but the demands of survival have hardly been conducive to the cultivation of refinements.

Beyond this, the varied people of the Southern frontier have one more battle to win: to find their own identity within the context of the larger American experience. Most of them are not likely to find it soon; their history, after all, has not left them much time to learn how to look. But from the universities as well as the public forums of political debate, the sounds of their emerging inquiry can be heard. The years to come should be as variegated—and probably as filled with tension—as their strenuous past.

This is the county courthouse. It was built in 1909. My office used to be on the second floor, but they moved it to the basement for me; I don't get upstairs as much as I did before my heart attack. I like to go to lunch at Klepper's, a nice little sandwich shop there on the square. It's crowded, but that way I get to talk to people.

The busy life of an Arkansas judge

Large parts of the South Central States remain remote from the bustle of big-city life. This is especially true of rural Arkansas, and one of the best ways to see one such area is through the eyes of a county judge.

The chief administrator of Boone County, in northwestern Arkansas, is County Judge John Roy Holt. Born in Lead Hill, 20 miles from the county seat of Harrison, Judge Holt has lived in Boone County all his life and knows most of the area's 16,000 people. Although he has had a heart attack, he keeps as busy as ever. Officially he has charge of the county roads, hospital and jail and presides over the county court. But he is also personal adviser to many of his constituents.

On this and the following pages, Judge Holt tells in his own words about his life, his friends and the day-to-day activities his job entails.

Photographs by Bruce Roberts

129

A stream of visitors on business and pleasure

An average of 35 people visit Judge Holt each day. They come to talk about everything, including their personal problems: "They want financial advice, or they'll say, 'My wife is talking about leaving me. I want you to talk to her,' or 'My girl wants to leave home. What shall I do?'"

The judge's heart attack occurred just as he came up for re-election to his third two-year term, and his friends did virtually all the campaigning; he won the election. To ease his workday, his office was then moved to the basement of the courthouse, but the illness had little effect on the judge's performance. Being a county judge is demanding but intensely satisfying. As he says, "I enjoy the work, being out in the open and getting something done."

Some of our retired men like to visit with each other around the courthouse. Sometimes I stop to have a word with them. I put benches for them inside for the wintertime. In the summer they can sit outside in the courthouse park. They like to talk and trade or sell knives to each other and pass the time off together.

Ray Henderson is the mayor of Everton. This is a little town over close to Valley Springs. When we have our equipment down there we grade their streets—they don't have blacktop—or spread their gravel. He's getting up a petition to get his roads taken into the state system so they can get regular service and has come for my advice.

This couple here this morning are retired. They were out-of-state people, I forget from where, moved here six years ago on a small pension. They're good people, and have their own home, but they've both had a lot of medical bills this year and they were seeking my advice on what their pension would cover.

130

Mayor Dene Hester of Harrison is one of our retired. He operated a successful clothes manufacturing business around Chicago. He was our mayor during the flood in 1961 but was defeated next election. Nobody blamed him for the flood, but there was disagreement about finding a solution. He ran again last time and won.

She's not from here originally, though she came here to work. Poor thing. Going to have that baby and no father. You have to help them. She wants to keep her baby and I admire her for that. I told her I'd try to arrange credit for her at the hospital. I can't always help, but if I can't I try to direct them to someone who can.

The judge's family: large but close knit

With the exception of an aunt and a sister in California, both sides of Judge Holt's family live in Arkansas, most of them in Boone County. During the Depression the Holt family business failed, and the judge, then a young man, went to work hauling railroad ties. "I never had much education," he says, "but I have learned a lot of things." In 1930 he met Ruth Davis. They went together for three years, then borrowed $40 and were married. When their first son, David Ray, was born, Judge Holt sold his saddle to pay the doctor. They have three children, two boys and a girl, and six grandchildren.

Years back the church ladies worked on this quilt, and they charged ten cents to anyone to have his name embroidered on it. Then they auctioned it off to a lady here in town, and later my wife bought it from her. My wife Ruth, the one in the middle, and these other ladies are looking for their family names. My father's name is on it.

We have a family reunion every year in Lead Hill. To my right is my aunt Marie Turner and to my left is Ruth with one of our daughter Judith's twins. My second son, Ross, is behind me and to his right is his wife Dotty. That's Judith in the polka-dot dress carrying the other twin. The rest of the family is following along.

Back in 1950 three of us organized this church and had it built ourselves. It's not fancy, but it's stood up well. I used to come here most every Sunday, but lately, since I was sick, I've been going to the church in Harrison. I still like to come out to Lead Hill, though, to see old friends and my sister and brother who live here.

These are my grandchildren, my daughter Judith's. That girl with the pretty smile is Kathy, who's just over two years, and the little ones are the twins, Ouida Annette and Clarence Jr., ten months old. Judith was training to be a nurse when she got married. We didn't want her to drop out, but there was no stopping her.

T. A. Raley and I—we always called him T. A.—were boys together. When we were in school we'd pull all kinds of pranks. I remember once T. A. and two or three boys took a saddle off a horse tied outside. They put that saddle on T. A. and he came up through the study hall, and of course you know what happened. He got whipped.

Garvin Dunlap and I were young fellows together. When I was going with Lucille [now Mrs. Green] before I met my wife, he was dating a cousin of hers. Once we went up to Springfield, Missouri, in an old Essex car to see them. We had seven flats on the way home. Garvin has a nice house and a lot of good-looking Hampshire pigs.

Childhood friends to visit and chat with

Judge Holt's friends, like his family, were born and raised in Boone County, and nearly all of them have remained there. Most of them grew up on farms and have been farmers all of their lives. Although the area shows few outward signs of increasing prosperity, it is no longer the poor country it was before World War II.

Most of the farms used to be marginal—the major crop, though a poor one, was cotton—but recently the county's agriculture has become more diversified. Livestock and dairy cows have been substituted for crops on many farms, and most farmers work closely with government advisers, a practice that has paid off: many of Boone County's residents now have healthy bank accounts, and a college education for the children is no longer rare.

Lucille Campbell Green teaches third grade in the Skyline Heights School in Harrison. When we were young she was a kind of sweetheart. Her grandfather didn't like me, so he'd get his pistol out and go to playing with it to scare me. When I was about 12 I'd bought a new suit, and I had to go over and show it to Lucille. I tripped running home and tore the suit. It like to broke my heart.

Pearl Devereaux Threet was the smartest girl in our school. It was always her papers I copied off. Her father was a minister, and had bees and sold honey all the time. She and her sister went to the Lead Hill School. Her husband Jim has always been a good, honest, hard-working fellow. Their daughter is a registered nurse, working in Little Rock. Both their sons have college degrees.

I like to visit Clayton Paddock. He was in business in Chicago before he came here and he has good business sense and we are lucky to have him. He's on our finance and planning commission. He is also a justice of the peace. Said some couple came up to him in the fields the other day and asked him to marry them right then and there.

I'm glad to get to that sawmill of Harold Estes up by Omaha [a small town 19 miles from Harrison]. I think the town used to do a little business with Harold before he started making just railroad ties. Sends them all the way up to Kansas City. He's worked hard to build up that mill and he's got a good business going.

We are mighty proud of Hillcrest Home. You know what the term "poor farm" means and all the awful things it signifies, and before the Mennonites came in here, ours was just about a poor farm. They came in about ten-twelve years ago and it is part of their religion to work to serve others, and I want to tell you they do it.

The advent of progress in Boone County

Although farming is still Boone County's most important occupation and many of the roads are dirt or gravel, there are numerous indications of change. Harrison is designated an urban area by the Bureau of the Census, and in 1967 the county airport got a new jet strip. A vocational and technical school provides training for jobs in factories at the industrial park taking shape behind the airport. The county hospital has some of the best modern equipment.

There was some opposition to one recent innovation: the telephone-equipped automobile that the judge now uses on his rounds. "Some folks said, 'Why don't he use a pickup truck?' I said, 'When I go to Little Rock with a delegation I don't want to take them in a pickup truck.' That shut them up."

Here I am with Fate Newman, who asked me to come out to Zinc to see where the bridge needs work. In some ways I don't like to go to Zinc. It was such a busy place and now it's a ghost town. Fate is an old resident who has been here years on top of years. He did a little farming, but he's not doing anything now, just visiting around.

7

The Quest
for Identity

For generations Americans have pondered the "mind of the South" or the "mind of New England" and even, more ambitiously, the "mind of America." This curiosity has produced a number of interpretive books, some dazzlingly perceptive and some little more than regional incantations. But none has been free of at least a taint of the confusion inherent in such a basically impossible undertaking. The various "minds" of America's regions are not only composed of many ideas, but of ideas that seem to contradict one another.

The confusion is no less when one attempts to analyze the South Central States. Any attempt to unravel the "mind of the Southwest" immediately gets tangled in the knotty fact that the region is at once "Southern" and "Western." The threads run in both directions—indeed, in many directions. Yet some general patterns can be detected. Perhaps the best place to look first is at the people themselves. What do they think they are?

In Dallas they have long looked upon themselves as staunch defenders of a set of traditional virtues

Astride a favorite five-gaited Tennessee Walking Horse, Lyndon B. Johnson surveys his 414-acre LBJ Ranch in the hill country of central Texas. Johnson has often used the ranch, which is a working cattle spread, to extend "Western hospitality" to foreign visitors.

generally associated with the U.S. South. Both the city's civic leadership and a large majority of its people have gained national attention for their determined, sometimes strident, defense of such old Southern verities as "states' rights" and "local self-government." Yet Dallas civic and commercial groups often print signs and advertisements urging visitors to enjoy their city's "Western hospitality."

Some years earlier, Lyndon Johnson, while still a Senator and thus directly responsible to his Texas constituency, carefully explained to national reporters that he was a Westerner. Johnson's Democratic colleague, Texas Senator Ralph Yarborough, followed a similar line when he announced in 1957 that he was not joining the "Southern caucus" of U.S. Senators, the group that historically has plotted hold-the-line strategy on all segregation issues.

One pattern that emerges, then, is that Texas public officials and business leaders seem to be trying to find new footing on somewhat non-Southern soil. Such changes of public posture are by no means limited to Texas. Already noted has been the election by Arkansans of that decidedly non-Southern specimen, New Yorker Winthrop Rockefeller, as governor. En route to the governorship, Rockefeller campaigned on a many-sided platform to "modernize" and "reform" Arkansas. Louisiana, too, is experiencing a change in its traditional politics: for the first time since Reconstruction days there is emerging a phenomenon that could be called the home-grown white Republican. For almost a century following the Civil War, Republicans comprised a tiny minority in the state. But recently some members of the urban middle class—generally young businessmen—have been setting up what are, in effect, Republican cells in their sections of New Orleans and Shreveport. This hardly constitutes a grassroots Republican movement; the countryside is firmly Democratic and there are only a handful of Republicans in the state legislature. But the nucleus of a revivified Republican Party has been created. Similarly, Oklahoma (which has never had a "Southern" past in a strictly historical sense) has nevertheless seen fundamental alterations in customs that were traceable to Southern inheritances. Foremost among these is the marked step away from religious fundamentalism implicit in the repeal of Oklahoma's timeworn law banning the sale of hard liquor.

But though these developments confirm the presence of a new pattern of attitudes in all four states, it remains difficult to define what these attitudes specifically are and what they may mean as portents of the future. For years, any alterations in the nature of Southern orthodoxy have been taken as proof—by casual observers—of the imminent arrival of an entity known as the "New South." With time, the phrase has acquired a variety of meanings, most of them heralding a new era of economic progress embodying at least some kind of racial accommodation. Both by Southerners and Northerners, the "New South" has been proclaimed many times in the years since Appomattox. Over and over again, however, the image of change has mysteriously vanished at the hands of more powerful though less discernible forces lurking beneath the surface of Southern life.

So the question recurs: is the latest "New South" as illusory as past ones or are the changes currently visible along the Southern frontier indicative of a truly "new" era across all the states of the old Confederacy?

Finding a concrete answer to this question is a perilous process. For a starter, there are many "Souths" and each has had its moments both of hope and of hopelessness. There is the patrician South of the Virginia tidewater country—the South of George Washington and Robert E. Lee, of planter civility and of long lines of gray-clad infantry charging across ruined fields, a tableau at once heroic and inevitably romantic. Almost as ancient

in lineage has been the South of the upcountry, the province of the white yeoman farmer whose various aspirations and fears have sometimes been a force for healthy economic change and at other times a bulwark of racism. Aside from these distinct Souths, there have been other sectional divisions—the "upper South" states of Virginia, North Carolina and Tennessee, which have generally been regarded as less resistant to social and racial adjustments; and the "lower South" states along the Gulf Coast, which have not been as flexible. And, finally, there is the "western South" of the trans-Mississippi country, the states of Texas and Arkansas.

Illustrating the elusiveness of these various descriptions is the fact that the state of Louisiana fits all of them generally—and none of them specifically. With its urban merchant classes in New Orleans and its rural gentry in the Mississippi delta, its upcountry Protestant farmers in the northern half of the state and its Roman Catholic "Cajun" farmers of the French-speaking southern parishes, its geographic juxtaposition between bitter-end Mississippi to the east and the more optimistic Texas to the west, Louisiana gives the appearance of having been a part of many worlds. And, indeed, all of the earnest heartbeats of these various Souths have pulsed from time to time in the state, but never in a way that conveyed a sustained flow of meaning. The attempt to understand "what the South really is" seems in Louisiana to yield the same pale uncertainty as in other Southern states.

Yet, in all the Souths that stretch from the Atlantic tidewater to the Mississippi delta, there is a common thread—a sense of thwarted intentions and tragic history that now supports a lean underlying pessimism about man and his possibilities. This sensibility is a most difficult thing to describe—or often even to see. It is frequently obscured by the white Southerner's hearty good-fellowship and by his fervent participation in religion, both personal and organized. But it flashes to the surface any time the racial status quo is threatened—often side by side with his sociability and his religiosity. During the integration troubles at the University of Mississippi in Oxford in 1962, visiting newsmen were astonished to hear the state's Lieutenant Governor, Paul Johnson, deliver a violent attack on all "race-mixers"—whether black or white, Northern or Southern—and then, his anger suddenly exhausted, abruptly turn and with sincere courtesy invite one and all to return again some other time and enjoy Mississippi's "Southern hospitality" when "things quiet down."

The writer Walker Percy, who lives in Louisiana,

has described the similar manner in which religion is harnessed to "canonize the existing social and political structure and to brand as atheistic any threat of change." By way of example, Percy cites the motives announced by a gentleman named W. Arsene Dick, the Mississippian who founded a society called "Americans for the Preservation of the White Race." Asserted Dick, in outlining the need for his organization to fight the race-mixers: "The trouble is they took God out of everything." Religion, as well as manners, is made to serve attitudes of racial orthodoxy.

Concludes writer Percy: "Some day a white Mississippian is going to go to New York, make the usual detour through Harlem, and see it for the foul cheerless warren it is; and instead of making him happy as it does now, it is going to make him unhappy. Then the long paranoia, this damnable sectional insanity, will be one important step closer to being over."

Scores of other writers have pondered this impulse toward negation in the Old South—indeed, the inquiry has produced some of America's most notable literature. In the process, novelists as diverse in style as Carson McCullers and William Styron have dramatized the sense of impending doom throbbing just underneath the surface of the South's social system.

But the suffocating blanket of pessimism stretching from the repressive political machine of the Byrd family in Virginia to the White Citizens' Councils in Mississippi tends to fray somewhere past the Mississippi River. On westward, something else is at work. Any attempt to understand the "mind" of Texans, Oklahomans, Arkansans and Louisianans must pause to take note of what this "something else" is.

It should at once be noted that this is less true of Louisiana and parts of eastern Arkansas than it is of the rest of the South Central region. Yet even these areas do not quite have the teeth-clenched militancy of, say, Mississippi. They, too, have at least a touch of "difference" to distinguish their style from that of the traditional "Deep South."

Stated simply, the people of the South Central region do not as a group view their situation pessimistically. Rather, they draw on a wholly different tradition of old-fashioned optimism that dates from the settlement of the frontier. This "difference" that is characteristic of the South Central region merits some study, for its effect in the decades ahead may be profound.

For the original Southwesterner, physical removal to virgin land was, simply and totally, a ratification

Eminent frontier historians

A probing scholar of the U.S. frontier, the late Walter Prescott Webb was one of the South Central region's most respected historians. Not afraid of controversy, he realistically depicted the hardships of frontier life and evolved a broad theory of the historical role of the frontier.

An imaginative social historian of the Southwest, J. Frank Dobie was, like Webb, for many years a professor at the University of Texas. Dobie called himself a "chronicler" of the past and was an avid collector of frontier folk tales involving cowboys, outlaws and other Westerners.

Some writers of the South Central States

Winner of the Pulitzer Prize for fiction in 1965, Shirley Ann Grau is a native of Louisiana and lives near New Orleans. Her prizewinning novel, *The Keepers of the House,* deals with bigotry in a Southern town. She has published two other novels and an outstanding volume of short stories.

Ralph Ellison, born and raised in Oklahoma City, is the author of one of the best novels of the 1950s, *Invisible Man,* the wild, sad story of a Southern Negro who comes to New York. One of the nation's most respected men of letters, Ellison is also the author of a perceptive book of essays.

The author of the poetic and haunting short novel *Pale Horse, Pale Rider,* Katherine Anne Porter was born in Texas. Miss Porter has written many fine short stories, some of which are set in her native state, and one full-length novel, *Ship of Fools,* which became a bestseller in 1962.

of his belief in the American Dream. Far from diminishing this feeling, the harshness of the frontier environment strengthened it so that it became the central ingredient in the peace of mind of the citizenry. No more than other Americans could the people of the frontier South be considered philosophers; in the name of a more pleasant future, their optimism was simply the most direct way of coping with the present. And with the frontiersman's sure instinct for making do, they used what resources they had—the availability of neighbors—to make the present as rewarding as possible. Camp meetings, folk dances, religious revivals, political rallies —anything that required people rather than money—took on such significance that cumulatively these public affairs came to be the cultural inheritance passed from one generation to the next.

It is this circumstance—call it folkway, regional memory or emotional legacy—that sets the states of the Southern frontier apart from those of the Deep South. It is a question of inherited style. The people of the South Central region remember the openness of the old West—the West the French settled in Louisiana, the Spanish in Texas and American frontiersmen everywhere. This West—the historical West—was a land of promise and possibility. Today, true enough, some of the white people

of Texas and Oklahoma and, a bit more frequently, those of Arkansas and Louisiana, still pay ritualistic homage to the slogans of the Confederacy, but for increasing numbers of them, individual self-respect is simply not bound up in an attempt to live by these slogans. The ties to the past are in many ways related to non-Southern events that are distinctly Louisiana experiences or Texas experiences, events having to do with bayous and frontier plains or with the French and Spanish past. At the time of the Civil War, Oklahoma had scarcely seen its first cattle herd, and statehood was still far off; Arkansas, too, was largely isolated from the passions that swept the Deep South. More and more there are indications that the people living in these states today are rather glad they have been spared an excess of emotional involvement in the Southern Cause. The baggage is too heavy.

So the reaction against the closed society of the South has yielded a reaching out to the openness of the West. This tendency can produce awkward moments. For example, Lyndon Johnson, then Vice President, placed his close friend, Texas Governor John Connally, squarely on the spot in 1963 when he loudly praised the Administration's civil rights program. Connally responded by endorsing parts of the program and opposing other parts. In so

Winner of the National Book Award in 1962 for his novel *The Moviegoer,* Walker Percy lives in Covington, Louisiana, outside of New Orleans. His novel describes the life of a despairing young New Orleans businessman. His excellent second novel, *The Last Gentleman,* appeared in 1966.

doing he avoided espousing either the classic Southern rhetoric of resistance or the point of view of his friend, the Vice President. "Texans are a unique people," Connally explained. Indefinite though it was, the statement made sense to most Texans. The Governor's remark meant that Texas is in transition and the attitudes of its people cannot be characterized as either Southern or Northern. Under the circumstances, emphasizing the state's "uniqueness" seemed as good a solution as any.

This blurring of political lines and social attitudes frequently produces a dense intellectual tangle. Throughout the four states, candidates from Left to Right promise voters that, once in office, they will conduct themselves "like our fathers before us." But since, depending on the time and the issue, "father" was both for and against fencing the range, for and against government aid to farmers, for and against international oil companies, for and against subsidies to railroads, for free enterprise but against "Eastern monopolies," for economic "progress" but against the sins of the cities that "progress" created—since "father" was of many minds on all these issues, it is abundantly clear that nobody can be truly certain how he would act. The legends of old—the old South, the old West, the old Creole days, the old Spanish period, the old Indian wars, the old Sooner times—all crowd in, overlap and contradict one another.

Happily, a massive sifting and sorting operation is now in progress. In recent years, regional scholars in the four states have been digging through the inherited legends to discover just how the successive waves of pioneers actually lived and interacted with one another. Implicit in this undertaking has been a common inquiry: what are we, as a people—and what have we wrought in some 300 years on the Southern prairie-plains? The scope of the work by regional historians is revealed by the titles of their books: *The American Cowboy, The Myth and the Reality* by Joe Frantz and Julian Choate, *Burs Under the Saddle, A Second Look at Books and Histories of the West* by Ramon F. Adams, *The Texas Republic, A Social and Economic History* by William R. Hogan and *The Southwest, Old and New* by W. Eugene Hollon. In addition there has been a spate of studies on the early Creoles and on such related offshoots as the Quadroon Balls of New Orleans, as well as the mammoth effort, now totaling some 88 volumes, of the University of Oklahoma's Civilization of the American Indian Series.

While Southwestern scholars have won acclaim for their painstaking efforts, the ideas expressed in their books have not always been pleasing to their regional public. Long after the cowboy had been accepted as a romantic figure and the archetype of pure Anglo-Saxon rugged individualism, natives of the region were dismayed to read in the works of even such sympathetic observers as Texan J. Frank Dobie that the cowboy was in many respects a conformist and that his life was hardly romantic, being largely a grim round of unremitting manual labor. Similarly, documented proof of the existence of Negro cowboys and Negro trail bosses has drawn at best uninterested responses from Southern traditionalists. The myth-dissecting cuts many ways: Negroes cannot really rejoice in their belated admission to the ranks of the cowboys and to the history of the old West—not when some of the same scholars have observed that the trade of cowboying was the janitor's job of the frontier, with long hours, low pay, and grueling and dirty tasks. The latter judgment, of course, undermines the entire legend of the mounted herdsman in the white hat, whatever his skin color might be.

Nor has the cowboy been singled out. Indeed, the cumulative effect of modern scholarship has rather thoroughly demolished the entire romantic portrait of triumphant frontiersmen casually winning their fortune in the trans-Mississippi West. In the letters and diaries that formed the source

A small town in Texas

This page contains excerpts from the opening pages of William Humphrey's 1965 novel, *The Ordways*. Humphrey, born in Texas in 1924, is an outstanding member of a group of powerful writers who have emerged in the South Central States in recent years. These younger writers are not "regional" writers in the old-fashioned sense. They often set their novels and stories in their native areas, but their true concern is with the nature of man everywhere.

Clarksville is in Texas—but only barely. Take a map and place the index finger of your right hand on Clarksville, your middle finger will rest in Oklahoma, your ring finger in Arkansas, and your little finger in Louisiana. It lies fifteen miles south of the Red River, on the road from the ferry which transported the first colonists to Texas. Standing on the edge of the blackland prairie, it was the first clearing they came to out of the canebrakes and the towering pines which choke the broad river bottom. Southerners, those first settlers were, and in the towns of northeast Texas, such as Clarksville, the South draws up to a stop. Mountain men, woodsmen, swampers, hill farmers, they came out into the light, stood blinking at the flat and featureless immensity spread before them, where there were no logs to build cabins or churches, no rails for fences, none of the game whose ways they knew, and cowered back into the familiar shade of the forest, from there to farm the margins of the prairie like a timid bather testing the water with his toe. The Texas of cattle herds and cowboys, of flat little sun-swept towns with low sheet-iron buildings strung out along a single main street, the Texas of the West, lies farther on, in time as well as space. The shady streets of Clarksville radiate from a spacious square, from the plaza in the center of which, bedded in wild roses, rises a tall marble shaft surmounted by a Confederate foot soldier carrying a bedroll on his back and a canteen at his side, resting his musket, and shading his eyes to gaze over the rooftops towards the southwest, in which direction the view is almost limitless.

The first colonists, and some later immigrants like my own great-grandfather, who drew back appalled from those vast and lonely prairies, went no farther, but settled in the town and in the farm hamlets which cling like children to its skirts. They felled timber and planted cotton and some brought in slaves while others did their own picking, and before long they were calling their town the long-staple-cotton capital of the world. Two blocks north of the public square they laid out another, and raised, of imported yellow stone, a courthouse eight stories high which to travelers on the oceanic prairie looked like a lighthouse. . . .

Thirty years ago, when I was a boy there, Clarksville was already an old, old town. In fact, thirty years ago, before the discovery of oil nearby, Clarksville was an older town than it is today. Shoals of autos thronging the streets now fill with bleat and roar the square where then the rumble of iron-bound wheels on bois d'arc paving bricks was heard and the snapping and crackling of a wagon bed carried like rifle shots. . . .

Then too an old custom, an annual rite, was still observed. The less well-to-do of Clarksville—which included the Ordways—were at most one generation removed from the farm, and all had country kin; and once a year, in late October, after crops had been gathered and after the first frosts had brought hog-killing time with presents from the farm of fresh pork sausage and sorghum syrup, after the west winds sweeping in off the prairie filled with the rustle of dry cornstalks and the rattle of empty cotton bolls had stripped the trees and dumped a blizzard of yellow leaves upon the streets before blowing themselves out, there came a Saturday when we got up early . . . put on old clothes, packed a lunch basket, and drove out of town to our ancestral homes for graveyard working day. . . .

For most . . . graveyard working day, though tinged with melancholy, was not so mournful an occasion as the name might suggest. The greater number found themselves reunited without recent loss. Old friends met, and though their conversations were weighted with sighs, though their eyes grew misty as they recounted the year's toll among their common acquaintance, though they said they too must soon follow after and doubted that they would meet again until they met in heaven, they were glad to be there and pleased to see one another. Younger gravetenders were not noticeably oppressed by the thought that others would someday do the same office for them. Many a mating in the community, later solemnized in the church, had had its beginning as boy and girl pulled weeds side by side on graveyard working day, and among the grove of trees behind the schoolhouse was one tall beech in the bark of which, high above my head, was carved a pair of hearts joined by an arrow and monogrammed with my father's initials and those of my mother's maiden name. . . .

material for these books, the same phrases recur again and again: "The times are hard. . . . We're not going to make a good crop. . . ." "The country is rough. . . ." "We can't find a good market. . . . Cotton [or cattle] prices are disappointing. . . ." There were too many floods or rustlers and not enough rain or railroads. After the railroads came, there were high freight rates to protest or high land prices charged by the agents of trunk lines. The complaints were endless and not without justification: the settlement of the West was a desperately tedious process in which the frontiersman's primary capital asset was his—and his wife's—capacity for hard work.

But no matter how severe the droughts or destructive the floods, the hard times were presumed to be temporary. Plans were eternally being made for "next year," which "had to be better" when "the railroad comes" or "prices go back up." This optimism was a sustaining force, the frontiersman's chief article of faith. And this faith, continuing today, sets the man of the South Central States apart from his neighbors in the Deep South.

There is one aspect of this regional optimism, however, that has produced less happy results. A robust but often naïve affirmation has coursed through the literature of the frontier South, giving rise to the improbable stories of the cattle trail and to comparable legends dealing with hundreds of other aspects of daily life—from the old Creole days in New Orleans to the lost treasures "buried right here in the county somewhere." The treasure stories themselves have taken on the romantic incrustations of other days: in different parts of the region, the source of mislaid riches has variously been ascribed to Spanish galleons, hard-pressed highwaymen, Lafitte's pirates or Confederate paymasters. A recurring theme of such literature has, of course, been its thunderously one-sided presentation of the Indians of the Southern plains. One has only to peruse half a dozen of the interminable "country histories" that have rolled off the presses of regional publishers to see how curiously uniform is the manner in which the red man is described. The history of Indian-white relations is, quite simply, reduced to a history of Indian "depredations." Indeed, the breathtaking provincialism of such accounts stands in notable contrast to the scrupulously honest and scholarly renderings by the region's best historians.

In sum, the picture painted by modern Southwestern scholars is clearly more searching and honest and simultaneously much richer in content than the one-dimensional caricatures of jocose cowhands on the Chisholm Trail or effete Frenchmen determinedly preserving gentility in the Louisiana wilderness. More than this, these new and more thorough interpretations are addressing a problem that the British historian D. W. Brogan once characterized in the following fashion: "The country that has a 'history,' dramatic, moving, tragic, has to live with it—with the problems it raised but did not solve, with the emotions that it leaves as a damaging legacy, with the defective vision that preoccupation with the heroic, . . . disastrous, . . . expensive past fosters." For a people to adopt such an expansive viewpoint as their own, a wide angle of vision is manifestly essential. And it is in this sense that outsiders may perhaps join with the residents of the South Central States in being optimistic about the latter's future. Modern myth-debunking Southwestern scholarship is but a reflection of the growing maturity of the people themselves. Particularly among the younger generation, there is an increasing lack of interest in the old legends of provincial glory. This may be partly traceable to the work of historians who have shown how insubstantial many of these legends appear to be, but it is also a measure of how irrelevant such nostalgia is to the questions young people are asking themselves. And these questions, quite simply, have to do with the problems of purpose and identity that beset 20th Century man wherever he lives.

This leads one to the emerging novelists of the South Central region. They write not as Southerners, nor as Westerners, nor even as Louisianans or Texans, but simply as civilized and anxious men in an age when all the old beliefs are being questioned. As such, they may offer as informative a guide as any to the condition of the "mind of the Southwest."

The afore-mentioned Walker Percy is not untypical. Descendant of a distinguished Mississippi delta family, Percy won the National Book Award for fiction in 1962 with his novel *The Moviegoer*, an urbane and sensitive account of man at bay in a sprawling modern metropolis. The city is New Orleans, which Percy knows intimately and describes deftly, but the book's value does not come from any specialized Southern connotations. The locale could be any city, for the traumas that skewer Percy's characters are those that imperil man, not merely Southern man.

Similarly, a novel by Texan William Owens describing growing up on a prairie farm (and characteristically entitled *This Stubborn Soil*) was applauded by one Texas reviewer for having "none of the suicidal longing for the lost village which seems to infect the writing of so many first generation urbanites." In short, the book was liked specifically because (despite its rural subject matter) it was *not* provincial, a circumstance that seems to link author, reviewer and public with an outlook decidedly different from that which has prevailed in the recent Southwestern past. Nor is this example an exceptional one. Authors Percy and Owens, and such other writers native to the region as Katherine Ann Porter, Shirley Ann Grau, Larry McMurtry and William Humphrey share at least one common point of view: while they all have a deep sense of Southern history, they have employed that tradition as an instrument of revolt against the region's romanticized legacies.

A handful of writers cannot be taken as typical examples of the current attitudes of 20 million people, nor are they so offered here. But insofar as these writers point to the future, to the directions in which the Southern frontier's culture as a whole is moving, they do seem relevant. In the region of the gulf prairie-plains, as elsewhere, writers have often been harbingers of the future. As far back as the 1870s, George Washington Cable's effort to set down the flavor of early New Orleans in his *Old Creole Days* outraged the city's first families, who found the uncouth French patois of Cable's characters at variance with their own recollections of pre-Civil War gentility. Cable languished in local disrepute until 1915 when the shrinking island of Creole survivors discovered that the most enduring portrait of their era was in Cable's writings. Then they honored him with a great reception at which he read from his own works.

Today, the time gap between an author's statement and public acceptance or understanding seems somewhat reduced. Negro Oklahoman Ralph Ellison's angry, prize-winning book of the 1950s, *Invisible Man*, included a shocking scene evoking the racist attitudes of whites in the narrator's boyhood hometown. Yet in the 1960s Ellison was invited back to the Sooner State to receive an engraved state medal as one of Oklahoma's most "distinguished" sons.

Viewing the question of race relations from the opposite side of the spectrum, Shirley Ann Grau, in her collection of short stories, *Black Prince*, performed the daring literary feat—for a Southern white writer—of "getting inside the mind" of her Negro protagonists. In a number of the stories in the collection the author views daily life in a segregated society from the agonizing emotional perspective of its Negro victims. That Miss Grau, who was born and brought up in New Orleans, could

accomplish this feat as brilliantly as she did reveals perhaps as much about the diminishing barriers— at least some of the psychological ones between the races as it does about her own remarkable talent.

The mind of the Southern frontier? In feeling for ground that is neither "Southern" nor "Western" but simply human, the novelists of the region seem to be clearly in advance of those politicians who seek a non-Southern identity by calling themselves Westerners. Yet, while novelists may be accurate recorders of private sensibility, politicians in democratic societies are often better barometers of the immediate possibilities of public policy. The cautious stance of office seekers is certain proof that, in their opinion, the mind of the Southwest has not yet been completely made up.

Still, the various portents, from businessmen and politicians, novelists and scholars, young people and average citizens, do point to a pattern of transition. Inexorably, the South Central region is loosening its ties to its provincial origins and, like much of the rest of America, is moving toward a more cosmopolitan view of itself and the world around it. The pace of this movement is unsteady and, in fact, varies widely within the region. But its presence is unmistakable. One has to look no further than the University of Texas. There the classics department has become famous both for its scholarship and for its lively approach to the teaching of its seemingly austere subject. Its 25 professors teaching or doing research full time make it the largest such department in the nation, and in one year an astonishing 1,600 students enrolled for one or more of its courses. All of this conjures up a picture of the sons of ranchers or of rough-and-ready oilmen studying Homer or Aeschylus or Tacitus or Virgil in the original languages—and, what is more, enjoying it. Such a picture is perhaps as revealingly symbolic of change as any single example that might be cited about the entire South Central region.

A bare 75 years have passed since the Sooners flooded into the unoccupied plains of Oklahoma, and little more than that since the frontier itself was made secure. The transition has been swift— too swift to provide settled certainties for a people now increasingly bunched together in jerry-built cities. As they wrestle with the tensions of the moment, they are still trying to figure out what they have done in the past and what it all means. But, in the process, it seems clear that they have already established another "New South." Amid the contradictions, there is evidence that this one, unlike so many others, may be here to stay.

Judge Roy Hofheinz, multimillionaire owner of the Houston Astros baseball team, sits in one of the antique chairs he chose for the ornate board room of Houston's Astrodome. Hofheinz has made his fortune in a variety of enterprises.

Spending money the Texas way

In Texas everything seems to be bigger, and personal fortunes are no exception: a Texas millionaire is likely to have even more millions than his counterparts elsewhere. Although some of these vast fortunes were made during the 19th Century from cotton or cattle, most Texas money has been made in this century, and almost all of it has come from oil. But while most rich Texans owe their fortunes to a common source, they spend their money in a wide variety of ways. Some endow entire museums or give large sums to hospitals or universities. Others take pride in assembling impressive personal collections of art or rare objects. For a large number of wealthy Texans, however, the greatest pleasure in having money is found in spending it on themselves; some sports lovers *(above)* can even root for what are almost literally their own home teams.

Large endowments
for the public good

In 1924 the Houston Museum of Fine Arts, the first such institution in Texas, opened its doors. The museum came into being largely through the efforts —and substantial donations—of millionaire lawyer Will Hogg, whose father, ex-Governor Jim Hogg, had founded the family's fortune in Texas' first big oil fields. During the 30 years that followed, such donations were the exception. But in the 1950s the endowment of public institutions began in earnest, and it has continued at an ever-increasing tempo.

San Antonio, for example, which had no art museum, did not begin by constructing one; it was handed one outright by millionaire Marion Koogler McNay, complete with pictures, a building and a large endowment to maintain both. Not all donations have been as munificent, but most have been impressive. Texas now has fine symphony orchestras, several new hospital wings, some with hundreds of beds, and a number of expanded university campuses. Many of these owe their existence primarily to huge benefactions from rich Texans.

Miss Nina Cullinan, an oil-fortune heiress, braves the rain to survey a gracefully arched work by the contemporary American sculptor Alexander Calder. Behind her is a wing of the Houston Museum of Fine Arts, toward which she contributed more than $430,000.

Michel T. Halbouty, an independent operator who has developed some 50 oil and gas fields, visits the nursery at Houston's St. Luke's Hospital that he provided for premature babies. The fully equipped 35-bed nursery cost Mr. Halbouty $125,000.

Dwarfed by an African-inspired mask, Mrs. John de Menil visits the Houston Museum of Fine Arts, to which she has made many donations. Mrs. de Menil is the daughter of Conrad Schlumberger, who helped found one of the world's largest oil engineering firms.

Miss Ima Hogg, daughter of the late Texas Governor, stands in one of the 19 antique-filled rooms of what was her family's home. Miss Hogg donated both house and collection, which spans three centuries of Americana, to the Houston Museum of Fine Arts.

Collectors of the rare and unusual

In Texas many moneyed men spend parts of their fortunes expanding private collections. A number of these collections are of paintings and sculpture, but some are of other rare objects, such as those shown on these pages. Troy Post, one of the few Texas millionaires whose money was made in a field other than oil (it was insurance), has an almost unrivaled collection of clocks. Everette DeGolyer Jr., while accumulating model locomotives, continues to add to his collection of railroad photographs at the rate of 1,000 a year. And Amon Carter Jr. has for more than 20 years been building a collection of currency that is the envy of other numismatists.

A collector of railroad memorabilia, Everette L. DeGolyer Jr. of Dallas has 200 scale models of locomotives. His 12,000 books and 160,000 photographs dealing mainly with railroads are housed at Southern Methodist University.

Dallas financier Troy V. Post sits amid a sampling of his collection of fine antique clocks. Most were made in the 18th and 19th Centuries but one, the intricately worked castlelike clock from Spain, at right, dates back to 1572.

Proudly displaying his collection of currency from all over the world, Amon Carter Jr. stands in the First National Bank in Fort Worth, in whose vault the coins and bills are kept. Carter inherited the Fort Worth *Star-Telegram* and a considerable fortune from his father.

Comforts and amusements for the rich

While many people have hobbies, the interests that engage wealthy Texans are often on a scale as large as life. Sports lovers may own an entire team; three professional football clubs—the Dallas Cowboys, the Houston Oilers and the Kansas City Chiefs— were founded by Texans at a cost of millions. Some Texas millionaires indulge their taste for distinctive homes, ranging from lavish, supermodern mansions to replicas of historic houses. Still others have a penchant for unusual modes of transportation, from private jet aircraft to specially built yachts.

Clint W. Murchison Jr., who helps manage his family's far-flung business interests—which include oil, real estate and insurance firms—is flanked by Mel Renfro (20) and Bob Hayes (22), two of the stars of the football team he owns, the Dallas Cowboys.

152

Houston millionaire C. H. "Pete" Coffield Jr. perches on the prow of his Mississippi-style side-wheeler, the *Texas Queen*, as he takes friends for an outing on a Texas lake. The 50-foot boat, which was meticulously executed by cabinetmakers, took two years to build.

H. L. (for Haroldson Lafayette) Hunt, whose estimated one-billion-dollar fortune makes him America's richest man, rocks on the front lawn of his Dallas mansion, which is an adaptation of historic Mount Vernon. Hunt's weekly income is said to be one million dollars.

8

Skyscrapers
on the Plains

The one undeniable fact about the South Central States today is growth. Like California, the states of the region are caught up in a convulsive process of tearing down and building anew that is changing the face of the land.

Civic enthusiasts in a place like Houston rarely sound any longer like eager promoters trying to hasten the arrival of a new boom. They are more likely to confess a certain awe about the one they are already in.

Throughout the region, statistics merely underline the obvious fact: the Southern plains are becoming cluttered with cities. These cities are among the fastest growing in the U.S. The nation's leader in population increase is Los Angeles, which recorded 750,000 new residents within its incorporated limits between 1950 and 1964. Of the next five leading cities, however, four are in the South Central region: Houston is second, Dallas third, San Antonio fourth and New Orleans sixth.

This surge in population seems even more pronounced when it is viewed in the context of all the states below the Mason and Dixon Line. Eight of the 15 largest cities in the southern half of the U.S. are in the states of Texas, Oklahoma and Louisiana. They include, in addition to the four mentioned above, the cities of Fort Worth, Oklahoma City, El Paso and Tulsa.

The problems that inevitably accompany such growth are now becoming apparent. Engineers speak of impending water shortages and offer intimidating blueprints for aqueducts hundreds of miles long. School systems are bulging—not merely expanding but doubling in enrollment every 10 to 15 years.

While growth is the rule in cities throughout the region, the story of Houston is something special. Since 1950 the population of the city's metropolitan area has grown an incredible 96 per cent, from 936,000 to more than 1.8 million. The city gained more people in the decade of the 1950s than did the entire states of Oklahoma, Wyoming and Utah put together. By the end of the 1970s the Houston area is expected to count some 3.25 million residents.

This phenomenal spurt, like that of New York City 75 years earlier, is traceable to a variety of causes. A basic one is the Houston Ship Channel, which snakes through 50 miles of bayou, river and bay to the Gulf of Mexico. Houston is the nation's

Dressed in traditional garb, a visiting rodeo rider looks out over glittering nighttime Dallas from the observation tower of Southland Center, one of the tallest buildings in the metropolis. Dallas is the insurance and banking capital of the South Central region.

This ornate structure, partly boarded up after a fire in 1913, once housed Dallas' Neiman-Marcus, now one of the world's most famous department stores. Neiman-Marcus has become so successful that it has recorded sales of $58 million for a single year.

Small craft tie up at docks on Buffalo Bayou at the foot of Houston's Main Street in 1910. Four years later the bayou was dredged to accommodate large oceangoing ships, becoming part of the Houston Ship Channel that has helped make the city a great port.

third port (behind New York and New Orleans) in annual tonnage. Much of this tonnage is connected with the petroleum industry, consisting not only of crude oil and its by-products but also of the yield of the subsidiary—and rapidly growing—petrochemical industry.

Chemical producers have been attracted to the "Chemical Crescent" of the Gulf Coast, which runs from Baton Rouge, Louisiana, to Brownsville in Texas. Houston has been especially favored because of its concentration of oil fields, its fortuitous supply of other raw materials—including natural gas and salt—its deepwater port and its refineries. The basic "feedstocks" of the petrochemical industry are oil, natural gas, refinery off-gases and natural-gas liquids. These are used to make ethylene, the undisputed monarch of the petrochemical kingdom; an ethylene pipeline system snakes through the Houston industrial area tying together a vast complex of chemical plants. The plants also produce other basic petrochemicals, including propylene, benzene and acetylene. The eventual consumer products include a variety of plastics and agricultural chemicals—everything from fertilizers to ballpoint pens and the polyethylene bags used by dry cleaners. Esoteric fertilizers composed of anhydrous ammonia and sulfur bases are being produced in

an increasing number of plants that have been drawn to the area by the fact that 75 per cent of America's sulfur is also produced in the "Crescent."

Ordinary salt is the vital ingredient of still other chemical processes that yield inorganic chemicals such as chlorine, soda ash and caustic soda. Even the Gulf of Mexico's sea water is put to industrial use. A cubic mile of this water produces more than 12 billion pounds of magnesium. Texas provides almost all the magnesium used in the United States and about 75 per cent of the Free World's supply.

The most recent boost to the Houston economy, of course, has been the Manned Spacecraft Center, located at Clear Lake, some 20 miles from the heart of the city. Around this project of the National Aeronautics and Space Administration have clustered hundreds of space-centered industries. By 1980 the Clear Lake area is expected to have 260,000 people, at least one of whom will probably have visited the moon.

Yet Houston's growth also rests on a number of less glamorous industries. Perhaps surprisingly, Harris County, which includes Houston, is Texas' second leading county in number of cattle, the port of Houston is the nation's No. 1 wheat exporter, and the Houston region as a whole is the source of nearly one third of the nation's rice.

People pack the streets and sit on porch roofs to get a view of the Mardi Gras parade in the 1890s in New Orleans. Mardi Gras is still celebrated with a parade, but Canal Street, where this picture was taken, has been almost totally revamped in recent years.

Despite this evidence of the continuation of agricultural production, the diversification that has resulted from new industrial ventures is the primary cause of the boom along the upper Texas Gulf Coast. Together, the oil and chemical industries have created raw materials for other, related industries. Some two thirds of the nation's synthetic rubber is produced here, for example.

All of these forms of industrialization have created one more product Houstonians would rather not talk about (except among themselves)—air pollution. Everyone from housewives to politicians and from athletes to businessmen has been drawn into an endless round of complaints, accusations and explanations. But as in so many other American cities, solutions are not yet much beyond the talking stage. The presence of the issue, however, illustrates perhaps more convincingly than industrial statistics ever could just how thoroughly the South Central States' old frontier environment has been altered. Things have proceeded a long way from the time of the "open range" and from the day in 1876 when Houston's free public schools opened with teachers who were paid at the rate of 10 cents per day per pupil.

The South Central region contains two other metropolitan areas of more than one million people

—Dallas (1,332,000 in 1965) and New Orleans (1,018,000). New Orleans, like Houston, owes its prominence to the advantages of its natural location. Its site near the mouth of the Mississippi River made it the most famous riverboat town of 19th Century America and developed the city as the great commercial trading center it has continued to be in the 20th Century.

But the emergence of the region's second-largest city—Dallas—has been (as its chamber of commerce boosters are notoriously fond of asserting) largely an act of will. Dallas cannot point to any "natural" origins comparable to Fort Worth's development as a military post or New Orleans' as a port. In fact, there is neither a natural nor a geographical reason for the existence of a city in the Dallas area. The city is in the center of the north Texas prairie country, its only distinguishing physical feature being the nearby Trinity River, which is hardly more than a good-sized creek by Eastern standards. The city, quite simply, is a product of the imagination and ingenuity of its local boosters, and this has been so since some of its early citizens managed to get two railroads to lay their tracks through town. In 1872 they paid the Houston and Texas Central, running north from Houston, to make a jog in their line and serve Dallas. The next year they

157

managed to get the state legislature to require the Texas and Pacific Railway, then being built, to put its main line through the city.

These twin feats, however, were hardly decisive—hundreds of similar towns grew alongside rail trackage on the plains. But Dallas seemed to nourish a special breed of adventurous traders and, later, oil promoters. The city really cashed in on the East Texas oil boom of the 1930s, the giant field creating hundreds of Dallas millionaires and undergirding the rise of a number of large banks that financed further oil explorations. The additional capital thus generated was available for developing the electronics and insurance industries that have made the city one of the national leaders in both fields. Despite the lack of a seaport, oil refineries or space facilities, the city's growth since World War II (its population more than doubled in the 20 years between 1945 and 1965) was only a shade less spectacular than that of Houston. Dallas is probably the nation's most staunchly conservative large city and probably its most thoroughly "white-collar" town as well. Few visitors are neutral about such a highly defined and well-organized city—people tend to like Dallas very much or to recoil from it in shock.

Urban sprawl in the South Central States is by no means restricted to the three cities of Houston, New Orleans and Dallas. Metropolitan San Antonio boasts more than 840,000 people (the former cow town has long since become a military center ringed with air bases), and Fort Worth has almost 680,000. The Oklahoma City metropolitan area can count some 635,000 residents and Tulsa more than 500,000. Arkansas' largest city is its state capital, Little Rock, with a metropolitan population of about 340,000.

All of which underscores the fact that the problem of "life in the city" has come to the Southern plains, as it has to most of the older regions of America. In a somewhat dazed effort to keep up with expanding school populations, Texas now supports almost two dozen state-financed colleges and universities, while junior colleges sprout to the dismay of state and local budget balancers. A similar rise in expectations—and expenses—is visible in Oklahoma and Louisiana and may assert itself in Arkansas.

Another consequence of urbanization—the expansion of big-city ghettos—is taking place with frightening speed, particularly in Houston, Dallas, San Antonio and New Orleans. Greater Houston will soon count almost as many resident Negroes—some 350,000—as its total population numbered a mere generation ago. And more than 300,000 Mexican-Americans live in San Antonio, most of them on the city's teeming West Side. Growing problems of jobs, housing and welfare thus must be added to the imposing tasks in the field of public and private education.

All of these imperatives press in on a people who but yesterday took special pride in their provincial institutions. The comfortable notion that the old, leisurely ways of doing things were best and would suffice is rapidly being eroded; now, from time to time, there is a whiff of crisis in the air.

Most fundamental of the problems facing the four states is the impasse in state government. Today, the organic laws of the South Central States are promulgated under procedures dictated by state constitutions that hark back to a now-departed agrarian era. Oklahoma's constitution dates from its year of statehood in 1907, and those of Texas and Arkansas date from the end of the Reconstruction era in the 1870s. Although Louisiana has rewritten its constitution several times, it remains out of date. The peculiarly constricting legacies of the post-Reconstruction period still hamstring Louisiana's state government in ways not dissimilar to those at work in Texas and Arkansas.

These outmoded documents are all understandable accidents of history, but their effects have been no less damaging in respect to the modern needs of the South Central region. The simple fact is that the decade of the 1870s in the American South was an emotionally violent and politically unfortunate period for anyone trying to fashion the basic documents of state government. The people of the South and of the Southern frontier had cordially loathed the post-Civil War regimes set up by the so-called carpetbaggers. These regimes, backed up by the bayonets of occupying Union forces, gave the former slaves full exercise of the franchise. Further, many of the Reconstruction governments were free-spending and corrupt and they left Southern state treasuries looted. They were not all bad—modern scholarship has called attention to the idealism that was implicit in their formation—but the fact remains that they were hated and feared by whites, especially because they had given the Negro the vote. As a result, the whole idea of powerful central state governments became suspect.

As a consequence, when federal troops were withdrawn and Reconstruction collapsed in the 1870s, state after state in the South wrote new constitutions designed to guarantee that their legislatures would never again "get out of hand." For example, in the new Texas state constitution of 1876—still the state's basic legal document—more than half of the 58 sections in the article dealing with the legislature placed limitations on its authority. One contemporary critic of the constitution likened the result to a horse that had been too tightly cinched. "The harness is so small, the straps drawn so tight, the check rein pulled up to the last buckle hole, and the load to draw so heavy, that the legislative horse will be galled from collar to crupper in the attempt to work, and the State wagon will go creaking along the highway of progress, in the rear of the procession."

These "Redemption" constitutions (the term derives from the feeling that Southern whites were "redeeming" their governments) were based, in the view of Southern writer George Washington Cable, on the concept of "pure government first, free government afterward." He called the Redemption philosophy a "twin fallacy" that could not produce "either free or pure government." In the decades that followed, what the people in the Southern half of the U.S. usually got from their immobilized legislatures was very little government at all.

Today, the millions of people in the South Central region's cities are struggling to find answers to the steadily escalating demands for metropolitan housing, education, transportation, public welfare and hospital services. But governments whose structures largely date back to the agrarian era simply are not geared to produce rational solutions to 20th Century needs. The old restrictions, always vexing, have now reached ridiculous proportions. Often, to enable themselves to pass a law, the legislators must first propose an amendment to the state constitution giving them the right to pass it. As one former aide to a Texas governor said in disgust, "In this state you have to pass a constitutional amendment to go to the bathroom."

In addition to these basic structural defects, state governments find themselves further hamstrung by a web of old rivalries that make cooperation and progress that much more difficult. The long history of passionate political battles between agrarians and urban businessmen has produced a bewildering assortment of political alignments and animosities in all four states.

Further complicating matters is the fact that new political forces are developing in the cities, building, as it were, on the unstable foundations of past grievances. Increasingly, political contests in the cities are being waged between liberal Democrats and conservative Republicans—both growing in strength at the expense of the old "states' rights" type of Democratic politician who has long presided over the rigid one-party political orthodoxy that the nation recognizes as a purely Southern phenomenon.

The confusing result is that the South Central region is moving from one-party to two-party politics by a circuitous route that, for the time being at least, will involve three parties—liberal Democrats, conservative Democrats and Republicans. The process may take years, but that it will eventually happen seems certain.

Though both Democrats and Republicans from the cities agree that the old, rural-oriented governmental institutions must go, a consensus on how to effect their departure has, until now at least, been unobtainable. The ancient constitutions—aimed at weakening the state government and decentralizing authority—gave much power to local courthouse cliques, and these old-style traditionalists are reluctant to yield any of their prerogatives to the growing cities. To do so would have the political effect of helping liberal Democrats and the new Republican Party, both of which would measure their gains out of the hide of the old states' rights orthodoxy. So the country boys stand pat in a way that continues to keep state government substantially immobilized.

The consequences of this conflict of forces are weird and often pathetic. In Louisiana, Governor John McKeithen's effort in 1966 to achieve long-overdue tax equalization threatened to upset a number of special arrangements, especially the ward-heeling power of the local assessors. Result: though McKeithen's goal was supported by business and taxpayer groups, the legislature, under pressure from the local assessors, backed off. Abandoned by almost every important political faction in the state, McKeithen withdrew his plan with the announcement: "I don't mind being hurt, but I'm not going to be destroyed."

Elsewhere, governors find themselves in the Mc-Keithen-like position of endeavoring to hold their friends while trying to win over their enemies. Tax legislation is the most certain cause of general non-agreement. The matter is made yet more acute, especially in Texas, Louisiana and Oklahoma, by the partisan concerns of out-of-state economic interests, including oil and natural-gas companies. These companies, eager to avoid higher taxes, exert powerful pressure to hold the line on spending for educational needs and other costly programs. This circumstance once moved a former Texas legislator, later a U.S. Congressman, to conclude that his state "will never get a civilized government responding to the people's legitimate governmental needs until all our natural resources are depleted and out-of-state oil lobbyists lose interest in us."

But though taxes continue as a focus of disagreement, even somewhat less controversial measures affecting such things as the consolidation of educational districts or cooperative water development frequently run into trouble. After watching an education bill undergo a whimsical remodeling by old-line politicos in an obscure but powerful committee, a Texas legislator concluded ironically: "There are two things folks should never be forced to witness —sausage being made and legislation being enacted." An observer of the Arkansas political scene similarly concluded: "Our system gives far too much power to local courthouse cronies and backwoods legislative types with hay in their hair. They are congenitally unresponsive to last year's problems, much less those coming up in the next decade. The system creates its own red tape and it is choking us all."

Yet, complaints such as these, coming as they do from local officials, are an indication that the old ways are threatened. Beyond this, the sheer pace of growth impels action: cities on the plains need water, and children throughout the region need classrooms. In one important particular, this growth has caused a fundamental and perhaps decisive break with the past by driving the courts to do what state legislatures for decades have been unwilling to accomplish. Court-ordered redistricting of state legislatures has tended to shift governmental responsibility from rural into urban hands—most dramatically in Texas, where the counties containing the four cities of Houston, Dallas, San Antonio and Fort Worth, which formerly had 35 representatives out of 150 and four state senators out of 31, in the mid-1960s had 51 representatives and 14 senators. Since these "city boys"—whether Democratic or Republican—tend to be more responsive to the needs of their urban constituencies, possibilities for creative change seem to be opening, despite the continuing ideological disagreements. The political aimlessness inherited from the past appears to be disappearing, though the underlying constitutional impasse remains.

Perhaps the most hopeful sign for the South Central region lies in an elusive kind of development that cannot be explained in political terms, or by statistics of population growth and economic progress, but rather comes out of the people themselves.

The people of the Southern frontier have had an enormously rich history. It has been fraught with violence and division, burdened by false romances and self-serving myths, and rent with provincial passion and a love-fear relationship with the land itself. The physical environment has been hostile and the history of interclan warfare almost always distracting. But, in contrast to the situation in some not dissimilar regions—the Balkans of Europe and the Old South of the United States—the burdens of history have not proved to be wholly insupportable. Various racial and governmental traumas remain, but the people's self-respect does not seem to be bound up in hanging on to them to the bitter end. By historian C. Vann Woodward's definition, they are "New South" people in the sense that the phrase sets apart "those whose faith lay in the future from those whose heart was with the past." In a way that differentiates them from their neighbors in the lower South, the people of Texas and Oklahoma, and also of Arkansas and Louisiana, look forward with hope, not backward in anger. The past is being sorted out by their own regional historians and its meaning being pondered by their own native writers. The people are coming to terms with this past, though the process is enormously painful for many. This evolution is perhaps more rapid than the nation perceives, though it is undoubtedly slower than many of its past and present victims deserve to expect.

Tension remains. As it has been for 300 years, much of it is racial. The land has felt the successive tread of Indians, Spaniards, Frenchmen, Southern Americans, Germans, Mexicans, Negroes, Italians, Irishmen—and Anglo-American plainsmen. All are still present, some in larger numbers than others, but none in a minority that could be called inconsequential. All know, dimly or with certainty, that none will find serenity in their homeland until they all can.

Today, by the thousands, a new generation is emerging from universities in Baton Rouge and Oklahoma City, Austin and New Orleans, Fayetteville and Houston. They bring a new style, rooted in attitudes undeniably different from those fashioned in the old days on the home place in the Louisiana bayous or in the Arkansas uplands. Undeniably, too, they carry part of the frontier— their many and varied frontiers—with them, as a tradition, but no longer as a rigid or exclusive way of life. Whatever their ethnic origins, the frontiers of their fathers and grandfathers have been dissolved by the onrush of American civilization. The new generation doubtless feels small need to be transfixed by nostalgia at the eclipse of the old by the new. Nor should they—for the idea of the Southern frontier has always contained an authentic admixture of old and new alike.

New one-family homes sprawl over hundreds of acres on the plain southeast of downtown Houston, whose skyscrapers loom in the distance. The nation's fastest-growing city except for Los Angeles, Houston built 122,619 housing units between 1960 and 1966.

A city growing in all directions

Houston, the largest city in Texas, is growing and spreading with breakneck speed. Still basically an oil town, it has spawned a multitudinous progeny of petrochemical enterprises; these, too, are based on the petroleum industry. The city's deepwater port handles about 4,000 cargo ships a year. Besides carrying Houston's industrial products to the world, these vessels transport the rich produce that flows into the city from its bountiful hinterlands. Recently the burgeoning city received another boost when the National Aeronautics and Space Administration built its Manned Spacecraft Center on Houston's outskirts. The wealth flowing from these many enterprises has produced an ebullience that finds expression in superb facilities for the arts, and, perhaps most characteristically, in the Astrodome, the largest covered sports arena in the world.

The impressive homes of powerful corporations

Central Houston's almost solid cluster of skyscrapers house some of the region's—and the nation's—most powerful business concerns. Most important are the oil companies that dominate the city's economic life; some of their offices have a distant view of a few of the derricks and wells from which their

HUMBLE OIL CO., largest U.S. producer of petroleum products, occupies the 44-story Humble Building. On the top floor is the Petroleum Club, where oilmen gather.

TENNECO INC., the largest gas transmission company in the world, occupies 70 per cent of its Tennessee Building. Other tenants include Anderson, Clayton & Company, a huge food and cotton merchandiser.

SCHLUMBERGER LIMITED does 85 per cent of the world's oil surveying. It occupies the Southwest Tower building *(behind scaffolding)*. Other tenants are Pennzoil and the Zapata Off-Shore Company.

profits flow. In Houston's tall buildings, too, are found the headquarters of the big independent oil operators. Oil industry satellites, such as manufacturers of surveying and drilling equipment and of a variety of heavy machinery, naturally gravitate to the city. Houston is also the nation's natural-gas center and the No. 1 producer of sulfur, so companies processing these products as well as petrochemical outfits also maintain offices in the city. Reflecting the widespread prosperity, the Houston skyline changes constantly as more and more skyscrapers rise dramatically out of the Texas plain.

GULF OIL runs its U.S. producing operations from the Gulf Building. Two of Houston's most successful independent oilmen, R. E. Smith and J. S. Abercrombie, also work here.

SHELL OIL has its exploration and production headquarters in this 22-story building. Shell is erecting a 50-story skyscraper behind the Tennessee Building, to be the tallest building west of the Mississippi.

TEXAS GULF SULPHUR, which produces one third of the U.S. supply of sulfur, has offices in the Houston Club Building along with the J. Ray McDermott Company, giant producer of offshore oil-well equipment.

FIRST CITY NATIONAL BANK, Houston's largest financial house, shares its building with Mitsubishi, a major Japanese export firm that sells heavy machinery to Houston industry.

TEXACO INC. maintains in this building the headquarters for all of its production operations in the Eastern U.S., all its U.S. refining operations and all its pipeline activities in the Western Hemisphere.

Wealthy Houston: lavish patron of the arts

Houston offers cultural activities as splendid as its businesses are powerful. As an outgrowth of its citizens' great wealth and lively philanthropic instincts, the city now has excellent museums, a symphony orchestra acclaimed as the Southwest's finest and a resplendent new center for the performing arts. So culture-conscious are Houstonians that one of the city's best hotels is virtually an art gallery.

A doorman in top hat and white gloves stands next to a statue from a Viennese palace that graces the entrance to the posh Warwick Club, in Houston's Warwick Hotel. The hotel's owner, oil tycoon John Mecom, has filled its rooms with rare European antiques.

A glittering concert hall, the Jesse H. Jones Hall for the Performing Arts opens in 1966 with a gala performance by the Houston Symphony Orchestra. The auditorium was a gift from a foundation established by Jones, Houston's leading citizen in the 1940s.

A maze of industries
lining the busy port

At the heart of Houston's commercial success is its Ship Channel, which connects the city with the Gulf of Mexico and the seas beyond. Opened in 1915 as a waterway wide and deep enough for large oceangoing vessels, it has enabled Houston to become the third-ranking U.S. port (after New York and New Orleans). The port of Houston can berth more than 100 ships at a time and handles so much freight from foreign countries that consulates have been established in the city by 38 nations. The Ship Channel's banks have become an enormous complex of industrial plants. Oil refineries have been joined by scores of petrochemical plants (which are interconnected by a 1,000-mile-long maze of pipelines) and by numerous other mills.

Tugs help a seagoing freighter to change directions in the Turning Basin, a narrow pool at the upper end of Houston's Ship Channel. Almost all the facilities offered by the man-made port are modern, mechanized and highly efficient.

The impressive bulk of the Signal Oil and Gas Company refinery takes on a somber beauty as it is mirrored in the waters of the Ship Channel at dusk. This plant alone, one of many in Houston, can process 70,000 barrels of crude oil a day.

The growing problems
of a modern boomtown

Between 1940 and 1965 Houston increased in area by 300 per cent, expanding with explosive speed into the surrounding open lands. This dramatic growth has brought the former frontier town some of the nagging problems that harass other big cities, such as smog, urban sprawl and the costly task of improvising a highway system able to handle an ever-increasing number of cars. Some 95 per cent of the residents of greater Houston must use automobiles to get around since the city has only a vestigial transit system; downtown, even prime pieces of real estate are set aside for freeways and parking lots. Smog is also a creeping threat. Worst of all, perhaps, is the invasion of once-green areas by industry and by the worst sort of roadside vulgarity.

A thicket of signs inviting the motorist to buy everything from shrimp-in-a-basket to motor oil lines a road near the Houston Astrodome. Lack of zoning laws has helped such garishness to flourish all over the city, even in residential communities.

Four major highways come together in a maze that Houstonians call the "Spaghetti Bowl." Houston's intricate highway system reflects the fact that there is one registered automobile for every 2.4 residents, women and children included.

Nerve center for
U.S. efforts in space

The Manned Spacecraft Center, 20 miles southeast of Houston, is the central U.S. control point for all flights aimed at a landing on the moon. The Houston area was picked by the National Aeronautics and Space Administration as a site for the center because it offered both land and modern service facilities. The center, with its office buildings and sophisticated laboratories, has pumped large sums of money into Houston's already booming economy through its payroll and construction expenditures. Around the center have grown up a new industrial complex and many residential communities built to accommodate the center's thousands of employees.

A playground featuring toy spaceships and simulated radar-tracking stations enchants children in one of the new developments near the spacecraft center. Shopping centers and a hospital have also been built for the growing suburban area.

The lights of the center go on as dusk creeps across the Texas prairie near Houston. The astronauts have their offices in the square three-story building in the center foreground. The Mission Control Center is in the large building in the rear, just right of center.

"The eighth wonder of the world"

The only completely enclosed sports arena ever built that is large enough to permit baseball and football games is the breathtaking Astrodome, proclaimed by its chief promoter, Houston's Judge Roy Hofheinz, "the eighth wonder of the world." The stadium seats a maximum of 66,000, more than many open major-league baseball parks, and has five restaurants, including the huge Domeskeller, which can accommodate some 2,000 guests. The dome itself is made of 4,596 plastic panels that let in some sunlight although they have had to be coated with gray paint to reduce the glare in baseball players' eyes. Since grass refused to grow on the enclosed field, it is now sodded with plastic "Astroturf." The arena's total cost was $38 million.

The mammoth Astrodome plays host to the Houston Livestock Show and Rodeo, an important annual event in the life of the city. The Astrodome's managers schedule many such special events —ranging from evangelist Billy Graham's "Crusade" to heavyweight title fights—in addition to University of Houston football games and the Houston Astros' regular baseball schedule.

Suggested tours

On the following pages nine maps show sections of the South Central States that are of particular interest to the tourist. No attempt has been made to show every road and town. Instead, scenic routes, parks, historic sites and other special features are emphasized. The text accompanying each map gives a description of the area. Opening dates and hours, especially for tours of business enterprises, should be confirmed locally, since they may vary with the season of the year. The nine areas covered are numbered on the small map below to correspond with the descriptive text.

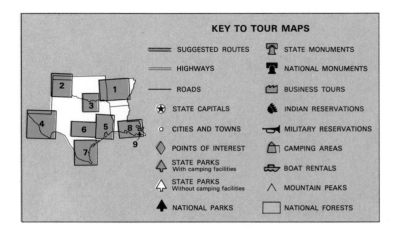

1. The mountain country

The section of Arkansas and eastern Oklahoma shown below contains not only Arkansas' capital city, Little Rock, and the important Oklahoma city of Tulsa, but also some of the loveliest and most varied natural scenery in the South Central States. Northwest and west of Little Rock lie two large national forests covering mountainous areas noted for their beauty. Near the foot of the Ouachita National Forest is the most famous of the Arkansas mountains' many old resort towns, Hot Springs. Between the two forests winds the Arkansas River, south of whose wide valley rise some of the highest peaks in the state, including Petit Jean and Mount Nebo. The area also has dozens of lovely lakes, such as Lake Ouachita, that offer choice boating, fishing and swimming.

Eastern Oklahoma offers both beautiful rolling country and a concentration of interesting historical sites, many of them, like the Choctaw Capitol Building and the Creek Indian Museum, having to do with the American Indians. Tulsa is also rich in material on the Indians, especially in its Gilcrease Institute and, in the nearby town of Claremore, the Will Rogers Memorial Park.

The burgeoning city of Little Rock boasts the Arkansas Territorial Capitol Restoration, which re-creates the early days in the life of the state. Forty-five miles northwest of the city by car lies Winrock Farms, Winthrop Rockefeller's model farm, which is open to visitors, as is Rockefeller's meticulously kept museum of antique automobiles.

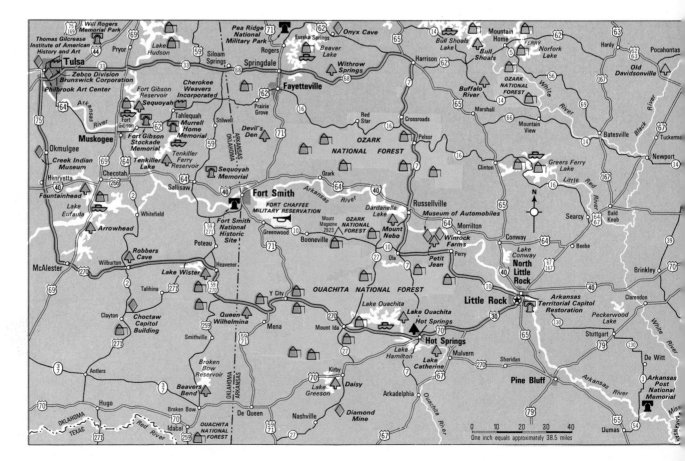

2. The Texas and Oklahoma Panhandles

Once an empty and desolate area where only outlaws and buffalo hunters lived, the panhandle section of northwestern Texas and western Oklahoma today has one large and important city, Amarillo, and a variety of interesting natural and historical sites. Near Amarillo lie the Alibates Flint Quarries, where some of the oldest traces of Stone Age man on the North American continent have been found. Also near Amarillo is a fascinating, if grim, reminder of the area's more recent, but far from peaceful, past—the Boot Hill Cemetery, where weathered red sandstone markers identify the graves of gunslingers who "died with their boots on." The Panhandle-Plains Historical Museum, just south of Amarillo, has exhibits and mementos that tell of these same outlaws as well as of the area's less violent former citizens. The most famous of all livestock auctions takes place in Amarillo three days each week; the city's extensive stockyards may be toured on any weekday, as may its large Texaco refinery.

South of Amarillo is the area's greatest natural wonder, the Palo Duro Canyon, whose brightly colored rock strata, carved by a branch of the Red River, have caused enthusiasts to call it "the world's most colorful canyon." The plains area north of the city is also worthy of a visit, offering the still visible remains of the old Santa Fe Trail, the black-lava-capped plateau called the Black Mesa, the No Man's Land Historical Museum, and The Buried City, the excavated remains of a Pueblo Indian village.

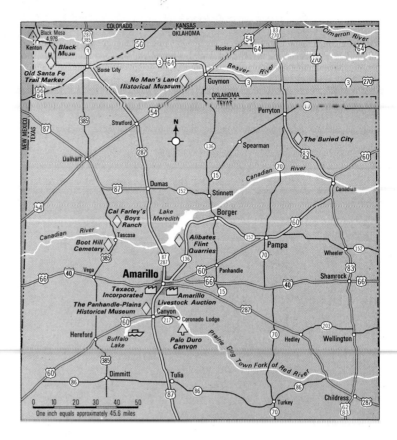

3. Fort Worth, Dallas and points north

If the South Central States have a central core, perhaps it is the area north of Dallas that straddles the Red River, the boundary between southern Oklahoma and north-central Texas. Here flat prairies merge with the highly productive Blackland, which in turn butts up against a green and hilly area farther west. Transitional both economically and socially, this central district has moved from being predominantly rural to urbanization, from a dependency on oil and cotton to industrial diversity.

Cultural activities in the area center around the Dallas-Fort Worth area. The Dallas Theater Center presents a year-round schedule of repertory. The city also has museums of natural history, science and fine arts, an aquarium and a botanical garden. Fort Worth, Dallas' rival for the reputation of being the cultural center of Texas, offers the Amon Carter Museum of Western Art, with an outstanding collection of paintings by Frederic Remington; its own botanical garden; and Casa Mañana, a theater-in-the-round that presents Broadway productions.

To the north of the two cities is a cluster of campgrounds; another is just across the Oklahoma border from the Hagerman National Wildlife Refuge. Eisenhower Birthplace State Park, which includes the house in which the former President was born, is in Denison. Nearby, the Denison Dam on the Red River has created Lake Texoma, with facilities for fishing, swimming, hunting and golf; in the northernmost section of the area Platt National Park draws health seekers from all over to its mineral springs.

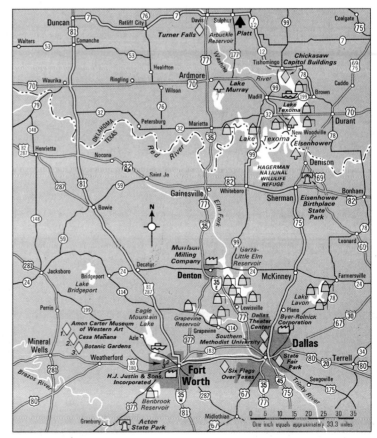

4. The Trans-Pecos

The westernmost part of Texas, out beyond the Pecos River, is a generally barren land that nevertheless, with its jagged brown mountains, dry river beds, stark mesas and vast horizons, has a peculiar grandeur all its own. Entering the area from the northeast, the visitor first comes upon the Monahans Sandhills State Park, almost 4,000 acres of shifting sand dunes in which Indian artifacts and the bones of prehistoric animals may be found. But the most awesome scenery is in the area's southernmost tip, at Big Bend National Park, where the Rio Grande has cut three separate, high-walled canyons. If the water is not too turbulent, hardy visitors can make a rough but beautiful boat trip down this part of the river. Less daring visitors can study the geology and history of the park by stopping in Alpine (on U.S. Route 90) at the Big Bend Historical Museum, north of the park itself.

Not far from Alpine are two forts—Old Fort Stockton and Fort Davis—that once protected Texas from warlike Indians. Proceeding farther westward, past such rugged peaks as Mount Livermore, the traveler will eventually reach El Paso. Just south of the city, which is almost as Mexican in atmosphere as Ciudad Juárez across the Rio Grande, there are several old and fascinating missions, relics of the time when Spain ruled this part of the world. Also in El Paso, the Aerial Tramway takes visitors to the top of the highest of the jagged hills that overlook the city, giving them a superb view of the great West Texas plains.

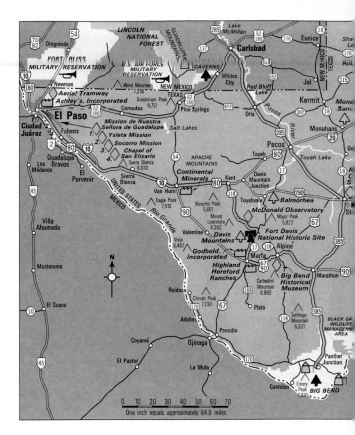

5. East Texas

East Texas is the dampest region of the state: the southeastern part is bayou country, rice is grown in the moist coastlands, and enough rain falls in the inland sections to support pleasant, green farmland. Within the section are four national forests, all with camping facilities.

On the fringe of this fertile land, along the coast of the Gulf of Mexico, is a triangle of industrial cities including Houston, Galveston and Beaumont. Houston is at the western edge of this complex and offers rich cultural facilities, the famous Astrodome sports stadium, and the Manned Spacecraft Center of the National Aeronautics and Space Administration. The area is bounded on the south by Galveston, which boasts miles of beaches and the best seafood restaurants in Texas, and on the east by the commercial centers of Beaumont and Port Arthur.

East of Houston is the San Jacinto Battlefield State Park, where a stone shaft higher than the Washington Monument commemorates a dramatic victory won by the Texans over the Mexican forces in 1836. North of Houston is the Sam Houston Memorial Museum in Huntsville, containing memorabilia of this famous Texan as well as of the early years of the area.

In Baytown, outside of Houston, visitors can observe petroleum refining at the Humble Oil & Refining Company. In Huntsville the Boettcher Lumber company is open for visitors, while farther north, in Palestine, Texize Chemicals, Incorporated, household and industrial cleaning agents manufacturers, offers a tour of its plant.

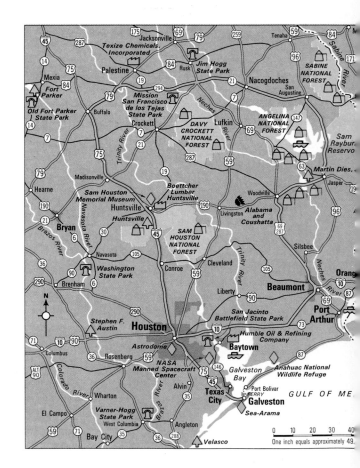

6. Central Texas and the Hill Country

The center of Texas geographically, this section is remarkable for the rich historical associations of San Antonio and for the state capital at Austin. The area's most beautiful scenery is the rolling Hill Country in its center, where towns such as New Braunfels and Fredericksburg still preserve the customs of the Germans who first settled them in the 19th Century.

San Antonio, once the seat of Texas' Spanish governors, is most famous for the Alamo, the historic mission where a small Texas force fought to the death against overwhelming odds during Texas' War for Independence. The atmosphere of San Antonio as it was under Spanish rule and in the early days of the Republic of Texas is preserved in a part of the city called La Villita, a block-square section of restored homes and shops. Just south of San Antonio is a string of four well-preserved 18th Century Spanish missions. Outstanding among them is Mission San José, which is one of the finest examples of Spanish architecture north of Mexico.

San Antonio's Lone Star brewery offers an interesting industrial tour, including a visit to a house the brewery now owns that once belonged to the writer O. Henry.

Driving northwest from San Antonio on Route 87 and turning onto Route 46, the traveler comes to the Frontier Times Museum in Bandera, with its valuable collection of Western paintings as well as thousands of artifacts, such as rawhide lariats, from the Old West.

Halfway between Fredericksburg, still inhabited mainly by descendants of the original German settlers, and Johnson City is the LBJ Ranch, built by Lyndon B. Johnson; driving past, the motorist can make out the ranch house itself through the surrounding trees. There are several interesting sights in the country west of the LBJ Ranch, among them the San Saba Mission and Presidio, a Spanish military stronghold built during the 1750s. The Presidio has been restored and looks much as it did when it was the center for a community of some 400 settlers. Also not far from the LBJ Ranch is the Longhorn Cavern, a cave so large that it is still unexplored in its entirety. Several miles are lit by electric lights, and there is a dining room and museum 75 feet below ground. To the east is Austin, the capital of Texas and the home of the University of Texas. The nation's largest fiber-glass boat manufacturer, the Glastron Boat Company, offers an interesting tour here. South of Austin is another large German community in New Braunfels; a tour of the New Braunfels Smokehouse is available. Bollman Industries, a wool-scouring plant, also offers tours.

There are numerous recreation facilities in this section of Texas, including state parks with camping facilities at Kerrville and elsewhere, golf at Bastrop State Park, and sulfur wells and unusual tropical plants in Palmetto State Park, east of San Antonio. There are fine lakes for boating, such as Buchanan Lake and Inks Lake State Parks.

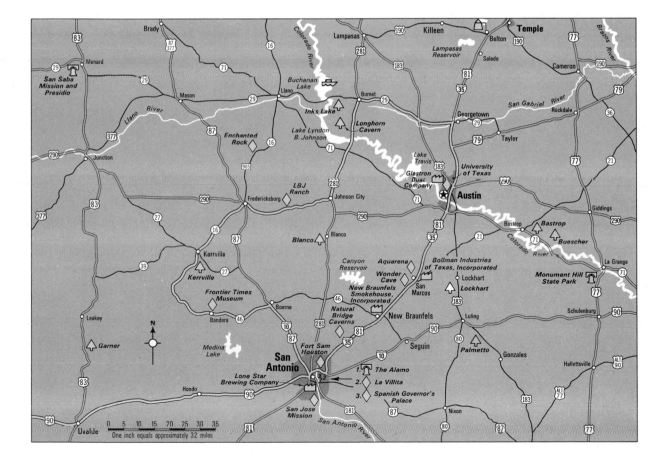

7. South Texas

South Texas (*below*) is a land of extensive beaches, fertile farms and sprawling ranches. It is also notable for its proximity to Mexico: in the town of Laredo, for example, travelers can visit Mexico simply by walking across a bridge over the Rio Grande into Nuevo Laredo. The road running south from Laredo along the Rio Grande Valley into Brownsville, near the Gulf of Mexico, is lined with palms and passes through lush citrus groves and vegetable fields, as well as leading the motorist through two state parks. North of Harlingen the Alberti Sea Foods Processing Corporation offers a tour of a shrimp-processing plant.

Across from Port Isabel, near Brownsville, lies the southern tip of Padre Island, whose beaches stretch north for more than 100 miles. The northern and southern ends of the island are developed and have tourist facilities, and parts of the island have good roads for travelers who come to search for driftwood or parts of wrecked ships, or simply to enjoy the excellent beaches. Leading north from Brownsville, toward Corpus Christi, Route 77 crosses the vast empire of the King Ranch, the fabulous preserve of the Kleberg family, which is one of the world's largest ranches. Kingsville is the center for the ranch community, and there one may tour the Running W Saddle Shop, which makes King Ranch-brand saddles and leather specialties, and which has a small museum of King Ranch memorabilia. Near Corpus Christi itself, visitors may tour one of the world's most modern and efficient water filtration plants, the O. N. Stevens plant.

8. The Louisiana Gulf Coast

The quiet town of New Iberia, in the center of Louisiana's sugar cane country, is an ideal starting point for a trip through the southern part of the state (*right*). Along the coast is bayou country, home of the Cajuns, a largely French-speaking people descended from the Acadians who were forced to abandon their settlements in Nova Scotia by the British during the French and Indian Wars. Longfellow immortalized these people and their plight in *Evangeline*, and both poet and poem are honored by the Longfellow-Evangeline State Park, a short drive north of New Iberia. Within a day's drive of the town are two of the state's principal cities, New Orleans and the capital, Baton Rouge. There are a number of state parks, most of which have camping facilities and, to the west, the Lacassine National Wildlife Refuge and the Rockefeller Wildlife Refuge.

Many splendid examples of ante-bellum architecture are also within easy range; Shadows on the Teche, in New Iberia, is perhaps the finest of these mansions. Because three fourths of the nation's sugar cane is grown in the area, there are several refineries nearby. Colonial Sugars Company, in Gramercy, offers guided tours on weekdays. On Avery Island, southwest of New Iberia, is the headquarters of the McIlhenny Company, manufacturers of Tabasco sauce. Aside from the tour of the facility, visitors are welcome to roam through the company's Jungle Gardens and Bird Sanctuary, which includes displays of tropical plants, huge flocks of egrets, cranes and herons, and a gold Buddha dating back to 1000 A.D.

9. Old New Orleans

The Vieux Carré, or Old Square, of New Orleans (*right*) offers something for every visitor, whether he comes seeking jazz music, good food or a chance to wander in the many blocks preserved nearly intact from the days when the French and the Spanish ruled the city. The best way to see the area is by foot, and travelers who have only a few hours should go to Jackson Square and walk in its immediate vicinity. Flanking Jackson Square, the two old apartment houses called the Pontalba Buildings stand out with their block-long balconies. The northwest side of the square has several public buildings: the Cabildo, which now houses the fine Louisiana State Museum; the St. Louis Cathedral, built in Spanish style; and the Presbytère, similar to the Cabildo but built as a residence for priests. Walking southwest on Chartres Street from Jackson Square the tourist passes the Little Theater, one of the country's oldest theaters; the Napoleon House, built as a refuge for the French Emperor; and Maspero's Exchange, a trading center built in 1788. Going northwest on Bienville Street the visitor will find the old Absinthe House, a memento-filled tavern reputedly patronized by the pirate Jean Lafitte. Another right turn, onto Bourbon Street, will take the visitor near two beautiful old homes, the Grima House and the Miro House. Nearby is Antoine's, one of the city's great restaurants. Jazz buffs should see Preservation Hall, where bands play nightly, and the New Orleans Jazz Museum on Dumaine Street.

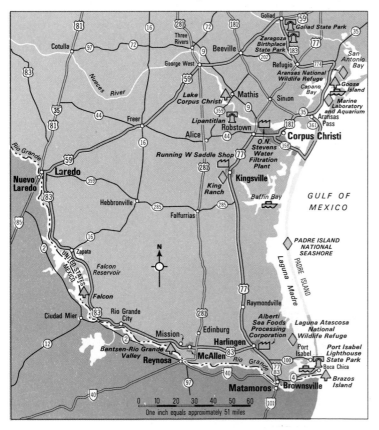

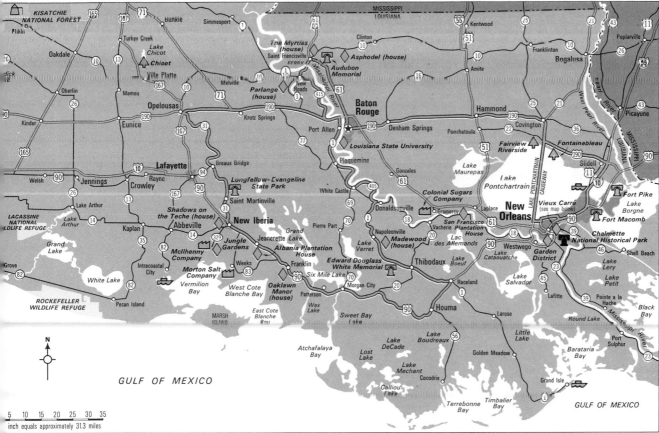

KISATCHIE
NATIONAL FOREST
Flikin
Oakdale
Oberlin
Kinder
Welsh
Jennings
Lake Arthur
Grand
Lake
Grove
White Lake
Pecan Island
ROCKEFELLER
WILDLIFE REFUGE
LACASSINE
NATIONAL
WILDLIFE REFUGE

Bunkie
Simmesport
Turkey Creek
Lake Chicot
Chicot
Ville Platte
Mamou
Opelousas
Eunice
Krotz Springs
Lafayette
Crowley
Rayne
Breaux Bridge
Abbeville
New Iberia
Saint Martinville
Shadows on
the Teche (house)
Kaplan
Lake Arthur
McIlhenny
Company
Jungle
Gardens
Morton Salt
Company
Intracoastal City
Vermilion
Bay
Weeks
West Cote
Blanche Bay
Oaklawn
Manor (house)
Franklin
Patterson
Wax
Lake
East Cote
Blanche Bay
MARSH
ISLAND

The Myrties
(house)
Saint Francisville
FERRY
Asphodel (house)
Audubon
Memorial
Parlange
(house)
New Roads
Melville
Baton
Rouge
Port Allen
Louisiana State University
Plaquemine
White Castle
Grand
Lake
Jeanerette
Albania Plantation
House
Six Mile Lake
Morgan City
Sweet Bay
Lake
Atchafalaya
Bay
Lost
Lake
Lake
DeCade
Lake
Mechant
Calliou
Lake
Cocodrie

MISSISSIPPI
LOUISIANA
Clinton
Kentwood
Franklinton
Bogalusa
Poplarville
Amite
Hammond
Ponchatoula
Covington
Denham Springs
Gonzales
Donaldsonville
Colonial Sugars
Company
Napoleonville
Lake
Verret
Madewood
(house)
Thibodaux
Lake
Boeuf
Raceland
Houma
Larose
Terrebonne
Bay
Timbalier
Bay

Picayune
Slidell
Fairview
Riverside
Fontainebleau
Lake
Maurepas
Lake
Pontchartrain
New
Orleans
Vieux Carré
(see map below)
Fort Pike
Lake
Borgne
Fort Macomb
Chalmette
National Historical Park
Shell Beach
Lake
Lery
Lake
Petit
Garden
District
Westwego
San Francisco
Plantation
House
Gramercy
Lac
des Allemands
Lake
Cataouatche
Lake
Salvador
Lafitte
Pointe a la
Hache
Black
Bay
Round Lake
Barataria
Bay
Port
Sulphur
Golden Meadow
Little
Lake
Lake
Boudreaux
Grand Isle

N

GULF OF MEXICO

GULF OF MEXICO

5   10   15   20   25   30   35
inch equals approximately 31.3 miles

BASIN   ST.
BASIN   ST.
NORTH   RAMPART   ST.
CANAL
ST.
IBERVILLE
BIENVILLE
CONTI
ST. LOUIS
TOULOUSE
ST. PETER
ST. ANN
DUMAINE
New Orleans
Jazz Museum
ST. PHILIP
URSULINES
NICHOLLS
BARRACKS
BEAUREGARD
SQUARE
GOVERNOR
ESPLANADE   AVE.
KERLEREC ST.
BURGUNDY   ST.
BURGUNDY   ST.
CABRINI
PLAYGROUND
DAUPHINE   ST.
DAUPHINE   ST.
Grima
House
BOURBON   ST.
VIEUX CARRÉ
BOURBON   ST.
ORLEANS
ST.
Absinthe
House
Antoine's
Miro
House
Preservation
Hall
SAINT ANTHONY'S
GARDEN
ROYAL   ST.
ROYAL   ST.
EXCHANGE   PLACE
Sieur George's
House
Saint
Louis
Cathedral
Beauregard
House
KERLEREC   ST.
CHARTRES   ST.
Napoleon
House
Cabildo
Madame
John's
Legacy
CHARTRES   ST.
Little
Theater
Presbytère
Mespero's
Exchange
Pontalba
Building
Pontalba
Building
JACKSON
SQUARE
Pontalba
Building
Ursuline
Convent
GOVERNOR NICHOLLS
DORSIERE ST.
BIENVILLE ST.
CONTI ST.
ST. LOUIS ST.
TOULOUSE ST.
ST. PETER ST.
PIRATES ALLEY
PERE ANTOINE ALLEY
ST. ANN ST.
MADISON ST.
DUMAINE ST.
ST. PHILIP ST.
URSULINES ST.
DECATUR   ST.
DECATUR   ST.
CANAL   ST.
U.S.
Customhouse
CLINTON ST.
NORTH PETERS ST.
IBERVILLE
CLAY
NORTH   FRONT   ST.
FOUNDERS
PARK
French Market
FRENCH MARKET PLACE
NORTH PETERS ST.
BARRACKS ST.
ESPLANADE AVE.
N

MISSISSIPPI   RIVER

0   0.1   0.2   0.3
One inch equals approximately 15 miles

179

Museums and galleries

Arkansas

Berryville
Saunders Museum, 113 E. Madison St. Famous gun collection. Mon-Sat 9-5; Sun 1-5.

Emmet
Arkla Village, U.S. 67. Re-created mid-1800 frontier town. Daily 9-5.

Hot Springs
I.Q. Zoo, 380 Whittington Ave. Zoo with exhibits of psychologically conditioned animal behavior. May-Sept: daily 9-5; Oct-Apr: daily 10:30-4:30.

Quartz Crystal Cave and Museum, 435 Whittington Ave. Collection of Southwestern minerals. Daily 8-6.

Little Rock
Arkansas Archives Department, Old State House. Antiques depicting history of state. Mon-Fri 8-4.

The Arkansas Art Center, MacArthur Park. Civic arts center; theater. Tues-Sat 10-5; Sun, hols 12-5.

Arkansas Territorial Capitol Restoration, 214 E. Third St. Building complex depicting Arkansas life in the 1820s. Tues-Sat 10-5; Sun, Mon, hols 1-5.

Museum of Science and Natural History, MacArthur Park. Historical exhibits. Tues-Sat 10-5; Sun 2-5.

Morrilton
Museum of Automobiles, Petit Jean Mt. Winthrop Rockefeller's collection of antique and classic cars. Apr-Oct: Tues-Sun 10-5; Nov-Mar: Wed-Sun 10-5.

State College
Arkansas State College Museum. Exhibits having to do with Arkansas and its military and natural history; herbarium. Mon-Fri 9-5; Tues-Thurs eves 7-9; Sun 1-5.

Louisiana

Arabi
Chalmette National Historical Park. Dioramas of the Battle of New Orleans; war museum and ante-bellum home. Daily 7:30-5.

Avery Island
Jungle Gardens. Three hundred acres of tropical plants. Daily 7:30-5.

Baton Rouge
Louisiana Arts and Science Center, 502 North Blvd. Good general collection; includes a children's museum. Tues-Sat 10-5; Sun 1-5.

Louisiana State University Anglo-American Art Museum, Memorial Tower. Exhibits showing impact of English culture on America. Sept-June: daily 10-4.

State of Louisiana Art Commission, North Blvd. and St. Philip St. Exhibits in contemporary art and photography. Mon-Sat 10-5; Sun 1-5.

Franklin
Oaklawn Manor, Irish Bend Rd. Fine 19th Century house; period furnishings. Daily 8-6.

Jeanerette
Albania Plantation House, U.S. 90. Historic home with renowned doll collection. Daily 9-3:30.

Marksville
Marksville Prehistoric Indian Museum. Archeological museum containing relics of early Indians; displays showing the story of man. Mon-Sat 10-4; Sun 10-6.

New Iberia
The Shadows on the Teche, 217 E. Main St. Restored ante-bellum mansion. Daily 9:30-4:30.

New Orleans
Isaac Delgado Museum of Art, Lelong Ave., City Park. Varied exhibits; Samuel H. Kress collection of Italian Renaissance painting. Tues-Sat 10-5; Sun 1-6.

La Pharmacie Française, 514 Chartres St. Pharmacology museum and old apothecary shop. Mon-Fri 10-4:30.

Louisiana Historical Association, Memorial Hall, 929 Camp St. Confederate relics and documents. Tues-Sat 10-4.

New Orleans Jazz Museum, 1017 Dumaine St. Extensive collection of jazz memorabilia. Tues-Sat, hols 10-5; Sun 1-5.

Shreveport
Louisiana State Exhibit Museum, 3015 Greenwood Rd. Exhibits showing Louisiana resources and agriculture; Indian artifacts and Civil War items. Mon-Fri 9-5; Sat 1-5; Sun 1-6.

The R. W. Norton Art Gallery, 4700 Block of Cresswell Ave. American and European painting and sculpture. Tues-Sat 1-5; Sun 2-5.

Oklahoma

Anadarko
Indian City, U.S.A. Re-creation of Plains Indian villages. Daily 9-6.

Bartlesville
Woolaroc Museum, Lake Murray State Park. Western paintings; exhibits showing the development of Southwest. Tues-Sun 10-5.

Fort Sill
U.S. Army Artillery and Missile Center Museum. Remarkable collection of U.S. Army equipment. Wed-Sun, hols 8-4:30.

Lawton
Museum of the Great Plains, Elmer Thomas Park. Human history and ecology in the Great Plains. Tues-Sat 10-5; Tues-Thurs eves 7-10; Sun 2-5. Closed many hols.

Norman
J. Willis Stovall Museum of Science and History, Asp St. Exhibits in natural sciences and classical art. Tues-Fri, hols 9-5; Sat 9-12; Sun 2-5.

Museum of Art, Jacobson Hall. American, Indian and Oriental art. Mon-Sat 9-5; Tues-Thurs eves 7-9:30; Sun 1-5. Closed Sun during Aug.

Oklahoma City
National Cowboy Hall of Fame and Western Heritage Center, 1700 N.E. 63rd St. on U.S. 40. Western art and memorabilia. Mon-Fri 9-5:30; Sun 1-5:30.

Oklahoma Art Center, Plaza Circle, Fair Park. American paintings, prints, sculpture. Tues-Sat 10-5.

Oklahoma Historical Society, Lincoln Blvd. Indian archives second only to the Smithsonian. Mon-Fri 8-4:30; Sat 8:30-12; Sun 1:30-4:30.

Ponca City
Pioneer Woman Museum, U.S. 77. Relics and mementos relating to the state's pioneer women. Mon, Wed-Sat 10-5; Sun 1-5.

Tahlequah
The Murrell Home. Restored ante-bellum mansion. Mar-Nov: Mon-Fri 10-5; Sat, Sun, hols 1-5; Dec-Feb: by appointment.

Tulsa
Philbrook Art Center, 2727 S. Rockford Rd. Exhibits in European, Oriental and Southwest art. Tues-Sat 10-5; Tues eve 7:30-9:30; Sun 1-5.

The Thomas Gilcrease Institute of American History and Art, 2401 W. Newton St. Fine collection of frontier and Indian art; history of Indian culture. Mon-Sat 9-5; Sun and hols 1-5.

Texas

Austin
Laguna Gloria Art Museum, 3809 W. 35th St. Works by Texas artists. Tues-Fri 9-3; Wed, Thurs eves 7-10; Sat 10-5; Sun 2-5.

O. Henry Memorial Museum, 409 E. Fifth St. Home of O. Henry; memorabilia. Mon, Wed-Sat 10-12, 2-5; Sun 2-5.

Texas Memorial Museum, 24th and Trinity Sts. Exhibits in Texas history and science. Mon-Sat, hols 9-5; Sun 2-5.

Bandera
Frontier Times Museum, two blocks north of Court House. Pioneer items and Indian relics. Tues-Sat 9-12, 1-5; Sun 1-5.

Canyon
Panhandle-Plains Historical Museum, 2401 Fourth Ave. Paintings by Southwestern artists; Oriental ceramics and European furniture. Mon-Sat 9-5; Sun 2-6.

Dallas
Dallas Health and Science Museum, Fair Park. Exhibits in anatomy, medicine, communications; planetarium. Mon-Sat 9-5; Sun, hols 2-6; June-Aug: Tues eve 5-9; planetarium shows: Sat, Sun 3 p.m.

Dallas Historical Society, Hall of State, Fair Park. Large collection of Texas memorabilia. Mon-Sat 9-5; Sun, hols 2-6; June 15-Aug 15: Tues eve 5-9.

Dallas Museum of Fine Arts, Fair Park. General collection; Texas folk art. Tues-Sat 10-5; Wed eve 5-9; Sun 2-6.

El Paso
El Paso Centennial Museum, W. College Ave. Exhibits in regional natural history; planetarium. Mon-Fri 10-5; Sat, Sun 1-5.

El Paso Museum of Art, 1211 Montana Ave. General collection with emphasis on American and Mexican art. Tues-Sat 10-5; Sun 1-5.

Fort Worth
Amon Carter Museum of Western Art, 3501 Camp Bowie Blvd. Works by Remington and

Russell; exhibits of Western art. Mon-Sat 10-5; Sun, hols 1-5:30; Sept-May, closed Mon.

Fort Worth Art Center, 1309 Montgomery St. Nineteenth and 20th Century American painting. Tues-Sat 10-5:30; Sun 1-5:30.

Houston
Contemporary Arts Association, 6945 Fannin St. Contemporary painting and sculpture. Mon-Fri 9-5; Sat, Sun 1-5.

Houston Museum of Natural Science, 1400 Hermann Loop Dr. Texas reptiles and amphibia; planetarium. Daily 9:30-5.

Museum of Fine Arts of Houston, Texas. 1001 Bissionnet Rd. Fine general collection of art from various cultures. Tues-Sat 9:30-5; Wed eve 7-10; Sun 12-6.

Huntsville
Sam Houston Memorial Museum, 1804 Avenue L. Memorabilia of Sam Houston and relics of the Texas revolution. Daily 9-5.

Laredo
Capitol of the Republic of the Rio Grande Museum, 1000 Saragoza St. Documents, guns and furniture. Wed-Fri 9:30-11:30; Sat, Sun

9:30-11:30, 2:30-4:30.

Pecos
West of the Pecos Museum, Inc., U.S. 258 at First St. Pecos and West Texas history. Hours vary.

San Antonio
The Alamo, Alamo Plaza. Restored mission; Texas relics. Mon-Sat 9-5; Sun 10-6.

Hertzberg Circus Collection, San Antonio Public Library, 210 W. Market St. Circus memorabilia. Mon-Sat 9-5:30.

La Villita. Reconstructed 300-year-old Spanish settlement where old arts and crafts are carried on and sold. Daily 8-6.

Marion Koogler McNay Art Institute, 6000 N. New Braunfels Ave. General collection. Tues, Wed, Fri, Sat 9-5; Thurs 9-9; Sun 2-5.

Witte Memorial Museum, 3801 Broadway. Exhibits covering natural history, Southwest history and regional art; historic houses. Mon-Fri 9:30-5; Sat, Sun, hols 10-6.

San Jacinto Monument
San Jacinto Museum of History Association, San Jacinto Battleground Park. Exhibits in Texas, Mexican and regional history. Tues-Sat, hols 9:30-5:30; Sun 10-6.

Local festivals and events

Arkansas
The Arkansas Folk Festival, Eureka. Singers and musicians from deep in the mountain country. Late Apr.

The Grand Prairie Grand Prix, Stuttgart. Sports-car races; entrants compete for trophies and points. Late Apr.

Arkansas-Oklahoma Rodeo, Fort Smith. Largest rodeo in the state. Late May.

Inspiration Point Fine Arts Colony Music Festival, Eureka Springs. Student concerts. Late June— early July.

Grape Festival, Tontitown. Celebration at height of the grape harvest. Aug.

Oil Belt Golf Tournament, El Dorado. Pro-Am golfers from tri-state oil area of Arkansas, Louisiana and Texas. Early Sept.

Arkansas Livestock Exposition and Rodeo, Little Rock. State's biggest annual event. Agricultural and industrial exhibits; entertainment. Early Oct.

World Championship Duck Calling Contest, Stuttgart. Prizes given to the best duck callers; entertainment. Late Nov.

Louisiana
Sugar Bowl, New Orleans. Football classic, parades and other festivities. Jan 1.

Mardi Gras, New Orleans. Traditional celebration that includes private deb parties and festive parades. Beginning on Jan 6 and ending on Shrove

Tuesday, the day before Ash Wednesday.

Crayfish Festival, Breaux Bridge. Crayfish-eating contest, French folk dances, parades. Every even year in Apr.

Holiday in Dixie, Shreveport. Week-long celebration, parades, flower and art shows. Apr.

Lafitte Pirogue Races, Lafitte. World championship races of canoelike craft over a four-mile course. May.

Contraband Days, Lake Charles. Celebration with a pirate theme; features mock invasions, parades and boat races. June.

Blessing of the Shrimp Fleet, Morgan City. Parades, street dances and a carnival. Sun before Labor Day.

Sugar Cane Festival, New Iberia. Dances, parades, and shows of boats, flowers and horses. Late Sept.

Louisiana Cotton Festival, Villa Platte. Cotton-growing exhibits, exhibits of Acadian life, folk dances of the area and an Acadian music festival. Oct.

Natchitoches Pilgrimage, Natchitoches. Tour of area homes in Louisiana's oldest town. Mid-Oct.

International Rice Festival, Crowley. Livestock show, Creole cooking contest, rice-eating contest. Late Oct.

Yambilee Festival, Opelousa. Celebration in honor of the yam. Late Oct.

Oklahoma
Rattlesnake Roundup, Okene. Prizes given for longest snake and greatest number caught; spectators may watch or participate. Late Mar—early Apr.

Eighty-niners Day, Guthrie. Celebration of the opening of new land to the homesteaders. Mid-Apr.

Northeastern Oklahoma Arts and Crafts Festival, Tahlequah. Displays and sales of native arts and crafts. Mid-Apr.

Dogwood Tours, Tahlequah. Guided tours of dogwood areas of northern Oklahoma and Arkansas. Late Apr.

Tri-state Music Festival, Enid. Student competition. Early May.

National Sand Bass Festival, Lake Texoma near Madill. Fishing contest, fish fry, races and dances. Mid-June.

International Brick and Rolling Pin Throwing Contest, Stroud. Contestants compete simultaneously in Stroud, Canada; Stroud, England; and Stroud, Australia. July 15.

American Indian Exposition, Anadarko. More than 1,000 Indians from 11 tribes participate for six days in parades, ceremonial dances and pageants. Mid-Aug.

Prison Rodeo, McAlester. Rodeo held in Oklahoma State Prison. All contestants are inmates. Early Sept.

State Fair of Oklahoma, Oklahoma City. Livestock and agricultural exhibits and entertainment. Nine days in late Sept.

Will Rogers Birthday Celebration, Claremore. An annual event with a

parade and memorial service at the gravesite. Nov 4.

Texas
George Washington's Birthday Celebration, Laredo. A five-day fiesta devoted to "Good Neighbor" policy. Feb 22.

Charro Days, Brownsville. A four-day costume fiesta, including colorful street dances. Thurs before Ash Wednesday.

Livestock Exposition and Fat Stock Show, Houston. Gigantic exposition and state's biggest rodeo, held in the Astrodome. Early spring.

All Texas Jazz Festival, Corpus Christi. Features professional as well as amateur entertainment. Early June.

Austin Aqua Festival, Austin. All types of water activities and contests. Early Aug.

Prison Rodeo, Huntsville. Wildly exciting rodeo, with the inmates in competition. Every Sun in Oct.

Texas State Fair, Dallas. The state's largest exposition, featuring varied exhibits and entertainment 16 days in Oct.

Cavoilcade, Port Arthur. A salute to the petroleum industry, featuring parades, contests and races. Late Oct.

Christmas Cotton Bowl Festival, Dallas. Features special entertainment and a basketball tournament, plus a football game on Jan 1. Late Dec—Jan 1.

Sun Carnival, El Paso. Art shows, bullfights, polo matches and horse races. Climaxed by football game on Jan 1. Late Dec—Jan 1.

Wildlife of the South Central States

A wide variety of wildlife flourishes in the South Central States. Many species are also found in other parts of the nation, but a few—the nine-banded armadillo and the collared peccary, for example—are seldom seen elsewhere. A sampling of the region's natural life is shown on these pages. In each case both the common and the scientific name are given. For further information, a number of useful specialized reference books on wildlife are listed on page 188.

Mammals

Evening bat

A denizen of woodlands, *Nycticeius humeralis* varies in color from rich, warm brown to dark chocolate. It eats insects and avoids its worst enemy, the owl.

Nine-banded armadillo

Dasypus novemcinctus, a well armored but peaceful animal, nests in burrows dug in thickets and grassy fields. It eats scorpions and other harmful insects.

Black-tailed jack rabbit

Largely a creature of the plains, *Lepus californicus* is among the most conspicuous small-game animals. Its diet consists mainly of herbs and grasses.

Eastern fox squirrel

This creature, *Sciurus niger*, the largest of the tree squirrels, prefers to live in oak or cypress woods. It eats berries, nuts and bark and is easily tamed.

Plains pocket gopher

A molelike rodent, *Geomys bursarius* is named for the pouches on the outside of its cheeks, in which it carries food, mostly bulbs and roots, to its nest.

Coyote

Having the appearance of a small, bushy-tailed shepherd dog, *Canis latrans* ranges throughout Oklahoma and Texas, from deserts to wooded mountains.

River otter

Lutra canadensis, playful and gregarious, lives in marshy areas or on riverbanks. Its webbed feet make it a strong and graceful swimmer; it can also run on land.

Collared peccary

The almost tailless, piglike collared peccary *(Pecari angulatus)*, called the javelina in the Southwest, travels in packs. It mainly eats berries and roots.

Fish and reptiles

Dolphin

One of the fastest ocean fish, *Coryphaena hippurus* prefers waters, such as those of the Gulf of Mexico, with a temperature of 70 degrees or warmer.

Southern flounder

Like other flatfish, *Paralichthys lethostigmus* begins its life like an ordinary fish, but soon starts to swim on one side; then the eye on the bottom migrates to the top.

Mangrove snapper

The mangrove snapper *(Lutjanus griseus)* changes color with its environment, varying from a red-brown to light gray. A salt-water fish, it prefers shallows.

Tripletail

Generally found in the Gulf of Mexico, *Lobotes surinamensis* is a bottom fish that feeds on shrimp and smaller fish. It may grow to 30 inches and weigh 25 pounds.

Eastern pickerel

A fresh-water fish, *Esox niger* lives in the quiet waters of weedy streams and ponds, lurking in ambush to seize its prey of smaller fish or frogs.

Spotted bass

The spotted bass *(Micropterus punctulatus)*, a favorite of fishermen, stays out of sight in shaded shallows by day, moving into open water by night to feed.

Horned dace

Also known as the creek chub, *Semotilus atromaculatus* is one of the larger relatives of the minnow. Some attain a length of one foot, a weight of two pounds.

Flathead catfish

One of the largest fresh-water fish, *Pilodictis olivaris* grows up to five feet long and may weigh 100 pounds. It is commercially fished in the lower Mississippi.

Alligator snapping turtle

Macroclemys temmincki, America's largest fresh-water turtle, lies on the muddy bottoms of streams and lakes wiggling its wormlike tongue to attract fish.

Mississippi diamondback terrapin

An excellent swimmer, *Malaclemys terrapin pileata* inhabits brackish streams and salt marshes. Its meat is considered a great delicacy in Louisiana.

Greater earless lizard

Holbrookia texana, a denizen of dry country, has protective coloration that blends so well with its surroundings that it is often virtually impossible to see.

Texas horned lizard

More commonly called the horned toad, *Phrynosoma cornutum* can eject a stream of blood from its eyes when alarmed. The survival value of this tactic is not known.

Banded gecko

A small lizard, the banded gecko *(Coleonyx variegatus)* prefers rocky areas where it can take shelter beneath rocks by day and feed on small insects safely by night.

Louisiana milk snake

The markings of *Lampropeltis doliata amaura,* which is nonpoisonous, mimic those of the venomous coral snake. It kills its prey by crushing it in its coils.

Western cottonmouth

An irritable and pugnacious snake, *Agkistrodon piscovorus leucostoma* is better known as the water moccasin. Poisonous, it is dark brown or black in color.

Western diamondback rattler

Extremely poisonous, *Crotalus atrox* grows to a length of seven feet. Despite its warning rattle, it accounts for a large proportion of U.S. snake-bite fatalities.

Birds

Brown pelican

The state bird of Louisiana, *Pelecanus occidentalis carolinensis* nests in coastal marshlands. It flies over the water, diving bill-first for fish.

Louisiana heron

The Louisiana heron *(Hydranassa tricolor),* noisy and active, is often seen running gracefully through tidal swamps and then spearing fish with its long, sharp bill.

White ibis

A permanent resident of Texas and Louisiana, *Eudocimus albus* nests in large colonies in bayous and grassy marshes. It feeds on crabs, small snakes and insects.

Fulvous tree duck

Dendrocygna bicolor, a long, gangly, gooselike duck, actually prefers paddies and ponds to trees. Its raucous squeal has gained it the nickname of Mexican squealer.

183

Black vulture

Soaring high in the air, the great eaglelike black vulture *(Coragyps atratus)* may sometimes be seen flying in large groups. Because of its penchant for carrion, it is an important sanitary agent.

Lesser prairie chicken

Easily distinguished by the red air sacs on either side of its neck, *Tympanuchus pallidicinctus* inhabits the prairies of Oklahoma and Texas, assembling in large flocks during mating season.

Wild turkey

A streamlined version of its fatter cousin, the barnyard turkey, *Meleagris gallopavo* inhabits the woodlands, thickets and prairie groves of the South Central States, where it is a favorite game bird.

Whooping crane

The tall whooping crane *(Grus americana)* stands nearly five feet high and has a wingspread of up to 7.5 feet. Nearly extinct, the entire species has not numbered more than 50 in this century.

Roadrunner

A member of the cuckoo family, *Geococcyx californianus,* the fast-running prairie bird of movie cartoon fame, is able to fly, but seeks safety most often by making good use of its long legs.

Scissor-tailed flycatcher

Muscivora forficata is the state bird of Oklahoma. It is an excellent flyer—its long, forked tail, which may reach nine inches in the male, gives it a greater maneuverability than almost any other bird.

Mockingbird

Both Texas and Arkansas have chosen the mockingbird *(Mimus polyglottos polyglottos)* as their state bird. It is able to mimic other birds and also the sounds of animals in its territory.

Black-capped vireo

Hard to see because of its predilection for staying close to cover, *Vireo atricapilla* is nevertheless a most obtrusive bird, its simple song being heard through the spring and summer.

Flowers and trees

Pickerelweed

The pickerelweed *(Pontederia cordata)* decorates ponds and shallow streams. It grows to a height of three feet, has large leaves and a four-inch spike of delicate blue-violet flowers.

Yellow lady's slipper

Growing in woodland bogs, *Cyripedium calceolus* is a relative of the orchid. The green- or purple-striped yellow blossoms, open from May to July, nod gently on the tips of two-foot stalks.

American lotus

Nelumbo lutea is a member of the water-lily family. It has large yellow flowers that may measure 10 inches across. Flowers and leaves are held above the water's surface by thick, tubular stalks.

Trumpet

An insect-eating plant, the trumpet *(Sarracenia flava)* is named for its tubular leaves. Insects, attracted by a sweet-smelling secretion of the leaves, crawl inside where they are trapped and digested.

Bluebonnet

A member of the pea family, *Lupinus subcarnosus* has a blossom that resembles the sun hats worn by pioneer women. These small, blue-purple flowers are arranged pyramidally.

Showy evening primrose

The showy evening primrose *(Oenothera speciosa)* grows in grasslands. It reaches a height of from six inches to three feet and puts forth a few one- to three-inch white flowers in May.

Prairie phlox

Also known as the hairy or downy phlox, *Phlox pilosa* prefers sandy slopes and prairies and requires little water. Its clustered flowers range in color from pale pink or violet to rich, deep purple.

Venus's looking-glass

Specularia perforliata, a plant that grows well in poor soil, bears two types of purple flower. Those at the bottom of the stalk are self-fertilizing, while the ones near the top must be cross-pollinated.

Pecan

A species of hickory, *Hicoria pecan* is a forest tree that is now widely cultivated to produce pecan nuts. Varieties have been developed that bear thin-shelled nuts, prized as a luxury food.

Redbud

Cercis canadensis has several common names, among them the Judas tree. Legend has it that the tree's blossoms took on their red-violet blush when Judas used the tree to hang himself.

Persimmon

The fruit of the persimmon tree *(Disopyros virginiana)* is about the size of a plum and is orange when ripe. Tough and astringent when immature, it ripens after the first frost.

Osage orange

The Osage orange *(Toxylon pomiferum)* was named for a tribe of Indians that prized the tree's tough and flexible wood—which is bright orange in color—for making bows and war clubs.

Southern magnolia

The state flower of Louisiana, *Magnolia grandiflora* is famed for large lilylike flowers that exude a sweet lemony odor. The tree is cultivated on city streets and in gardens in the Gulf States.

Eastern cottonwood

This graceful tree *(Populus deltoides)*, also called the necklace poplar, grows along the streams and rivers of plains areas. Prized as a shade tree, it is often planted in cities.

Sassafras

Sassafras albidum grows leaves of three different shapes. A useful tree, its roots are boiled to make tea, its leaves are added to soup for flavor, and its aromatic oil is used in soap.

Bald cypress

A majestic member of the pine family, *Taxodium distichum* prefers swamps, where it grows to 150 feet. The "knees" at the base of its trunk, connected underwater, help anchor the tree.

Statistical information

State nickname, date of admission, capital

Arkansas: Land of Opportunity; admitted 1836 (the 25th state); Little Rock.

Louisiana: Pelican State; admitted 1812 (the 18th state); Baton Rouge.

Oklahoma: Sooner State; admitted 1907 (the 46th state); Oklahoma City.

Texas: Lone Star State; admitted 1845 (the 28th state); Austin.

Population

By state (U.S. Census, 1965 preliminary estimate):
Texas: 10,551,000.
Louisiana: 3,534,000.
Oklahoma: 2,482,000.
Arkansas: 1,960,000.

By city (region's 10 largest cities are listed below, followed by their population and rank in the U.S. according to the estimate of the *1967 Editor and Publisher Market Guide*):

Houston	1,197,167	6
Dallas	854,363	9
San Antonio	722,893	13
New Orleans	675,217	17
Oklahoma City	369,973	39
Fort Worth	365,887	42
El Paso	344,199	47
Tulsa	292,041	51
Austin	235,979	59
Shreveport	183,932	74

Land areas

Texas: 262,840 square miles.
Oklahoma: 68,887 square miles.
Arkansas: 52,499 square miles.
Louisiana: 45,106 square miles.

Bodies of water

Principal lakes, including man-made ones

Lake Pontchartrain (Louisiana): 630 square miles; maximum depth, 15 feet.

Eufaula (Oklahoma): 160.16 square miles; maximum depth, 87 feet; man-made.

Texonoma (Texas and Oklahoma): 149.06 square miles; maximum depth, 94 feet; man-made.

Bull Shoals (Arkansas): 111.31 square miles; maximum depth, 243 feet; man-made.

Ouachita (Arkansas, Missouri): 62.65 square miles; maximum depth, 207 feet; man-made.

Texarkana (Texas): 46.56 square miles; maximum depth, 39 feet; man-made.

Principal rivers (lengths in miles)

Note: Only the states in the South Central region that these rivers flow through are named.

Mississippi (Arkansas, Louisiana): 2,348.

Rio Grande (Texas): 1,885.

Arkansas (Arkansas, Oklahoma): 1,450.

Red (Oklahoma, Louisiana, Texas): 1,018.

Canadian (Oklahoma, Texas): 960.

Brazos (Texas): 870.

Colorado (Texas): 840.

Pecos (Texas): 735.

Important engineering feats

World's largest indoor arena: Harris County Sports Stadium, also known as the Astrodome, Houston, Texas. Capacity 45,000 for baseball, 66,000 for football.

Largest dome in the U.S.: Atop the Astrodome, Houston. Outer diameter 710 feet.

Longest twin concrete trestle: Lake Pontchartrain Causeway, Louisiana. Length of bridge, 28,550 feet; total length of causeway, 24 miles.

Some U.S. superlatives

First and second in petroleum production: Texas and Louisiana.

Largest state among the 48 contiguous states: Texas.

Nation's largest privately owned ranch: King Ranch, 823,000 acres in Texas.

First recognized beef breed developed in Western Hemisphere: Santa Gertrudis, bred at the King Ranch.

Greatest number of farms with greatest acreage: Texas, with 205,109 farms and 141,714,031 acres.

Agricultural statistics (1964)

	Number of farms	Acreage (in millions)	Principal commodities
Arkansas	79,898	16.5	Cotton, rice.
Louisiana	62,467	10.4	Sweet potatoes, sugar cane, rice, cotton.
Oklahoma	88,726	36.1	Wheat, cattle, cotton, peanuts.
Texas	205,109	141.7	Cattle, sheep, rice, cotton.

Minerals, petroleum and natural-gas production (1965)

	Number of producing wells at end of 1965	Principal minerals
Arkansas	6,672	Petroleum, bauxite.
Louisiana	39,464	Petroleum, sulfur, salt.
Oklahoma	87,100	Petroleum, helium, zinc, gypsum, cement, lead.
Texas	225,772	Petroleum.

Pronunciation glossary

Amarillo (am ah RILL low). City in northern Texas.

Arapaho (uh RAP ah hoe). Tribe of Southwestern Indians; town in Oklahoma.

Atchafalaya (ah CHA full ee uh). Bay and river in southern Louisiana.

Balcones Escarpment (bal CO nis). Geological fault about 200 miles long, in Texas.

Baton Rouge (BAH ton ROOJ). City in southeastern Louisiana.

Bayou (BY oo). A secondary watercourse or tributary to a larger river, common in Louisiana.

Bogalusa (beau gah LOU sah). City in southeastern Louisiana.

Brahman (BRAY mun or BRAH mun). A cattle breed.

Chalmette (shall MET). Small village in southeastern Louisiana; also a national historical park in same locale.

Choctaw (CHOCK taw). Indian tribe and county in Oklahoma.

Helena (heh LEE nuh). City in Arkansas; town in Oklahoma.

Kiowa (KI uh wuh). Town and county in Oklahoma; name of tribe of Indians.

Lake Pontchartrain (PON chuh tran). Shallow lake in southeastern Louisiana.

Laredo (luh RAY doe). City in southwest Texas.

Llano Estacado (LAH no ess tah CAH doe). The "Staked Plains" of West Texas.

Lubbock (LUH buck). City and county in northwestern part of Texas.

Nacogdoches (nah kuh DOE chess). City and county in East Texas.

Natchitoches (NAK i tosh). City and parish in central Louisiana.

Nueces (new AY sis). River and county in southern Texas.

Ouachita (WOSH i toh). County in Arkansas; parish in Louisiana; river in Arkansas and Louisiana; mountains in Oklahoma and Arkansas.

Palo Duro (PAH luh DOO row). Canyon and creek in northern Texas.

Pedernales (ped er NAH less). River in south-central Texas.

Plaquemine (PLAQUE mine). Town, parish and bayou in central Louisiana.

San Jacinto (SAN huh SIN toh). River, county and site of battlefield in East Texas.

Sequoyah (suh COY uh). Name of the inventor of Cherokee alphabet; county in eastern Oklahoma.

Tahlequah (TAH luh quah). City in Oklahoma.

Texarkana (tex sar KAN uh). Dual city in northeastern Texas and southwest Arkansas.

Thibodaux (tib uh DOE). Town in southeastern Louisiana.

Waco (WAY co). City and small lake in Texas.

Credits and acknowledgments

Maps for front and back end papers by Jeppesen & Company, Denver, Colorado, and for pages 174 through 179 © by The H. M. Gousha Company, San Jose, California. Maps on pages 40 and 76 by Lothar Roth.

The sources for the illustrations that appear in this book are shown below. Credits for the pictures from left to right are separated by commas, from top to bottom by dashes.
Cover—A. Y. Owen.
Front end papers—Drawings by Richard Boland.
Chapter 1: 8, 9—A. Y. Owen. 11 —Map by Lothar Roth from *Climates of the States*, U.S. Weather Bureau, Department of Commerce. 17—A. Y. Owen. 18, 19—Stonehill Studio—A. Y. Owen, Grant Heilman. 20, 21— A. Y. Owen except top right Stonehill Studio. 22, 23— Stonehill Studio—Ralph Crane, Eastex Incorporated. 24, 25— Stonehill Studio—A. Y. Owen. 26, 27—Ralph Crane, Stonehill Studio—A. Y. Owen. 28, 29— Stonehill Studio, A. Y. Owen. 30, 31—Ralph Crane, A. Y. Owen, Stonehill Studio. 32, 33— Stonehill Studio, A. Y. Owen.
Chapter 2: 34, 35—Culver Pictures, Inc. 37—The Bettmann Archive. 42—Culver Pictures, Inc., De Venny Wood Studio courtesy San Jacinto Museum of History Association. 44— Drawings by Don Spaulding. 47, 48—Lee Boltin. 49—Left Clarence John Laughlin; right Lee Boltin. 50, 51—Lee Boltin except top second from left Clarence John Laughlin. 52 through 55— Lee Boltin.
Chapter 3: 56—A. Y. Owen cour- tesy Division of Manuscripts, University of Oklahoma Library. 59—The Smithsonian Institution, Office of Anthropology, Bureau of American Ethnology Collection, Oklahoma Historical Society. 64 —Map by Lothar Roth adapted from *A Guide to the Indian Tribes of Oklahoma* by Muriel Wright, University of Oklahoma Press. 67 —The Bettmann Archive. 68 through 73—A. Y. Owen courtesy Division of Manuscripts,

University of Oklahoma Library except 69 bottom right and 71 bottom right A. Y. Owen courtesy Oklahoma Historical Society.
Chapter 4: 74—Leonard McCombe. 78, 79—Erwin E. Smith courtesy Library of Congress and Mrs. L. M. Pettis. 80—Drawing by Sam Savitt. 81—Drawing by Otto van Eersel. 82—Drawing by Leslie Martin. 83—Map by Lothar Roth adapted from *The King Ranch* by Tom Lea, courtesy of King Ranch. 85 —Joern Gerdts. 86, 87— Drawing by Arno Sternglass, Shel Hershorn from Black Star except bottom left and right Shelly Katz. 88, 89—Drawing by Arno Sternglass. 90—Joern Gerdts. 91—John Loengard. 92, 93— Joern Gerdts. 94, 95—Diagram by Matt Greene.
Chapter 5: 96—Ralph Crane. 98 —*Dallas Morning News*. 99— Freelance Photographers Guild Inc., United Press International. 101, 102—Texas Mid-Continent Oil and Gas Association courtesy of Charles Simons. 103—Map by Lothar Roth adapted from *Principles of Petroleum Geology* by William L. Russell, McGraw-Hill Book Company, 1960, courtesy of The American Institute of Mining, Metallurgical and Petroleum Engineers. 104— Diagram by James Alexander. 105—Map by Lothar Roth adapted from *Oil and Gas Fields of the United States* by Sophie D. Vlissides and Barbara A. Quirin, Department of the Interior, U.S. Geological Survey, Washington, D.C., 1964. 107 —Drawing by James Alexander adapted from *The Petroleum Handbook*, Shell International Petroleum Company Limited, London, 1966. 109 through 117 —A. Y. Owen.
Chapter 6: 118—Jim Nickless. 120—Culver Pictures, Inc. 121 —The Bettmann Archive. 124— Drawing by Otto van Eersel. 125 —Recipes adapted from *Original Picayune Creole Cook Book*. 127—Drawings by Don Spaulding. 129 through 137— Bruce Roberts from Rapho Guillumette.
Chapter 7: 138—Stan Wayman. 141—Bill Malone. 142, 143— Howell's Photo Service, Ben Martin, Walter Bennett, J. W. Guillot. 144—Excerpts from *The*

Ordways by William Humphrey, copyright 1964 by William Humphrey, reprinted with the permission of Alfred A. Knopf, Inc. 147, 148—Shel Hershorn from Black Star. 149—Shel Hershorn from Black Star except right Ralph Crane. 150, 151— Shel Hershorn from Black Star. 152, 153—Shel Hershorn from Black Star except bottom right Ralph Crane.
Chapter 8: 154—Ralph Crane. 156, 157—Courtesy Neiman-Marcus, courtesy Houston Chamber of Commerce, Collection of Leonard V. Huber. 161—Ralph Crane. 162, 163— Inger McCabe from Rapho Guillumette. 164, 165— Bert Brandt, Ralph Crane. 166, 169—Inger McCabe from Rapho Guillumette. 170, 171—Bert Brandt for TIME, Inger McCabe from Rapho Guillumette. 172, 173 —Ralph Crane. 182 through 185—Drawings by Rudolf Freund. Back end papers—Drawings by Richard Boland.

The editors of this book wish to thank the following persons and institutions for their assistance: Dillon Anderson, former Special Assistant to the President for National Security Affairs, Houston; Robert H. Brewer, Manager Industry and Commerce, Houston Chamber of Commerce; Vince G. Brigante, Sugar Industry Consultant, New Iberia, Louisiana; Vaughn Bryant, Director of International Relations for the Port of Houston; Ben Burnside, Charolais rancher and Southwestern agricultural and livestock leader, Longview, Texas; Governor John Connally of Texas; Jack Crowson, Director of Public Relations, Fort Worth Stockyards; Robert E. Cunningham, Stillwater Engraving Service, Oklahoma; John Cypher, Director of Information, the King Ranch, Kingsville, Texas; D. A. Deterling, *The Progressive-Farmer*, Dallas; Frederick J. Dockstader, Director of the Museum of the American Indian, New York City; McFadden Duffy, Louisiana Wildlife and Fisheries Commission, New Orleans; Leland Duvall, Agricultural Director, *The Arkansas Gazette*, Little Rock; Glenn Faris, Secretary General, National Cowboy Hall of Fame, Oklahoma City; Bedford Forrest,

High Plains Research Foundation, Plainview, Texas; Jack Haley, Director of Manuscripts, University of Oklahoma Library, Norman; Alf Jernigan, Assistant General Manager, East Texas Chamber of Commerce, Longview; Dean Krakel, Director, National Cowboy Hall of Fame, Oklahoma City; Tom Lea, author-artist, El Paso; Paula McSpadden Love, Curator, Will Rogers Memorial Museum, Claremore, Oklahoma; Charles McCarthy, editor, *Daily Iberian*, New Iberia, Louisiana; Watt Matthews, General Manager, Matthews Ranch, Albany, Texas; Mrs. E. A. Mueller, former Secretary, Boys Camp, Marfa, Texas; Sandy Neal, rancher, Van Horn, Texas; Charles Odell, Beef Specialist, Neuhoff Packing Company, Dallas; William Patout Jr., Managing Director of Sugar Plantations of William Patout and Sons, Patoutsville, Louisiana; Patrick Patterson, Director, Woolorac Museum, Bartlesville, Oklahoma; William Poe, editor of the *Sugar Journal*, New Orleans; Carroll Pouncey, Amarillo Chamber of Commerce, Texas; Elaine Proctor, Director of Information, Thomas Gilcrease Institute of American History, Tulsa; Jay Rose, Director of Information, Humble Oil and Refining Company, Houston; Paul Rossi, Director, Thomas Gilcrease Institute of American History, Tulsa; John Shelton, Area Resource and Development Agent, University of Arkansas Agricultural Extension Service, Harrison; Glenn Shirley, author-historian-collector, Oklahoma State University, Stillwater; Henderson Shuffler, Director, Texana Library, University of Texas, Austin; Charles Simons, Texas Mid-Continent Oil & Gas Association, Dallas; Virginia Smyth, Librarian, American Petroleum Institute, New York City; Texas Agricultural and Mechanical College, College Station; Texas State Department of Agriculture, Livestock Division, Austin; United States Department of Agriculture, Livestock Division, Austin; Dick Wilson, editor, *The Cattleman Magazine*, Fort Worth; Walker Wilson, Charolais rancher, Overton, Texas; Muriel H. Wright, Research Specialist, Oklahoma Historical Society, Oklahoma City; Albert Yeargan, Regional Manager, Stetson Company, Dallas.

Bibliography

* Available also in paperback.
† Available only in paperback.

General and historical reading

Dale, Edward Everett, and Morris L. Wardell, *History of Oklahoma*. Prentice-Hall, 1948.

Fletcher, John Gould, *Arkansas*. University of North Carolina Press, 1947.

Foreman, Grant, *A History of Oklahoma*. University of Oklahoma Press, 1942.

Gittinger, Roy, *The Formation of the State of Oklahoma, 1803-1906*. University of Oklahoma Press, 1939.

Goodwyn, Frank, *Lone-Star Land*. Alfred A. Knopf, 1955.

Harlow, Victor E., *Oklahoma History*. Harlow Publishing Company, 1961.

Hogan, William Ransom, *The Texas Republic, a Social and Economic History*. University of Oklahoma Press, 1946.

Hollon, William Eugene, *The Southwest: Old and New*. Alfred A. Knopf, 1961.

McCleskey, Clifton, *The Government and Politics of Texas*.* Little, Brown & Company, 1963.

McReynolds, Edwin C.:
Oklahoma: History of the Sooner State. University of Oklahoma Press, 1964.
Oklahoma, the Story of Its Past. University of Oklahoma Press, 1961.

Morris, Willie, ed., *The South Today*.* Harper & Row, 1965.

Richardson, Rupert N., *Texas, The Lone Star State*. Prentice-Hall, 1958.

Smith, Henry Nash, *The Virgin Land: The American West as Symbol and Myth*.* Harvard University Press, 1950.

Steen, Ralph W., *The Texas Story*. Steck-Vaughn Company, 1960.

Webb, Walter Prescott, ed., *The Handbook of Texas*, 2 vols. The Texas State Historical Association, 1952.

Woodward, C. Vann, *The Origins of the New South, 1877-1913*.* Louisiana State University Press, 1951.

Special topics

Arnold, Oren, and John P. Hale, *Hot Irons: Heraldry of the Range*. The Macmillan Company, 1944.

Asbury, Herbert. *The French Quarter*.† Pocket Books, 1949.

Atherton, Lewis, *The Cattle Kings*. Indiana University Press, 1961.

Branch, Douglas, *The Cowboy and His Interpreters*. Cooper Square Publishers, 1961.

Clark, James A., and Michel T. Halbouty, *Spindletop*. Random House, 1952.

Cotterill, Robert S., *The Southern Indians*. University of Oklahoma Press, 1954.

Day, Donald, *Will Rogers: A Biography*. David McKay Company, 1962.

Dobie, J. Frank:
Cow People. Little, Brown & Company, 1964.
Guide to Life and Literature of the Southwest.* Southern Methodist University Press, 1952.
The Longhorns.* Little, Brown & Company, 1946.

Early, Eleanor, *New Orleans History*. Rinehart & Company, 1943.

Ford, Gus L., ed., *Texas Cattle Brands*. Clyde C. Cocherell Company, 1958.

Foreman, Grant:
The Five Civilized Tribes. University of Oklahoma Press, 1934.
Indian Removal. University of Oklahoma Press, 1956.
The Last Trek of the Indian. University of Oklahoma Press, 1946.

Frantz, Joe B., and Julian Ernest Choate, *The American Cowboy: The Myth and the Reality*. University of Oklahoma Press, 1955.

Friend, Llerena B., *Sam Houston, The Great Designer*. University of Texas Press, 1954.

Gard, Wayne:
The Chisholm Trail. University of Oklahoma Press, 1954.
Rawhide Texas. University of Oklahoma Press, 1965.

Harris, William Foster, *The Look of the Old West*. Viking Press, 1955.

Hodge, Frederick Webb, ed., *The Handbook of American Indians North of Mexico*, 2 vols. Pageant Books, 1960.

James, Marquis, *The Raven, A Biography of Sam Houston*. Bobbs-Merrill, 1929.

Josephy, Alvin M., *The Patriot Chiefs*. Viking Press, 1961.

Knowles, Ruth Sheldon, *The Greatest Gamblers: The Epic of American Oil Exploration*. McGraw-Hill, 1959.

Lea, Tom, *The King Ranch*, 2 vols.

Little, Brown & Company, 1957.

Long, Huey P., *Every Man a King*.* National Book Company, 1933.

Lynn, Stuart M., *New Orleans*. Hastings House, 1949.

Masterson, James R., *Tall Tales of Arkansaw*. Chapman and Grimes, 1942.

Meyers, John M., *The Alamo*. E. P. Dutton and Company, 1948.

Morrison, Hugh, *Early American Architecture*. Oxford University Press, 1952.

Owens, William, *This Stubborn Soil*. Charles Scribner's Sons, 1966.

Post, Lauren C., *Cajun Sketches*. Louisiana State University Press, 1962.

Rister, Carl C., *Oil! Titan of the Southwest*. University of Oklahoma Press, 1949.

Russell, William L., *Principles of Petroleum Geology*. McGraw-Hill, 1960.

Sandoz, Mari:
The Cattlemen. Hastings House, 1958.
Cheyenne Autumn. Hastings House, 1961.

Sanford, Trent Elwood, *The Architecture of the Southwest*. W. W. Norton & Company, 1950.

Shirley, Martha Lou, ed., *Deltas*. Houston Geological Society, 1966.

Smith, Erwin E., and J. Evetts Haley, *Life on the Texas Range*. University of Texas Press, 1952.

Thorp, Raymond W., *Bowie Knife*. University of New Mexico Press, 1948.

Wagon, Kenneth A., Reuben Albaugh, and George H. Hart, *Beef Cattle Production*. The Macmillan Company, 1960.

Wallace, Ernest, and E. Adamson Hoebel, *The Comanches, Lords of the South Plains*. University of Oklahoma Press, 1964.

Webb, Walter Prescott, *The Great Plains*.* Blaisdell Publishing Company, 1959.

Wellman, Paul I., *Death on Horseback*. J. B. Lippincott Company, 1947.

Widmer, Jack, *The American Quarter Horse*. Charles Scribner's Sons, 1959.

Wilson, Charles Morrow, *The Bodacious Ozarks*. Hastings House, 1959.

Wissler, Clark, *Indians of the United States*. Doubleday and Company, 1966.

Wright, Muriel H., *A Guide to the Indian Tribes of Oklahoma*.

University of Oklahoma Press, 1957.

Natural setting and wildlife

Anthony, Harold E., *Field Book of North American Mammals*. G. P. Putnam's Sons, 1928.

Check-List of North American Birds. Committee of the American Ornithologists, 1957.

Conant, Roger, *A Field Guide to Reptiles and Amphibians*. Houghton Mifflin Company, 1958.

Hylander, Clarence J., and Edith Farrington Johnston, *The Macmillan Wild Flower Book*. The Macmillan Company, 1954.

La Monte, Francesca Raimonde, *North American Game Fishes*. Doubleday and Company, 1946.

Matthews, F. Schuyler, *Field Book of American Wild Flowers*. G. P. Putnam's Sons, 1955.

Migdalski, Edward C., *Angler's Guide to the Salt Water Game Fishes*. The Ronald Press, 1958.

Moldenke, Harold N., *American Wild Flowers*. D. Van Nostrand Company, 1949.

Oberholser, Harry C., *The Bird Life of Louisiana*. Department of Conservation, 1938.

Palmer, Ralph S., *The Mammal Guide*. Doubleday and Company, 1954.

Peterson, Roger Tory, *A Field Guide to the Birds of Texas*. Houghton Mifflin Company, 1960.

Sargent, Charles Sprague, *Manual of the Trees of North America*, 2 vols. Dover Publications, 1949.

Guidebooks

Federal Writers' Project:
Arkansas: A Guide to the State. Hastings House, 1940.
Louisiana: A Guide to the State. Hastings House, 1941.
Oklahoma: A Guide to the Sooner State. University of Oklahoma Press, 1941.
Texas: A Guide to the Lone Star State. Hastings House, 1940.

Fodor, Eugene, ed., *Fodor Shell Travel Guides U.S.A.; South Central*. David McKay Company, 1967.

Mobil Travel Guide: The Southwest and South Central Area. Simon and Schuster, 1967.

Texas Almanac and State Industrial Guide, 1966 1967.* A. H. Belo Corporation, 1965.

Index

Numerals in italics indicate an
illustration of the subject mentioned.

PRODUCTION STAFF FOR TIME INCORPORATED
John L. Hallenbeck (Vice President and Director of Production),
Robert E. Foy, Caroline Ferri and Don Sheldon
Text photocomposed under the direction of Albert J. Dunn and Arthur J. Dunn